Writing Africa in the Short Story

AFRICAN LITERATURE TODAY 31

Editor:	Ernest N. Emenyonu
Assistant Editor:	Patricia T. Emenyonu
Associate Editors:	Jane Bryce
	Maureen N. Eke
	Stephanie Newell
	Charles E. Nnolim
	Chimalum Nwankwo
	Ato Quayson
	Kwawisi Tekpetey
	Iniobong I. Uko
Reviews Editor:	James Gibbs

T0313524

HEBN Publishers PLC

JC JAMES CURREY

GUIDELINES FOR SUBMISSION OF ARTICLES

The Editor invites submission of articles on the announced themes of forthcoming issues. Submissions will be acknowledged promptly and decisions communicated within six months of the receipt of the paper. Your name and institutional affiliation (with full mailing address and email) should appear on a separate sheet, plus a brief biographical profile of not more than six lines. The editor cannot undertake to return materials submitted, and contributors are advised to keep a copy of each material sent. Please note that all articles outside the announced themes cannot be considered or acknowledged. Articles should be submitted in the English Language.

Length: Articles should not exceed 5,000 words.

Format: Articles should be double-spaced, and should use the same type face and size throughout. Italics are preferred to underlines for titles of books. Articles are reviewed blindly, so do not insert your name, institutional affiliation and contact information on the article itself. Instead, provide such information on a separate page.

Style: UK or US spellings are required, but be consistent. Direct quotations should retain the spellings used in the original source. Check the accuracy of citations and always give the author's surname and page number in the text, and a full reference in the Works Cited list at the end of the article. Italicize titles of books or plays. Use single inverted commas throughout except for quotes within quotes which are double. Avoid subtitles or subsection headings within the text.

Citations: Limit your sources to the most recent, or the most important books and journals, in English. Cite works in foreign languages only when no English-language books are available. Cite websites only if they are relatively permanent and if they add important information unavailable elsewhere.

For in-text citations, the sequence in parentheses should be (Surname: page number). No year of publication should be reflected within the text. All details should be presented in the Works Cited list at the end of the article. Consistency is advised. Examples:

Cazenave, Odile. *Rebellious Women: The New Generation of Female African Novelists.* Boulder, CO: Lynne Rienner Publishers, 2000.

Duerden, Dennis. 'The "Discovery" of the African Mask.' *Research in African Literatures.* Vol. 31, No. 4 (Winter 2000): 29-47.

Ukala, Sam. 'Tradition, Rotimi, and His Audience.' *Goatskin Bags and Wisdom: New Critical Perspectives on African Literature.* Ed. Ernest N. Emenyonu. New Jersey: Africa World Press, 2000: 91-104.

Ensure that your Works Cited list is alphabetized on a word-by-word basis, whether citations begin with the author's name or with an anonymous work's title. Please, avoid footnotes or endnotes. Do not quote directly from the Internet without properly citing the source as you would when quoting from a book. Use substantive sources for obtaining your information and depend less on general references.

Copyright: It is the responsibility of contributors to clear permissions.

All articles should be sent to the Editor:
Ernest N. Emenyonu, African Literature Today
Department of Africana Studies
University of Michigan-Flint
303 East Kearsley Street
Flint MI 48502
USA
Email: eernest@umflint.edu
Fax: 001-810-766-6719

Reviewers should provide full bibliographic details, including the extent, ISBN and price, and submit to the Reviews Editor:
James Gibbs, 8 Victoria Square, Bristol BS8 4ET, UK • jamesgibbs@btinternet.com

AFRICAN LITERATURE TODAY

1-14 were published from London by Heinemann Educational Books and from New York by Africana Publishing Company

*Backlist titles available in the US and Canada from Africa World Press
and in the rest of the world from James Currey, an imprint of Boydell & Brewer*

Note from the publisher on new and forthcoming titles
James Currey Publishers joined Boydell & Brewer Ltd in 2008.
African Literature Today continues to be published as an annual volume under the James Currey imprint.
North and South American distribution:
Boydell & Brewer Inc., 68 Mount Hope Avenue, Rochester, NY 14620-2731, US
UK and International distribution:
Boydell & Brewer Ltd., PO Box 9, Woodbridge IP12 3DF, GB.
Nigeria edition: HEBN Publishers Plc

Call for papers

Writing Africa in the Short Story

AFRICAN LITERATURE TODAY 31

James Currey is an imprint of
Boydell & Brewer Ltd
PO Box 9, Woodbridge,
Suffolk, IP12 3DF (GB)
and of
Boydell & Brewer Inc.
668 Mt Hope Avenue,
Rochester, NY 14620-2731 (US)
www.boydellandbrewer.com
www.jamescurrey.com

HEBN Publishers Plc
1 Ighodaro Road, Jericho,
PMB 5205, Ibadan, Nigeria
Phone: +234 2 8726701
info@hebnpublishers.com
hebnpublishers@yahoo.com
http://www.hebnpublishers.com
www.facebook.com/pages/HEBN-PublishersPlcs
www.twitter.com/HEBNPublishers

© Contributors 2013
First published 2013

British Library Cataloguing in Publication Data
is available on request from the British Library

ISBN 978-1-84701-081-0 (James Currey paper)
ISBN 978 978 081 2171 (HEBN paper)

The publisher has no responsibility for the continued existence or accuracy of URLs
for external or third-party internet websites referred to in this book, and does not
guarantee that any content on such websites is, or will remain,
accurate or appropriate.

Papers used by Boydell & Brewer are natural, recycled products
made from wood grown in sustainable forests.

Designed and set in 10.5/12 pt Berkeley Book by
Kate Kirkwood Publishing Services, Cumbria, UK
Printed in Great Britain
by CPI Group (UK) Ltd, Croydon CR0 4YY

Dedication

Chinua Achebe
Joins the Ancestors

1930–2013

We, at *African Literature Today*, mourn the death of Chinua Achebe, one of the greatest writers of all time. He chose for his moment of transition (11.51 pm, 21 March), not a mere coincidence, during the 2013 annual conference of the African Literature Association (20-24 March) at Charleston, South Carolina, USA. His novel, *Things Fall Apart* (1958), initiated the Heinemann African Writers Series which laid the foundation for what today is known as African Literary studies, which is the central focus of *African Literature Today*'s publications. We convey our condolences to the family of Prof. Chinua Achebe at this difficult time. We mourn his death, we celebrate his legacies!

Things Fall Apart, one of the greatest novels in living memory, like the Comet that its creator was, appeared and streaked into the heavens and stayed there, and as we all know, it will for ever stay, palpable and immoveable. Achebe executed for the world to behold, a mandate of destiny that will remain out there without parallel. Chinua Achebe, bards come and go, but we know here that the courage and dignity which you exhibited over the years, will like the stories you told so well, endure in our sight like the grand iroko tree in our consciousness upon whose greenery you remain, majestic and grand in well-deserved immortality.

Like the inimitable character in your *Things Fall Apart*, we bid you farewell in your own words:

> If you had been poor in your last life, we would have asked you to be rich when you come again. But you were rich. If you had been a coward, we would have asked you to bring courage. But you were a

fearless warrior. If you had died young, we would have asked you to get life. But you lived long. So we shall ask you to come again the way you came before!

Chinua Achebe, the Eagle on the Iroko, the Comet of African Literature, your kind appears once in a century. We say, 'Go in Peace'. Most worthy son, may the ancestors cheer you with drums into the Hallowed Hall of Illustrious Ancestors!!

***

STOP PRESS/ TRIBUTE TO KOFI AWOONOR 1935–2013

As we were going to press we heard the terrible news that Ghanaian poet Kofi Awoonor, one of Africa's pioneer and most versatile writers of the twentieth century, was among those killed during the shootings in the Westgate Mall in Nairobi on 21 September. We will carry a full tribute on his life and work in the next volume of *ALT 32: Politics & Social Justice.*

***

Contents

Notes on Contributors

Mary Jane Androne, Professor of English, is Co-Director of Africana Studies at Albright College in Reading, Pennsylvania. Her current scholarship centres on African and African American women writers and her publications include articles on Tsitsi Dangarembga, Mariama Bâ, Julie Dash, Nawal El Saadawi, and Ama Ata Aidoo.

Juliana Daniels is a Lecturer in the Department of English Education at the Community University College, Takoradi. Her research interests include women's writings and children's literature. She is currently working on heroines in West African war novels.

Blessing Diala-Ogamba, Associate Professor of English at Coppin State University, Baltimore, Maryland, teaches courses in World Literature (African, Asian, Latin American, and British writers). Her research interests are women's and children's literature.

Louisa Uchum Egbunike is a PhD candidate in the Africa Department at the School of Oriental and African Studies (SOAS), University of London. She is also one of the organisers of the annual Igbo Studies Conference held at SOAS.

Eve Eisenberg is a doctoral student in the Department of English at Indiana University-Bloomington, where she also teaches. Her dissertation which she hopes to defend in 2014, discusses rewriting as a genre of Africa and its diaspora.

Maureen Eke, Professor of English at Central Michigan University, Mount Pleasant, teaches courses in African Diaspora Literatures, postcolonial literatures and theory as well as women's writing. She has published widely on African Literature and Cinema.

Imene Moulati teaches at Saad Dahleb University in Algeria. A recent Fulbright scholar at Central Michigan University, Mount Pleasant, her research interests include trauma literature, psychoanalysis and postmodern philosophy.

Tinashe Mushakavanhu read for a PhD in English at the University of Kent, England. He graduated with a first class honours in English from Midlands State University, Zimbabwe and became the first African to receive an MA in Creative Writing at Trinity College, Carmarthen, Wales. He co-edited *State of the Nation: Contemporary Zimbabwean Poetry* (2009). He is currently a part-time lecturer in English at Africa University, Zimbabwe.

Stephanie Newell, Professor of English at the University of Sussex, England, teaches postcolonial literature. She has published widely on African popular literatures and literary history. Her recent books include *West African Literatures: Ways of Reading* (2006) and *The Forger's Tale: The Search for Odeziaku* (2006).

Vincent O. Odamtten is a Professor in the Department of English at Hamilton College, New York. He published an acclaimed book *The Art of Ama Ata Aidoo* (1994), and has contributed articles to *The Encyclopedia of African Literature* (2003) as well as a number of critical anthologies, including *FonTomFrom – Contemporary Ghanaian Literature, Film and Culture* (2000), *Of Dreams Deferred, Dead or Alive: African Perspectives on African-American Writers* (1996), and *Language in Exile: Jamaican Texts of the 18th & 19th Century* (1990). He edited the volume, *Broadening the Horizon: Critical Introductions to Amma Darko* (2007), and also contributed an article to *Essays in Honour of Ama Ata Aidoo at 70,* edited by Anne V. Adams (2012).

Regina Okafor, formerly Senior Lecturer in the Department of Modern Languages and Literatures at the University of Port Harcourt, Nigeria, currently teaches in the Department of World Languages and Cultures at Howard University, Washington, DC. She has published journal articles on African Literature.

Rose A. Sackeyfio is an Associate Professor in the Department of English at Winston Salem State University, North Carolina. She completed a PhD (1992) in Education at the Ahmadu Bello University, Zaria, Nigeria where she taught for ten years. Her scholarship and research pursuits examine the literature of African and African American women. She has published critical essays that explore various aspects of the lives of African women in a global arena.

Hellen Roselyne Shigali is a Senior Lecturer in the Department of Literature, Theatre and Film Studies, Eldoret University, Kenya. Her publications include *Alternative Conceptualization of Empowerment: African Gender Perspective* (2010).

Iniobong Uko is a Professor of English, and currently Director of Pre-Degree Studies, University of Uyo, Nigeria. Her research interests are women's writing and a cross-cultural study of African and Diasporic women's writings. She has participated in several women's activities and initiatives in Nigeria and abroad, and has published extensively in journals and books in Nigeria, Ghana, Germany, the US and UK. She is the author of the seminal book, *Gender and Identity in the Works of Osonye Tess Onwueme* (2004).

Lindsey Zanchettin is a PhD candidate at Auburn University, Alabama, with a focus on African and African Diaspora literatures, feminist theory and women's studies. Her dissertation examines notions of expatriatism in the texts of women writers from Africa and the Diaspora.

Editorial

'Once Upon a Time Begins a Story...'

... A CHALLENGE FACING CRITICS OF AFRICAN LITERATURE in the 80's is facing the neglected frontiers of our literary and critical endeavors. We all have, up to now, neglected the short story as a genre worthy of critical attention, even though there is already a respectable body of short stories written by our most celebrated writers. Whatever the case may be, our critics must be reminded that the short story as a genre is still stillborn on the African literary scene. To deliver this baby, to ensure the healthy birth of the short story (through vigorous response) into the mainstream of the African literary scene is a major challenge facing critics of African Literature. (Nnolim 1982, 51-6)

The above outcry was taken from an article, 'The Short Story as a Genre, with Notes on Achebe's "The Madman"' by my friend and colleague, the erudite scholar, Charles Nnolim. Three decades later, nothing has changed; the critical gap in the criticism of African Literature decried by Nnolim remains unaddressed, unfilled. If anything, the gap has become wider and deeper. It is as if no serious critic even took notice of Nnolim's call for urgent action. National and international conferences and colloquiums continue to be held in Africa and elsewhere to address issues and challenges associated with the novel, poetry, and drama in African literature, with virtually no attention paid to the short story. This abysmal lack of interest is also true of the attitudes of teachers, publishers and educators in general in Africa. These concerns are the factors that motivated this special volume of *African Literature Today*, on 'Writing Africa in the Short Story.'

Through the study and analysis of selected authors and their works *ALT 31* takes a close look at the African short story to re-define its own peculiar pedigree, chart its trajectory, critique its present state and examine its creative possibilities. Do the African short story and the novel match complementarily or do they exist in contradistinction in terms of over-all success and the informing antecedents within the driving purview of culture and politics, history and/public memory, legends, myths and folklore? What in a capsule is the state of the African short story in terms of foundations, aesthetics, energy, literary and linguistic strengths or weaknesses as a form, seen from the perspectives of chosen authors and their short stories?

Nowhere else was 'story' more socially revered as culturally significant and purposeful than in the traditional African society where it was used for the dual functions of acculturation and entertainment. From time immemorial, Africans designed 'the story' as a vehicle for cultural transmission and continuity. The story (tale/folktale) was the source of 'raw' (authentic) African values and the elders structured its form and sharpened its message such that it became a coherent and reliable vehicle for childhood upbringing, social transformation, and the conveyance of esteemed norms, values, and virtues transmitted by word of mouth from generation to generation. No other culture ever used 'the story' in quite this pointed and methodical manner in its preliterate era for serious didactic and yet light-hearted entertainment purposes.

Elsewhere (Emenyonu 1978), I had elaborated on the place, nature, and purpose of the 'tale' (a tool for social transformation and acculturation), and, the artist (both a technician and visionary) in the traditional African society. The artist knew his/her society—its pace, pulse, dreams, and realities—and through his/her artistic creations, sought to provide some fulfillment for the audience. The artist was for the audience, the educator, entertainer, philosopher, and counselor. He entertained as he instructed and endeavoured to make the values and beliefs portrayed in each tale come alive. The African society at the time did not derive its entertainment from books. Imagination was developed through oral narratives. Logic was inculcated through proverbs and riddles. Good speaking habits were learnt from experienced practitioners who embellished their language with imagery, folk idiom, and witticism. Through these, the young had to learn and appreciate the basic ideas of life, the community's fundamental values, their systems of personal relationships and their sense of humor. The traditional artist had a clear conception of the immediate society, its problems and needs, and reflected these in the course of narration, projecting through the ethical formulas in each tale a direction for the society and the individuals caught in the dilemmas of humanity.

The traditional African society had a large stock of tales in the form of legends and fairy tales and these were constantly exploited by the narrators to add life and excitement to their tales. They were at liberty to use animals and birds as illustrations , but these were used in such a way that they seemed to be endowed with human powers. The narrators imitated the sounds of the animals brought into the stories to enhance the entertainment of the audience. At the end of the day's work , people young and old were ready to relax with stories that gladdened the heart or challenged the intellect. Mothers, fathers, uncles and aunts took turns to entertain. The stories were told as they came to mind. When the adults retired for the night or on occasions in their absence, the children in turns, told stories that came to their minds making sure that no one repeated a story that had already been told. The stories, whether by adults or children, need not always be folktales. They could be stories of actual events which are considered humorous or delightful. Or they could be stories that the narrator simply felt the audience would like to hear. The most important factor was that the stories allowed the audience to draw some conclusions based on moral or ethical considerations.

A narrator with some experience might use a number of stylistic devices in telling a story. The devices could take the form of proverbs and sayings, woven into the body of the story itself. These devices could constitute a summary of the vital issues in the story. When proverbs, imagery or symbolism appeared in the stories, they helped to make the stories more challenging, and the process of understanding the full impact of the stories was a further exercise for the faculties of the children — an exercise which if successfully completed , added to the entertainment and fun which the stories could bring. This scenario is the antecedent of the modern short story in Africa.

'Once upon a Time, a man harvested green vegetables that filled seven baskets from his farm, and gave them to his mother to cook for him. The broth that his mother served him could fill only three baskets. The man accused his mother of theft and killed her. Then he cooked seven freshly harvested baskets of green vegetables. When he emptied the broth, the vegetables could fill only three baskets. He killed himself!!'

'Once upon a Time, the King of all the animals that inhabited a forest (where they had become easy prey to hunters), summoned all the

animals to an early morning meeting in his house. He did not reveal the agenda which was to pick by a unanimous process, a single animal to offer to human beings to use for food, sacrificial, and other purposes when needed. On the appointed morning, all the animals showed up at the king's palace except chicken who pleaded a previous engagement as the excuse for inevitable absence but was willing to abide by whatever decision was reached at the meeting. She thus became the unanimous choice!!'

'Once upon a Time, when the world was divided into two – the earth and the sky – there was acute famine on earth but surplus food in the sky within the reach of only the winged creatures who looked enviably robust and full of energy in the midst of universal suffering and hardship. The turtle notoriously "famous" for his wit and cunning had his plan of averting imminent death from starvation. He cajoled the birds into lending him each a feather which glued to his body would enable him to fly. When all was set to go to the sky, he convinced the birds that all earth's creatures visiting other spaces were, by an ancient law, required to take on new names to use in the alien territory. His own name was – "All of You". When they arrived at their destination and their hosts served them superfluous dishes, and they were about to eat, Turtle asked the hosts matter-of-factly, "who is all this food for?" Response – "All of You". With this, he cheated the birds of all the food except revolting dry bones. But he paid a dear price when the birds plucked off his body the feathers each had lent him. It wasn't at all funny when he fell from the sky to earth. He has till today a cracked shell to show for it.'

'Once upon a Time, when the world was still young and was inhabited by human beings and animals in sweet harmony; there was no suffering, no sickness and no death. All creatures could live forever. This was boring to some creatures especially such little ones as ants and squirrels, but the big animals along with human beings had no problem with the situation. All the same, a meeting was called to reach an irrevocable consensus. The big creatures were in the majority and a message was crafted to the Creator of the Universe to continue to allow life without death on earth. The Dog, the fastest animal at the time, was despatched to deliver the majority decision to the Creator in his abode. The small creatures however, for what it was worth, prepared their minority opinion and despatched the not- so- fast frog (who would leap the enormous distance) to deliver it to the Creator. Dog had no reason to worry, so he decided to take a nap along the way. He was still sleeping when Frog leaped his way *to the abode of the Creator and delivered the minority opinion. That was how death came to be a permanent phenomenon in the world today. And the Dog lost his place among the animals in the forest. Human beings took him in out of compassion and from time to time the dog aided them in the hunt for "enemy" animals in the forest. That is why today the dog is found in human homes instead of the forest with most other animals!'*

The story-hour (or simply 'Story Telling') was an important feature of the school curriculum in colonial Africa but the early European missionaries had other things in mind beyond relaxing the mind, challenging the intellect, or providing humorous or didactic entertainment. Using the structure known to the children, the missionaries in the schools they founded constructed short narratives about things in the African environments, but wove into them biblical information and religious instruction. In some cases they invented entirely new tales in which they provided didacticism and moral tags that reflected Christian morality and ethics. A few samples would make the point. A narrative on hunting as an important occupation ended with: *'A famous hunter was Nimrod whose story we read about in the Bible. Esau the brother of Jacob was also a hunter.'* Another narrative on trading as another important occupation began with: *'Trading is a good occupation if embarked upon with the fear of God and honesty',* and ended with: *'To cheat your customer is bad. One who fears God should desist from such. Jesus Christ urges you to do unto others as you would that they do unto you.'* A similar narrative targetting riverine inhabitants ended with: *'Our Lord Jesus Christ asked four fishermen to be his disciples. Do you know their names? They were Andrew, Peter, James and John. Do you know what he charged Peter and Andrew to do when he called them? He said,"follow me and I will make you fishers of men".'* (Emenyonu 1978, 26). Unknowingly, therefore, the children in the missionary schools were effectively learning as much of the Christian religion as could be taught in any formal religious class. Such was the importance as well as the impact of the short story tradition in Africa recognized over the ages.

Sadly, although 'the short story' has not lost its pedagogical value and aesthetic appeal in Africa, urbanization and modern technology have eroded its essence and impact, and this is what makes its 'recovery' and 'reinvention' both a cultural and intellectual necessity on the continent of Africa. Story-telling can be reinvented and adapted to coexist harmoniously with modern technology which can indeed facilitate and increase its appeal for the young within the school system at all levels.

Modern African writers have not ceased to let the story serve its age-long purposes. Some of the best stories in contemporary world literature have come from the pens and imaginations of highly talented African writers. They have not ceased to use the story to teach morals, castigate criminal offenders, remind the young about the perils of intransigence, insubordination, belligerent defiance of authority, the folly of negating ancestral sanctions as well as the wisdom of respect for old age, the belief in worthy traditions and the sanctity of moral order. The younger generation of African writers in particular, have used the short story to comment on various aspects of life in modern African societies: the senselessness of violence, war, religious bigotry, racism, corruption and all forms of injustice meted to any human group especially women and the disenfranchized 'others' in Africa as anywhere else in the world. They have canvassed in their stories set in today's Africa, a new sense of direction, moral regeneration, social integration, racial tolerance, and equality of all human beings under the law. This is what makes the neglect of the short story in Africa by scholars, critics and teachers, all the more deplorable in the field of African literature. And the time is now to begin actively and noticeably to reverse the trend.

So far in the new millenium, the most significant driving force in the revival of active interest in the African short story is 'The Caine Prize for African Writing', founded in the UK in the year 2000 (when the maiden prize was also awarded) in memory of Sir Michael Harris Caine. Worth £10,000 sterling (about US$15,000), the prize is awarded annually for the best short story by an African writer resident anywhere in the world, published in the English language. Since its inception, the prize has been won four times by Nigerian writers, twice each by Kenyan, Zimbabwean and South African writers, and once each by Sierra Leonean, and Sudanese writers. Notably, the maiden prize in 2000 was won by the Sudanese writer, Leila Aboulela (discussed in this volume), with her story, 'Fair in Harare'. Five finalists were short-listed for the 2013 prize – four Nigerian writers (Tope Folarin, Abubakar Adam Ibrahim, Elnathan John, Chinelo Okparanta), and Pede Hollist (Sierra Leone), Tope Folarin was announced as the winner for his short story 'Miracle'. The Prize has had the full support of Africa's four Nobel laureates for literature so far (Wole Soyinka 1986, Naguib Mahfouz (11

December 1911–30 August 2006) 1988, Nadine Gordimer 1991, J.M. Coetzee 2003), listed as 'Patrons of the Prize'.

'The Caine Prize' has more than any other institution in the 21st century, inspired and enhanced the enthusiasm for the African short story, projecting in the process new and exciting voices in contemporary imaginative creativity in Africa. Over the years since its inception entries for the Prize have continued to rise as with the number of African countries represented. This provides a good starting point for the revival of vital interest in the African short story by teachers, literary scholars, the general reader, and most especially, the critics of African Literature. The winning stories can be read and discussed in classrooms by teachers (to inspire budding writers), and assiduously analysed and critiqued by literary scholars (for impact and necessary publicity). The thirteen stories so far which have won the the Prize are substance enough for use in creative writing and literary criticism classes, as well as workshops in colleges and universities. It is in reading these stories, discussing and critiquing them that their impact can be fully realized, and the salient contributions of 'The Caine Prize' to African Literature in the 21st century can be deservedly appreciated.

This volume of *African Literature Today* embodies twelve articles on the short stories of authors from nine African countries – Algeria, Botswana, Egypt, Ghana, Nigeria, South Africa, Sudan, Uganda, and Zimbabwe, and an interview of a veteran of the short story genre in African Literature. Together with the thirteen winning stories of 'The Caine Prize', this volume of *African Literature Today*, highlights some major achievements of contemporary African short story writers. Perhaps teachers and literary critics can take it from here and move the essential discourse forward!

WORKS CITED

Emenyonu, Ernest. *The Rise of the Igbo Novel*. Oxford University Press, 1978.
Nnolim, Charles. 'The Critic of African Literature: The Challenge of the 80's'. Owerri, Nigeria: *Afa Journal of Creative Writing, No 1, 1982*.

'Real Africa' / 'Which Africa?'

The Critique of Mimetic Realism in
Chimamanda Ngozi Adichie's Short Fiction

EVE EISENBERG

People are expecting from literature serious comment on their lives.
They are not expecting frivolity. They are expecting literature to say
something important to help them in their struggle with life. That
is what literature, what art, was supposed to do: to give us a second
handle on reality so that when it becomes necessary to do so, we can
turn to art and find a way out. So it is a serious matter. That's what I'm
saying, and I think every African writer you talk to will say something
approaching what I have just said – in different forms of words, except
those who have too much of the West in them, and there are some
people, of course, who are that way. But the writer I am referring to is
the real and serious African writer. I think you will find them saying
something which sounds as serious, as austere, or as earnest as what I
have just said.
(Chinua Achebe in Rowell 1990: 88)

A great deal of postcolonial literary criticism about African
literature naturalizes the notion that African writers produce
literary artwork whose primary function is the exposure of the
atrocities of the colonial era – and the lingering effects of that era
– in order to redress injustice via a true account of history. The
idea is that, once people know this true story of their own history,
they shall be more able to resist the psychological and sociocultural
effects of imperialism and its attendant racist dogma. In the words
of the epigram above, the 'serious', 'austere', 'earnest', and above
all the 'real' African writer, who does not 'have too much of the
West' in her, meets the 'expectations' of 'the people' by producing
literature that has a positive, direct, material impact on the lives of
African readers.

According to this figuration of the relationship between literature and politics, the African writer is a resistance activist, the
artwork itself an act of resistance; predictably, much academic

writing about African literature therefore examines what and how texts resist. While many factors contribute to this tendency to read for resistance, arguably one of the most influential is Chinua Achebe's widely read non-fictional account of why he wrote his canonical 1958 novel *Things Fall Apart*. He famously claimed to have written the novel in order to counteract racist representations of African people in Western literature, particularly Joyce Cary's *Mister Johnson* and Joseph Conrad's *Heart of Darkness*.[1]

Therefore when literary critics and journalists describe Chimamanda Ngozi Adichie's relationship to Chinua Achebe within a kind of 'father-daughter' narrative, they discursively figure her authorial persona according to this image of the African writer as resistance activist.[2] When we imagine Adichie as Achebe's literary 'heir', we picture her as an artist who takes up her pen in order to present a 'true image' of African people and the African past in order to contest racist misrepresentations and erasures. Adichie's frequent and explicit references to Achebe in her fiction, the periodization of African literary history currently dominant in the academy (which views Achebe as part of a canonical 'first generation' of independence-era activist-writers to and against whom later writers reply[3]), and other factors, contribute to this tendency to imagine a progenitor-heir relationship between the two writers. Adichie thus appears to *descend* from Achebe – her writing an extension or extrusion of his oeuvre – and/or to be obliged to *dissent* from him. Thus critics often view Adichie as having 'cleverly reworked' Achebe (Bryce 2008: 62), while journalists often focus on the biographical parallels between the two writers in order to frame Adichie as 'the new face of Nigerian literature' because she is seen to be stepping into a place made for her by Achebe (Murray 2007: M1).

Elsewhere, I argue that the writers/intellectual characters in Adichie's novels represent alternative ways of receiving and creating 'political art' in the postcolony. Using Jacques Rancière's theories of politics and aesthetics, I have claimed that Adichie's novels model new ways of communing around and through African intellectual and artistic enterprises. Something different, however, happens when Adichie invokes Achebe in her short fiction. Whereas the length and complexity of the novel form permit Adichie to fully explore the ideological formation of the African writer, and thus to think through and model alternative routes to authorial 'interpellation', the short story's length restriction paradoxically frees Adichie from the obligation to provide the closure of positive, resistant, 'politically efficacious' answers.

The writing characters in Adichie's short stories 'Jumping Monkey Hill'[4] and 'The Headstrong Historian'[5] problematize a discourse of African literary history that figures the possibilities of political activism within a realist-mimetic understanding of the relationship between art and politics. These stories employ Achebe as a kind of shorthand, a way of invoking a dominant meta-narrative discourse of the African author, one that circulates both within and outside the academy. In these short stories, Adichie's references to Achebe illuminate the problems for African authorship that arise from conceptualizing literary-creative possibilities according to an ideological figuration of the author as resistance activist. By virtue of their formal brevity, these short stories powerfully foreground problems rather than imagining the fullness of solutions. In foregrounding problems without offering solutions, the stories thus resist the very call to literary-political activism about which they speculate.

However, at first glance it appears that Adichie accepts as natural the notions that 'true' narratives of Africa counteract racist misrepresentations in prior fiction; that representing scenes of atrocity against African people constitutes a positive political action which will engender corresponding, positive, and direct political change; and that the African fiction writer's role obliges her to employ her special cultural status in order to voice protests against injustice. Often Adichie seems to do precisely those things we would expect of someone who accepts her role as 'Achebe's heir'.

For example, in her introduction to the Everyman Library's 2010 single-volume collection of Achebe's *Things Fall Apart*, *No Longer at Ease*, and *Arrow of God*, Adichie cements her place in Achebe's lineage, in part simply by being the writer of the introduction to a collection of Achebe's novels, but more meaningfully by both paralleling her own development as a writer with Achebe's, and by representing his oeuvre as the catalyst for her self-recognition as an authentically African writer. Adichie narrates Achebe's well known story about how 'the Nigerian character' in Joyce Cary's *Mister Johnson* was 'unrecognizable to [Achebe]' and then parallels that seminal experience of Achebe's – the experience of the inability to recognize himself or his culture in fiction that was supposed to represent them – to her own:

The strangeness of seeing oneself distorted in literature – and indeed of not seeing oneself at all – was part of my own childhood. I grew up in the Nigerian university town of Nsukka in the 1980s, reading a lot of British children's books. My early writing mimicked the books I was reading: all my characters were white and all my stories were set in England. Then I read *Things Fall Apart*. It was a glorious shock of discovery, as was *Arrow of God*, which I read shortly afterwards; I did not know in a concrete way until then that people like me could exist in literature. Here was a book that was unapologetically African, that was achingly familiar, but that was, also, exotic because it detailed the life of my people a hundred years before. ('Introduction' 2010: vii-ix)

Adichie enunciates an affective connection between herself and Achebe via the experience of the 'strangeness of seeing oneself distorted in literature', an enunciation that constructs authorship as that which is motivated by an insufficiency in prior literature (an insufficiency of representation), and thus as that which is motivated by the subjective experience of reading and of a failure to recognize and to identify.

She sustains this discursive construction by framing her own 'early writing' as an act of 'mimicry', suggesting that she has had (at least) two phases as a writer: the 'early' phase, in which she only 'mimicked' because she 'did not know in a concrete way…that people like [her] could exist in literature,' and a post-reading-Achebe phase in which, we are meant to understand, she transcended mimicry and now produces original artwork. She thus frames Achebe's oeuvre – particularly *Things Fall Apart* and *Arrow of God* – as ideologically transformative, as hailing agents that authenticated (via demonstrations of African characters and authorship) her theretofore inauthentic interpellation as an African writer.

There are other examples that would seem to support the assertion that Adichie is Achebe's 'heir,' or at least that she understands and performs her role as a writer according to Achebian principles about African authors and their obligations. In her 2009 TED talk, Adichie's comments about her early experiences as a reader of British fiction echo an Achebian understanding of the relationships between representation, African self-perception, and global stereotypes about Africa.[6] Her 2004 op-ed piece for the *New York Times*, 'The Line of No Return', both exposes institutional racism and speaks directly to Nigerians about matters of political power and self-perception; the op-ed thus resonates strongly with Achebe's 1983 treatise *The Trouble With Nigeria*, as well as with his more general, abiding concerns about the dehumanization of African people and the need for African writing to address the problem.[7]

A reader of Adichie's introduction to Achebe's Umuofia trilogy who has also paid attention to her other non-fiction talks and essays (as well as Achebe's), could be forgiven for anticipating that Adichie's fiction would reflect Achebian politics and principles, including – and perhaps even most prominently – his well-known conceptualization of the direct, resistant relationship between art and politics. We can see, however, a significant and meaningful disjuncture between Adichie's public performance of her authorial persona, and the manner in which she invokes Achebe in order to depict a relationship between art and politics in her short fiction. This disjuncture suggests that Adichie wrestles not with the content of Achebian political propositions, but with the apparent obligations of the African fiction writer.[8] The objection seems to lodge itself not against simply *being obligated*, but against the foundational assumptions that discursively figure literature's political efficacy as mimetic, and which thereby render African literature vulnerable to appropriation and exploitation by neocolonial publishing elites.

By using the term 'mimetic,' I invoke Jacques Rancière's work, in *The Emancipated Spectator* (2009) and *The Politics of Aesthetics* (2006), on the relationship between politics and art. Rancière argues that literature is political not because it exposes atrocities 'mimetically' and thus motivates better behaviour, but because it makes visible new modes of 'community' via a new 'distribution of the sensible' (*Aesthetics* 2006: 14-15).[9] For Rancière, there is a 'gap at the heart of mimetic continuity,' a 'rupture of the harmony that enabled correspondence between the texture of the work and its efficacy' (*Spectator* 2009: 62). Rancière describes a 'representative' or 'mimetic regime of the arts,' a theory of meaning-making dependent upon 'a regime of concordance inherent in representation' (60). According to Rancière's view of the representative regime of the arts – the regime of Molière and Voltaire, a more or less modern regime – for representation to be mimetic, signs themselves could not be arbitrary; signs were understood to be perfectly unambiguous, 'because they possessed a grammar which was regarded as the language of nature itself' (60). According to this regime, art could motivate its audience to 'appropriate emotion' because it was part of an unbroken unity; art was political – and politically efficacious – because it could transmit, transparently and mimetically, universal and 'natural' truths that would resonate with the audience (60).

Thus, for Rancière, it would be reasonable to expect that, with the Derridean, postmodern attack on the 'naturalness' of the sign, we would abandon theories about the political efficacy of art that depend on the stability and universality of the sign and of the audience receiving it. Yet despite our having dispensed, putatively, with the theory of a mimetic 'continuum' of 'the stage, the audience and the world':

> Most of our ideas about the political efficacy of art still cling to that model. We may no longer believe that the exhibition of virtues and vices on the stage can correct human behaviour. But we are still prone to believe [...] that the photography of some atrocity will mobilize us against injustice. (*Spectator* 61)

In other words, then, despite a post-Derridean rejection of the transparency of the sign, Rancière's 'we' continues to understand art's 'political efficacy' according to a more or less mimetic understanding of meaning-making and of audience. Rancière's 'we', I would argue, includes those who read African literature as that which exposes atrocity in order to redress injustice; this 'we' therefore also includes those who imagine the African author to be obliged to produce artwork that enacts positive, calculable political change in a direct, mimetic manner.

Adichie's short story 'Jumping Monkey Hill' invokes Achebe in order to call to mind, and then to critique, the discourse of African authorship that emphasizes the mimetic exposure of atrocity as a primary obligation of the literary-creative enterprise. In the story, a group of writers from seven different African countries has gathered for a two week arts-foundation-sponsored workshop, held at the Jumping Monkey Hill resort near Cape Town, South Africa. On the second evening, after supper, all of the writers except for the Ugandan (who is too busy 'toadying' to the British organizer of the workshop) gather in a gazebo and talk, a little drunkenly:

> about the war in Sudan, about the decline of the African Writers Series, about books and about writers. They agreed that Dambudzo Marechera was astonishing, that Alan Paton was patronizing, that Isak Dinesen was unforgiveable. The Kenyan put on a generic European accent and, between drags at his cigarette, recited what Isak Dinesen had said about all Kikuyu children becoming mentally retarded at the age of nine. They laughed. The Zimbabwean said Achebe was boring and did nothing with style, and the Kenyan said that was a sacrilege and snatched at the Zimbabwean's wineglass, until she recanted, laughing, saying of course Achebe was sublime. The Senegalese said she nearly

vomited when a professor at the Sorbonne told her that Conrad was really on *her side*, as if she could not decide for herself who was on her side. Ujunwa began to jump up and down, babbling nonsense to mimic Conrad's Africans, feeling the sweet lightness of wine in her head. (102, emphasis in original)

Tellingly, when Adichie represents African writers speaking about their trade, Achebe enters the conversation, not just as a deity against whom 'sacrilege' can be committed, but in a dual role: as the producer of 'sublime' writing, and as the author who used his pen to contest Conrad's racist depiction of Africans. It is a conversation, moreover, not only about good and bad writers, but about good and bad representers of Africa; the reference to Achebe occurs as a response to a recitation of Isak Dinesen's racist remarks. Yet Achebe could be said to have been present in the conversation even before that moment, for the African Writers Series was truly Achebe's, while it existed and, even during the period of its 'decline', would represent something extremely meaningful to a group of young African writers.[10] In 'Jumping Monkey Hill,' then, a story about Ujunwa and the story she is writing during the workshop, Achebe materializes as the lens through which these writers understand their literary world, its obligations and possibilities; even 'laughing' sacrilege against him will be confronted, and not by Ujunwa, the one Nigerian author present – for Achebe transcends his national origins in his role as the progenitor of African literature.

The passage also draws attention to a relationship between performance and authorial personae. Just as if 'Isak Dinesen' were a well-known script, her comments about Kikuyu children can be acted out, the persona of 'the elite European writer' a role available for performance by anyone who happens to know the lines. Ujunwa, too, puts on a performance, mocking the notion that Conrad could be read as non-racist by demonstrating how *Heart of Darkness* would imagine her, as an African, to behave: '[jumping] up and down, babbling nonsense.' The juxtaposition of references to performance with references to writing and authorship suggests that, for Adichie, there is an element of performativity to African authorship, perhaps one also suggested when the Zimbabwean who criticized Achebe 'recanted, laughing, saying of course Achebe was sublime.' The phrase 'of course' suggests that the Zimbabwean, in making her initial comment about Achebe, recognizes that she has departed from a particular script, one to which she will now return, the script whose words demand the performance of reverence for

Achebe and for his position at the 'sublime' apex of the African literary world.

Later in the story, the Zimbabwean deviates from the script again, a deviation which exposes a set of limits and expectations imposed on African writers. Hers is the first story reviewed by the participants in the workshop, a story about an urban husband and wife who are simultaneously religious and superstitious, a narrative which strikes Ujunwa as very 'true.' Yet the workshop's organizer – the British Edward, who has secured the funds for the workshop, and who came by his 'love' of African literature during his Oxford days – critiques the story by saying that 'there was something terribly passé about it when one considered all the other things happening in Zimbabwe under the horrible Mugabe' (107). Ujunwa wonders, 'What did he mean by 'passé?' How could a story so true be passé?' (107). 'True' or not, Edward, and the Western publishing elites whom he represents, obviously expect the Zimbabwean to produce a text that clearly and mimetically represents atrocity; moreover, she is expected to represent the atrocities specifically associated with her national origins, an expectation emphasized by Adichie's choice of identifying all the writers (except for Ujunwa) solely by their nationalities. In a literary world delimited by a discourse of Achebe's famous enterprise, the enterprise of producing literature that takes direct, corrective action against injustice, an African writer is off-script if she performs the role of an artist who is not representing for the purpose of resisting.

'Jumping Monkey Hill,' then, exposes the manner in which Achebe's construction of a discourse of resistant literature is itself open to (re)re-appropriation; for Edward, African literature is only truly African if it reveals atrocity. When the Senegalese writer produces a story about the death of her girlfriend,

> Edward chewed at his pipe thoughtfully before he said that homosexual stories weren't reflective of Africa, really.
>   'Which Africa?' Ujunwa blurted out.
>   The black South African shifted on his seat. Edward chewed further at his pipe. Then he looked at Ujunwa in the way one would look at a child who refused to keep still in church and said that he wasn't speaking as an Oxford-trained Africanist, but as one who was keen on the real Africa and not the imposing of Western ideas on African writers. [...]
>   'This may indeed be the year 2000, but how African is it for a person to tell her family that she is homosexual?' Edward asked. (107)

A story by an African person that depicts African sexualities as varied and complex is deemed inauthentic, not by an African person, but by an 'expert' knower of Africa, one who defends 'real' African culture by pointing out how African same sex desire can only happen as the result of Euro-West influence.

By contrast, Edward heartily approves of the Tanzanian's story, which depicts 'the killings in the Congo' with 'prurient violence' (109). The incident with the Zimbabwean's short story so distresses Ujunwa that, for a time afterwards, she cannot write. By the end of the story, however, she has come to understand what it is that Edward wants to see – depictions of violence and chaos in Africa – so that when he criticizes her own story (about a young woman's experiences with sexual harassment as she hunts for a job in Lagos) on the hypocritical grounds that it has too obvious an 'agenda', and that it is 'implausible', she has no difficulty defending herself by explaining that, in fact, her story is a roman à clef, that all but one of the details in the story are true events from her own life (114).

The story ends with Ujunwa stalking tearfully, but with a grim pride, out of the writing group and back to her cabin. The final line of the story is: 'She was looking forward to calling her mother, and as she walked back to her cabin, she wondered whether this ending, in a story, would be considered plausible' (114). Ending the story in this manner has several effects: on one level, the self-reflexivity of the line (a line about the ending of a story that serves as the ending of a story), and the fact that it occurs in juxtaposition with a purportedly fictional short story that is in fact about true events, naturally raises questions about whether or not 'Jumping Monkey Hill' narrates some version of events Adichie herself experienced. On another level, though, the line draws attention to Edward's opinions about what is plausible and implausible, fitting and inappropriate, in African fiction.

In this respect, the story emphasizes not the fact that Ujunwa's story is a roman à clef, but rather the position of the African writer from whom only certain narratives are being solicited. Moreover, the line draws attention to the fact that it is not necessarily Africans who are regulating what is authentically African and what is not; the 'Oxford-trained Africanist', the evaluator whose expertise is authenticated by his self-professed 'keenness' for 'real Africa', is the one who makes the decisions about which African writing will be published, will receive awards. It is Edward, reading from an Achebian epistemic perspective, yet with insidious racism, who will make the Tanzanian's pruriently violent depiction of the Congo 'the lead story' in the next issue of the literary magazine (109). The Tanzanian understands very well, in fact, how it all works: he tells Ujunwa that 'Edward was connected and could find them a London agent; there was no need to antagonize the man, no need to close doors to opportunity' (113).

In this story about stories, then, the depiction of atrocity, far from having any political capacity to redress injustice, has become part of what troubles the African literary world. Achebe enters the story as the deified canonical figure whose famous representation of the atrocity against Umuofia informs how African writers perform their authorial personae. Yet, in the world of the story, Achebe's grand legacy has become a normative set of controls, laying out a limited range of possibilities for African writers, and serving as a kind of instruction manual for people like Edward, who gain from Achebe – especially from his extra-fictional statements – the mantle of benevolent expertise from within which they regulate African literary production.

This outcome seems especially perverse when one considers that Achebe's original goal involved depicting the richness and internal complexities of Igbo lives and culture; if Edward has his way, African writers take the place of Cary and Conrad, producing stereotypical, mono-dimensional 'images of Africa' rather than richly complex 'Achebian' stories. Therefore it is important to note that Adichie invokes Achebe not to critique him, but to expose the manner in which he can be and has been appropriated, not through any fault of his own, but because the discourse of the resistant-mimetic cloaks racist neo-imperialism when it seems benevolently to publish from an Achebian episteme.

Whereas Adichie invokes Achebe in 'Jumping Monkey Hill' in order to critique the discourse of mimetic realism by exposing how easily its representations of atrocity are – and have been – exploited in order to misrepresent 'the real,' her references to Achebe in 'The Headstrong Historian' help her to ask an even more fundamental question about representation in the postcolony. By isolating historical revision and separating it from fiction writing, the story foregrounds and vexes the assumption that post-independence recuperative rewriting constitutes an act of effective resistance. The story's ambivalent ending raises more questions than it answers, questions about just what kind of positive change such rewriting enacts.

'The Headstrong Historian' is something of a *kunstlerroman*, but it concerns the development of an historian rather than a writer. An omniscient third-person narrator relates Nwambga's life story, which presumably begins in the late 1800s or early 1900s, from her early life in the small village when she first falls in love with Obierika, to her struggles with fertility, to her difficult decision to send her only son to a missionary school so that he can learn and later use English to help his mother turn to the British district courts for assistance in a long-standing land dispute. Most of the story deals with Nwambga, but the final quarter turns to her grand-daughter, Grace, and quickly outlines, in broad strokes, the events in her life that cause Grace to become a historian, and to adopt the use of the Igbo name her grandmother gave her: Afamefuna.

Adichie borrows a prominent, memorable phrase from an Achebe novel in order to situate Afamefuna/Grace within a recognizable narrative: the story of the African intellectual who confronts cultural imperialism via a recuperative, revisionary interaction with a racist text. Within the story of her development as a thinker and as a writer, Afamefuna/Grace goes to a missionary-run school and reads a textbook with a chapter entitled 'The Pacification of the Primitive Tribes of Southern Nigeria' ('Headstrong' 215). We can compare this fictional chapter title from Adichie's short story to the final line of Achebe's *Things Fall Apart*. Achebe's line concerns the district commissioner, who, having '[driven] him [Okonkwo] to kill himself,' muses to himself that the Okonkwo incident might take up one paragraph in one chapter of his book: '[The district commissioner] had already chosen the title of the book, after much thought: *The Pacification of the Primitive Tribes of the Lower Niger*' (*TFA* 208-9). Thus the district commissioner's account dismissively reduces the grandeur of Okonkwo's tragedy to a mere paragraph, a sidelight to the central story of the commissioner's successful 'pacification'. In a slightly altered form, then, Achebe's district commissioner's degrading account of his time in Nigeria reappears as a metonym of the imperial record in Adichie's 'The Headstrong Historian.'

Adichie interweaves Achebe references into the narrative of Afamefuna/Grace's development as an intellectual and as a writer; paradoxically, these references to Achebe signal his absence from the fictional world of Adichie's story. *Personal*, direct experience and observation – rather than an experience of having read Achebe – motivates Afamefuna/Grace to become a historian; the story of a London-educated Nigerian who resigns a post 'in disgust' at the idea that African history might be added as a subject at an educational institution

> would cause [Grace] to make a clear link between education and dignity, between the hard, obvious things that are printed in books and the soft, subtle things that lodge themselves in the soul. It was Grace who would begin to rethink her schooling [....]. It was Grace who [...] would become haunted by the image of a destroyed village and would go to London and to Paris and to Onicha, sifting through moldy files in archives, reimagining the lives and smells of her grandmother's world, for the book she would write called *Pacifying with Bullets: A Reclaimed History of Southern Nigeria.* ('Headstrong' 217)

There is no indication that, in the world of the story, Achebe or his texts exist or have ever existed; Afamefuna/Grace experiences Okonkwo's story as it has been transmitted to her via the district commissioner's narrative, presented to her as part of her education. This in turn suggests that 'The Headstrong Historian' takes place in the same world as *Things Fall Apart*, a fictional world in which Achebe, as the author of the ur-text, cannot himself exist. Therefore Afamefuna/Grace's drive to become a historian emerges from stimuli other than an encounter with Achebe's novel's implicit call for a truer rendering of African history, and other than an encounter with Achebe's famous extra-fictional demands for such histories. By removing Achebe – his entire oeuvre, fiction and non-fiction – Adichie separates the intellectual, political 'goal' of *Things Fall Apart* – a truer rendering of history for purposes of positive political change – from the novel form, which in turn permits Adichie to study the goal in isolation.

By isolating the goal from its famous Achebian form, Adichie redistributes the responsibility for correcting the lies in the colonial record, and in other racist representations of Africa and Africans. The repetition of the phrase 'It was Grace who' (repeated ten times in two and a half pages) has several effects: on the one hand, it highlights the fact that Nwambga's son, Anikwena/Michael, has become part of a lost generation, torn irreconcilably between his family and the missionary education that has taught him to despise all things African; it will not be Anikwena/Michael who will contest what he is taught by the British missionaries through a reclamation of true history. Perhaps most importantly, the repetition of the phrase also emphasizes the absence of Achebe himself: the story suggests that, in a world without Achebe, it is Afamefuna/Grace, or someone like her, who recognizes the powerful injustices embedded in Western writing about Africa, and who takes up a pen to contest them. The repetition of the phrase implies that this impulse to correct and reclaim should not be understood to be something that Achebe created or that only he could – or would – innovate; the phrase's repetition emphasizes that even in an alternate reality, one that lacks Achebe, these lies would not go unchallenged. Adichie's story defrays some of Achebe's legend in order to proclaim faith in the African drive to know and to speak the truth: it is not only the great, canonical fiction writer who could and would take on this corrective task.

The layers of writing and rewriting, then, quickly imbricate within the story's narrative structure. On one level, Adichie signals Achebe by incorporating a version of the final line of his novel in the final short story in her collection; moreover, the story itself resonates with other connections to Achebian themes and plots, such as concerns about female fertility, decisions to send children to white-run missionary schools, and a recurrence of names such as Okonkwo and Obierika. At another level of allusion, Adichie takes up an Achebian concern about African self-perception and how the tendrils of cultural imperialism, making transit via the British/ missionary educational system, continue to put a kind of self-hating pressure on African intellectuals and on how they perceive their own histories.

On yet another level, after coming to an awareness of the injustices perpetrated via the slander of Africa in the British educational system – and, emphatically, the libel in its written texts: 'the hard, obvious things that are printed in books and the soft, subtle things that lodge themselves in the soul' – Afamefuna/Grace sets out to 'reclaim,' via rewriting, the misre(dis)membered history of her own people. She does so with an explicit allusion to a prior (and highly problematic) text: the chapter of a history textbook she read while in school, presented to her, with all its inaccuracies and racism, as a true account of her homeland and her people. Afamefuna/Grace's explicit, appropriative allusion thus calls attention to two others: to Adichie's allusion to Achebe (to her appropriation of his line), and to Achebe's well-known claim that he wrote *Things Fall Apart* as an antidote to the racist representations of Africans which he found in Western fiction about Africa.

Because of this accretion of rewritings, the story thus serves as a kind of literary thought experiment, a venue within which to consider the roles and effects of reading, writing, and recuperative rewriting; to think not only about Afamefuna/Grace's project of remembering, but also about Achebe's project in *Things Fall Apart*; and also, self-reflexively, to consider Adichie's own place as a writer who takes up a pen in a literary world profoundly imprinted by Achebe – his oeuvre and his extra-fictional statements about why he wrote his most famous work.

The story ends on an ambivalent note: despite having received 'faculty prizes,' having become recognized internationally as an expert 'about the Ijaw and Ibibio and Igbo and Efik peoples of Southern Nigeria,' despite being 'surrounded by her awards, her friends, her garden of peerless roses,' '[it] was Grace who, feeling an odd rootlessness in the later years of her life … would go to the courthouse in Lagos and officially change her first name from Grace to Afamefuna' (217-18). Despite her unquestionable professional success, despite the apparent international recognition of the truth of her work, and as a bodily contrast to the story's foregrounding of her 'headstrongness,' Afamefuna/Grace's story concludes with her sensation of 'an odd rootlessness.' None of the headstrong historian's writing can bring back what has been lost in the colonial encounter – the 'roots' that have been severed. Remembering history may be a worthy enterprise, but it cannot restore lost lives, lost generations – it cannot 're-member' the body, cannot put the strong 'head' back together with the lost 'roots'. There are limits, in this story, to what corrective rewriting can be expected to do; and, because the story is itself a metonym of *Things Fall Apart*, there is also an implicit critique of Achebe's canonical novel and its political efficacy – or, more precisely, a critique of the metanarrative that has sprung up around that novel and Achebe himself, the metanarrative of the literary text as the restorer of lost worlds.

Afamefuna/Grace demonstrates, via her inchoate, emotional acknowledgement of her writing's failure to restore lost roots – a failure to enact a certain kind of tangible change – what Rancière calls the 'gap at the heart of mimetic continuity,' a 'rupture of the harmony that enabled correspondence between the texture of the work and its efficacy' (*Spectator* 2009: 62).

Afamefuna/Grace's sense of 'an odd rootlessness,' following, as it does, her exposure of 'atrocity' in her history of Southern Nigeria, marks a hard boundary, an unbridgeable gap: representation, no matter its discipline or form, is not and can never be resuscitation. I do not mean that Afamefuna/Grace's work lacks meaning or importance; clearly her decision to change her name signals a powerful drive to reclaim an identity the colonizer would have preferred to erase. The 'odd rootlessness' at the end of the story subtly signifies not utter failure, but rather the absence of the most fully satisfying outcome – the restoration of lost roots that Afamefuna/Grace feels all the more strongly now that she knows in great detail how those roots came to be severed through a 'pacification with bullets'.

The self-reflexive quality of the story, with its echoes and echoes of allusive intertextuality, offers a different kind of hope, even as it refuses to proclaim a happy ending for the headstrong historian, nor for all those writers and rewriters who have seen themselves as activists, their texts material acts of resistance. If fiction cannot regrow lost roots, nor by exposing atrocity end it, Adichie's short story demonstrates that fiction can provide a powerful lens through which to view the roots, the garden, and the gardener. If signs cannot transparently and mimetically transmit to a universal audience the full 'reality' of lost worlds, they can still expose through the 'falseness' of fictional worlds truths about the processes and outcomes of the search for the historical 'real'.

Whereas 'The Headstrong Historian' self-reflexively isolates an intellectual goal from its original form in order to explore the goal itself, 'Jumping Monkey Hill' emphasizes form in order to query the limits – and possibilities – of fiction. The self-reflexivity of this story about a story means that when Ujunwa stalks away from what Edward and his cronies offer, temporarily she becomes transposed upon Adichie, and the possibility of alternate African literary worlds become visible. The very fact that Adichie's story exists, that we are reading it, and that it exposes Edward instead of acquiescing to his demands, demonstrates that there is a place for African literature beyond the limitations of stereotypes, even as the story implicitly calls for more such 'unlimited' places. 'The Headstrong Historian', too, offers its own hopeful possibility in the form of Afamefuna/Grace's name change: through her work, Afamefuna/Grace avoids her father's psychological dilemma of Anglophilic self-hatred, and instead finds joy, pride and a strong sense of self in her Igbo heritage.

Yet despite the fact that both stories offer glimpses of hope, neither produces the fullness or the closure of triumph. Afamefuna/Grace's 'odd sense of rootlessness' shadows her life's work, and Ujunwa's future – as a writer of non-stereotypical African stories – remains unclear. These short stories foreground problems rather than solutions; they hint at hopeful possibilities yet promise none, outlining the edges of discursive problems without offering a roadmap for their avoidance. Instead of offering themselves up as what Achebe calls 'a second handle on reality' to 'to help [people] in their struggle with life,' these stories self-reflexively question the role of writing as a utilitarian, political tool in the ongoing anti-colonial resistance effort, and simultaneously resist the call to behave as utilities.

Through the writing characters in her short fiction, Adichie troubles the narrative of African literature that informs the conditions within which African writers work, even as she performs her Achebian heritage in various extra-fictional scenarios. However, it is not true that the disjuncture between Adichie's fiction and her extra-fictional persona necessarily constitutes a paradox or some kind of hypocrisy. Instead I would argue that Adichie seems to have responded to a call for her to perform her role as Achebe's heir, and that, in doing so, she has also taken on the responsibility for examining and critiquing what that heritage entails. The disjuncture reveals that she is especially concerned with redefining and expanding the discursive boundaries of African literature. Her short fiction, I believe, tears down walls in order to open up new spaces for African literary production. Despite the fact that an Achebian conceptualization of mimesis contributes to the construction of these discursive boundaries, the act of attacking the limits on creativity seems to me a truly Achebian enterprise at heart: Achebe, after all, is a great imaginer of richly complex worlds, and a staunch proponent of African writing and writers. But if Adichie is his 'heir', she does not march unquestioningly in the footprints he has left.

NOTES

1 See Achebe's essay 'An Image of Africa: Racism in Conrad's *Heart of Darkness*,' published originally in 1977 in the *Massachusetts Review*, and now reprinted often, including in W.W. Norton's widely used scholarly edition of *Heart of Darkness*.

2 Chimamanda (chih-mah-MAHN-dah) Ngozi (nn-GOH-zee) Adichie (ah-DEE-chee-ay)

3 This narrative of African Literary history features prominently in two highly influential texts: Kwame Appiah's 'Is the Post- in Postmodernism the Post- in Post-colonial?' (*Critical Inquiry*, 1991), and Neil Lazarus' *Resistance in Postcolonial African Fiction* (Yale UP, 1990); it is also visible in a great deal of literary criticism before and since, and often invoked in discussions of Achebe's roles as canonical author and as editor of Heinemann's now-defunct African Writers Series.

4 Published first in 2006 in *Granta* and later in Adichie's 2009 short story collection *The Thing Around Your Neck*

5 Published first in the *New Yorker* in 2008, and also in *The Thing Around Your Neck*

6   The full text of Adichie's TED conference presentation, including a video recording of her talk, are available at the following URL: http://www.ted.com/talks/chimamanda_ adichie_the_danger_of_a_single_story.html

7   The full text of Adichie's op-ed is available at the following URL: http://www. nytimes.com/2004/11/29/ opinion/29adichie.html

8   There is some excellent criticism that ably demonstrates the ways in which Adichie seems to share many of Achebe's beliefs and ideas. A good example of this kind of critical work is Chima Anyadike's essay 'The Global North in Achebe's *Arrow of God* and Adichie's *Half of a Yellow Sun*' (*The Global South*, 2008). While I want to caution against reading Adichie uncritically as 'Achebe's heir', Anyadike's essay and others like it certainly offer compelling evidence that the two writers ascribe to similar beliefs, such as a figuration of 'global northernness'.

9   My work on Adichie's novels focuses on how she 're-distributes the sensible' in order to facilitate the possibility of alternative communities and subjectivities; in this essay I am more concerned with how Adichie's short stories problematize mimesis.

10 See James Currey's 'Chinua Achebe, the African Writers Series and the Establishment of African Literature' in *African Affairs* (2003) for an account of Achebe's role as editor of the series and as a prominent figure in African literary publishing.

WORKS CITED

Achebe, Chinua. 'An Image of Africa: Racism in Conrad's *Heart of Darkness*.' *Heart of Darkness: Authoritative Text, Backgrounds and Contexts, Criticism*. Ed. Paul B. Armstrong. 4th ed. New York: W.W. Norton & Co., 2006. 336-348.

—— *The Trouble with Nigeria*. Enugu, Nigeria: Fourth Dimension Publishers, 1983.

—— *Things Fall Apart*. 1958. New York: Anchor, 1994.

Adichie, Chimamanda Ngozi. 'The Line of No Return.' *NewYorkTimes.com*. The New York Times Company. 2004. Web, 10 Jun. 2011.

—— 'Jumping Monkey Hill.' *The Thing Around Your Neck*. New York: Alfred A. Knopf, 2009. 95-114.

—— 'The Headstrong Historian.' *The Thing Around Your Neck*. New York: Alfred A. Knopf, 2009. 198-218.

—— 'The Danger of a Single Story.' *Ted.com*. TEDGlobal. Oxford University, Oxford, UK. 23 Jul 2009. Web/Lecture. 10 Jun. 2011.

—— 'Introduction.' *The African Trilogy: Things Fall Apart; No Longer at Ease; Arrow of God*. New York: Everyman's Library (Alfred A. Knopf, Inc.) 2010. vii-xiv.

Anyadike, Chima. 'The Global North in Achebe's *Arrow of God* and Adichie's *Half of a Yellow Sun*.' *The Global South* 2.2 (2008): 10.

Appiah, Kwame Anthony. 'Is the Post- in Postmodernism the Post- in Postcolonial?' *Critical Inquiry* 17.2 (1991): 21.

Bryce, Jane. '"Half and Half Children": Third-Generation Women Writers and the New Nigerian Novel'. *Research in African Literatures* 39.2 (2008): 49-67.

Lazarus, Neil. *Resistance in Postcolonial African Fiction*. New Haven: Yale University Press, 1990.

Murray, Senan. 'The New Face of Nigerian Literature?' *BBC News*. Abuja: BBC, 2007. Web. 10 Jun. 2011.

Rancière, Jacques. *The Politics of Aesthetics: The Distribution of the Sensible*. Pbk. ed. London; New York: Continuum, 2006.

—— *The Emancipated Spectator*. Trans. Elliott, Gregory. London: Verso, 2009.

Rowell, Charles. 'An Interview with Chinua Achebe.' *Callaloo* 13.1 (1990): 15.

Writing Apartheid

Miriam Tlali's
Soweto Stories

MARY JANE ANDRONE

Miriam Tlali is a short story writer who shapes the genre to record voices from the Soweto community. In so doing her fictional forms emerge from the politics of apartheid, from the dialogue, debate, argument and rhetoric of the struggle. Her forms not only serve as a protest against the ways individual lives are deformed by the realities of the oppressive laws and restrictions but they emerge from that conflict and become vehicles expressing the injustices black South Africans faced daily. In describing the setting of her first novel, *Muriel at Metropolitan* (1975) Miriam Tlali claims the store is 'like a kind of stage where the whole of the South African scenario was being played out' (Jolly 1998: 144). In a sense, this allusion to the dramatic captures the essence of Tlali's writing where the use of dialogue and the recording of voices constitutes so much of the content of her novels, stories, interviews and journalism. The evolution of Tlali's forms reflects her decision to foreground voices in her texts from the first person *Muriel at Metropolitan* (republished in 2004 as *Between Two Worlds*, Tlali's original and preferred title) to *Amandla!* which draws heavily on various discourses – dialogue, debate, speeches and pamphlets – to *Mihloti* and *Soweto Stories*[1] which are interviews, first person journalistic accounts and stories Tlali bases on conversations with people who came to her with their experiences of township life. All these genres reflect Tlali's intention to write literature which conscientizes her readers through a realistic rendering of the ways apartheid deforms the lives of black Africans. Her use of voices and her ability to create unique genres which stay within the realist tradition, bring to mind Lewis Nkosi's discussion of 'Postmodernism and Black Writing in South Africa', where he states 'there is an unhealed split between black and white writing, between on the one hand an urgent need to document and bear witness and on the other the capacity to go on furlough, to loiter and to experiment' (Nkosi 1999: 75). While Tlali's texts clearly 'document and bear witness,' I would also argue that her use of voices in shaping new genres suggests that her writing is experimental and bears many of the hallmarks of postmodernism. In discussion with other *Staffrider* colleagues, Tlali makes this statement on the writer's need to experiment:

> [I]n exercising his creative vision [the writer] should be free to acquire his knowledge, not only to imitate, but to divert or dissent from accepted tradition. His way should be open to unknown spheres, and set the pace of advancement. That is what I believe creativity is. We must continue to explore and never forget our main task of being engaged in a psychological battle for the minds of the people.
> (*Ten Years of Staffrider* 306)

In allowing her characters to tell their own stories, Tlali's narrators disappear or recede so there is a minimum of authorial intervention – a trait Njabulo Ndebele (1994: 20) sees as a hallmark of African storytelling tradition. In drawing deliberately on the oral traditions in township life and including heterogeneous elements – African phrases, folktales, proverbs – she invents genres which include both realistic and postmodernist elements. As Cherry Clayton observes in commenting on *Soweto Stories*, 'Such manipulations of Western genres set up their own ironies. She adapts the more impersonal Western interview to the township situation of dialogue, laughter and interruptions making it resemble a play script' (Clayton 1990: 129). The sources for Tlali's forms, then, emerge from African contexts, including not only the African storytelling Ndebele alludes to, but also township drama, political debate and oratory and the intimate conversations and lively exchange which is carried on privately and publicly. Tlali's genres have their roots in the historical struggle itself which created a space for voices to be heard and which offered disparate discourses and opposing points of view. In this sense Tlali's heterogeneous forms parallel postmodern genres without the emphasis on indeterminacy of meaning which, as Nkosi (81) argues, is an inappropriate goal for literature which is written to seek deliberate political change.

Another distinctive aspect of Tlali's stories in both *Mihloti* and *Soweto Stories* is the way she foregrounds women's experiences; while deconstructing patriarchy, she also offers a detailed rendering of women's agency which defies the political and gender constraints that circumscribe their lives. The empowering strategies many of Tlali's African women invent confirms Maria Lugones' assertion that 'through travelling to other people's 'worlds' we discover that there are 'worlds' in which those who are the victims of arrogant perceptions are really subjects, lively beings, resistors, constructors of vision ... (Lugones 1990: 150). And Tlali's Soweto is a functional community where despite the unjust circumstances apartheid imposes, the Africans who live there are lively subjects who actively resist the system.

My purpose in addressing these works is to see them not only as powerful first hand testimonials on apartheid but also as stories which go beyond historical, political moments and locations and connect Tlali's vision with other women internationally who also witness the political events of their countries and subvert them by presenting the voices of particular women situated with-in oppressive circumstances. Chandra Mohanty sees the 'inter-national links between women's political struggles' as essential if women are to gain solidarity globally and argues that 'the links, the relationships between the local and the global' should be foregrounded across cultures (Mohanty 1995: 260). Caren Kaplan defines 'transnational feminism' as a critical practice insuring the preservation of the particularities of individual women's positions as well as allowing them to see 'beyond national and ethnic borders' to find intersections and common ground with other feminist voices. This is useful in approaching Tlali's works since it is a framework that includes Tlali's political agenda alongside her rendering of women's voices (Kaplan 1992: 119). Both Caren Kaplan and Kenneth Harrow (1993) discuss women's testimonials as 'outlaw genres' or 'resistance literature' which through their emphasis on 'collective' achievement subvert the status quo because they destabilize the societal conditions which promote notions of individual achievement.

Mihloti (Tears), Tlali's heterogeneous 1984 collection includes testimony, travelogue, interviews and fiction. Some of these pieces were published earlier in *Staffrider*, the African journal devoted to black writing, and reveal Tlali's move away from the realist mode of *Muriel at Metropolitan* and *Amandla!* as well as continuing her political emphasis.

In 'Detour into Detention' Tlali details a horrific event which happens to her and ninety-two other people travelling to Steve Biko's funeral. As she unfolds the action surrounding her, the reader detects the hallmarks of a fiction writer. The carefully modulated tone, the telling descriptions of the actions and behaviour of the police and their victims and the final triumph of the prisoners' voices exchanging the lines of a hymn, testify to the vision and talent of the fiction writer. It is unlikely that the South African police who unjustly arrested ninety-two Africans on 24 September 1977 waiting to be bussed to Steve Biko's funeral in King Williams Town even imagined that a black African woman writer was among them or that one of the women beaten by the police that day would be Desmond Tutu's wife. Tlali's first hand witnessing of these events as she records them in 'Detour into Detention' is a powerful testimonial on all of the ways blacks were routinely abused under apartheid. She witnesses a near rape on the van transporting them to Meadowlands Prison, intervenes to help a young woman suffering a devastating beating and recounts the inhumane conditions within the prison itself – the bad food, cramped conditions and insistent harassment from jailers. Tlali's tone in this initial article in *Mihloti* is not resigned or detached but it is not an overtly angry piece of political rhetoric either. She describes the scene in the police station:

> All around were movements of arms towards parts which had been hurt. Hands were holding pieces of tissues, handkerchiefs, torn pieces of clothing, gaping wounds on eyes, foreheads, skulls, necks, ears – everywhere the human body can be struck. There was blood everywhere – on our clothes, shoes, some dripping on to the floor. (*Mihloti* 1984:14)

In striking a balance between an accurate reporting of atrocities and celebrating the bonds between prisoners which culminate in their holding their own funeral for Biko as it is being played on television in the guards' quarters, Tlali manages to memorialize this collective experience as both an occasion for 'tears' and as a significant act of resistance which testifies to the solidarity of the women and men so unjustly detained on that day. As they overhear the broadcast of the actual funeral, the women sing hymns and freedom songs and offer their own testimonials:

> As if by some telepathic transmission, when the voices of the detained females rose towards the blue skies above, singing the hymn: '*Senzeni na; Senzeni na?* (What have we done, What have we done?) The same hymn was repeated simultaneously on the other side by male detainees. (*Mihloti* 38)

This moment of resistance and solidarity becomes the victory none of the arrestees had expected.

Tlali's journalistic pieces which record voices and witness events are important predecessors to the development of her stories since they determine the shape of the fiction in *Soweto Stories*. In speaking about her role as a writer Tlali refers to herself as a 'a cultural worker' and sees her writing as 'guided by the moral power of her community' (Lenta 1992: 109). 'Detour Into Detention' is Tlali's witnessing of a remarkable event, but it is not an account of her individual struggle on this occasion as much as it is a record and a celebration of the collective experience of all those who were there with her. In her article, 'Not Just A Personal Story': Women's *Testimonios* and the Plural Self,' Doris Sommer articulates the political motivation behind the collective persona of Latin American women's testimonies:

> [T]hese intensely lived testimonial narratives are strikingly impersonal. They are written neither for individual growth nor for glory but are offered through the scribe to a broad public as one part of a general strategy to win political ground (Sommer 1988: 109).

Tlali's account has a similar political motive. It is written to expose apartheid, to record the way in which this experience united those ninety-two people who were detained and confirmed them in their opposition to the practice of unjustified arrests. The day after the funeral they were released and left there singing freedom songs, resolving to refuse to pay whatever fines the government might levy.

In the opposed vignettes in *Mihloti*, 'Leah Koae' and 'Lilian Ngoyi,' Tlali contrasts two women, both part of the resistance, both agents in promoting social and political change. Again she serves as a scribe allowing each woman to speak for herself and to define her life in her own words. Leah Koae, a township mother and dressmaker, is an active agent in restricted circumstances. She reveals an amazing array of business and technical skills as she talks with her daughter, Miriam Tlali, and another friend around her kitchen table laughing over customers, discussing pattern making, evaluating fabrics and equipment and strategizing about economic and professional survival. Tlali's interview with Leah Koae in *Mihloti* illustrates how a woman who is a 'resistor' and a 'subject' is able to flourish despite the reality of political oppression and her story exemplifies how township discourse shapes the genre. Here Leah, her friend Freda, and Miriam Tlali talk about everything from millinery techniques and sewing equipment to business practices and the negative effects of apartheid on black township enterprises. The conversation is interspersed with humorous remarks on Leah's oversized customers, current township plays, customers who never pay, and Leah's vision of a future sewing school she hopes to open. This conversation with its interruptions and frequent laughter brings to mind observations Paule Marshall makes when she identifies the source of her creativity as the 'Poets in the Kitchen' recalling her West Indian mother and her friends talking in the kitchen 'endlessly, poetically, and with impressive range' (Marshall 1997). When Marshall describes this talk as 'highly functional' because 'it restored them to a sense of themselves,' 'served as an outlet for the tremendous creative energy they possessed,' and a 'refuge from the vast complexity and power of America,' she identifies some of the ways Tlali also sees women's discourse in private settings. Although there is plenty of complaint and dissatisfaction with the restrictions township life imposes, in this lively banter Leah Koae's 'art' thrives and her sense of humour and involvement in community life suggest her resilience and resourcefulness.

Tlali's tribute to Lillian Ngoyi, who led 30,000 women to march on Praetoria's Union Buildings and later served as President of the ANC's Women's League is also recorded in Ngoyi's own words. If Tlali serves as a scribe for Leah Koae, here she literally recalls Lillian Ngoyi's oral narrative to her shortly before Ngoyi's death, detailing her memories of the radical issues women fought for and debated at the 1955 Conference on Women in Switzerland. Although she never states it explicitly, the ideology underlying Tlali's narrative forms in both *Mihloti* and *Soweto Stories* is that the struggle is a collective one. Individual women contribute in their own ways – through their roles as workers, public leaders, friends, and mothers – but that it is only through collective effort that the struggle goes on.

Tlali's role as a journalist and the interviews she conducted is an important stage in her development as a fiction writer and her works in *Soweto Stories* reflect her practice of listening to and recording actual voices. Again, whether in private settings or public arenas, Tlali's stories emerge from the historic struggle and are shaped by the exchange of ideas and the expression of emotion that apartheid inevitably elicited.

Tlali takes these anecdotes, incidents, memories and conversations and shapes them into the mosaic of tales which comprise *Soweto Stories*, a fictional commemoration of a dark era.

Tlali's use of conversation, discussion and argument recurs throughout *Soweto Stories* where political and personal debate, consolatory exchanges and public chants and songs constitute so much of the action. Michael Vaughan and Margaret Daymond both discuss the dialogic potential of conversation. Vaughan sees conversation as 'a medium of counsel, a critical interchange at a spontaneous level' and therefore a form which has the ability to 'incorporate experiences and perspectives that are divergent and contradictory' (*Staffrider* 315). Daymond claims 'Tlali's stories are dialogic in two senses: they absorb social conflict into themselves by recording the many ways in which people actually talk about their lives; they are often told in a structured exchange of voices that is disruptive of the status quo' (Daymond 1996: 234). This disruption is particularly apparent in 'Metamorphosis' which records the conscientization of a young African man Velani who struggles to resolve the competing directives of his wife Mavis who insists that 'we are all black . . . we are all oppressed. An attack on one must be an attack on all' (*Soweto Stories* 79) and his uncle who has changed his African name from Mbuti Mkhabela to Boetie McCabel and passes for coloured in Eldorado Park outside of Soweto who urges him to flee saying, 'Soweto is a jungle. I don't know what you want there. You should come to Eldorado Park. We coloreds here are safe' (*Soweto Stories* 96). Throughout the story Tlali juxtaposes African phrases and township vernacular with the standard English of the narrator and Velani, her central character. The interplay of voices, languages and slang suggests the ways in which the struggle requires the coming together of people of various classes, levels of consciousness and political energy. In this sense Tlali's use of a range of voices and opinions achieves clarity and offers a definite political stance which is unlike the effects of postmodernist forms which relish indeterminacy and multiple possibilities for meaning. Unity is difficult but 'Metamorphosis' argues for the unanimity of the people and for the need for collective action despite the complexity of the township communities. Effective action in this story, as in so many of Tlali's works, comes from the whistles, the private arguments and the organization of determined women who have a clear sense of mission.

'Travelling,' 'land' and 'bodies', particularly women's bodies, are the tropes that unite the ten works which comprise *Soweto*

Stories. Through these motifs Tlali reveals the ways in which gender and apartheid work together to constrict women's lives and demonstrates how all black Africans are controlled when their land is taken and their bodies exploited. In nearly all these stories people are en route – they are travelling by train, bus, car or on foot – or they are sitting in train or bus stations, police headquarters or in other public places waiting for transportation. The sources for many of these vignettes of Soweto life came from interviewing women, recording their stories and converting them into fiction. Published in 1989, *Soweto Stories* reflects the influence of Tlali's forms in the earlier *Mihloti*, for, although they are fiction, the stories bear the imprint of Tlali's interest in documenting and bearing witness in the sense that they are first-hand observations that come from the 'testimony' of the people. What they all reveal is the profound dislocation apartheid imposes on black Africans living in Soweto townships and the precise ways in which women, in particular, must devise elaborate strategies to negotiate the complicated terrain in going about the most routine aspects of their lives. Deprived of homes, forced into public spaces and controlled by laws requiring passbooks, travel documents and permits, the effort required to travel to jobs, visit relatives in another township or to cross borders, these characters constantly calculate times, check documents, worry about vagrancy laws, anticipate unfriendly officials and negotiate crowds. In an extreme illustration of the way the difficulty of travel emblemizes the position of blacks under apartheid, a disabled old woman, Jessie, complains to her husband that he must hire a wheelbarrow to take her to the superintendent's office every two months in order to collect her pension money.

One devastating example of how little land black Africans may occupy comes in 'Point of No Return,' a story about the 1950's, as a young man justifies his political resistance to his wife by telling her that the 'turning point' in his political commitment came on the day a white supervisor jeered at the new house his family had just built in area soon to be restricted and tells his father 'You should have built it on wheels!' (*Soweto Stories* 132). In 'Dimomona' Tlali goes back to Sophiatown in 1932 to suggest the way in which the present injustices can be traced back in South African history. In this story a young man Boitumelo loses his job and is imprisoned for four months as he is arrested in his own latrine for not having his passbook on him. While he is away his pregnant wife gives birth to twin boys, a joy that is quickly eclipsed by his release from prison, the loss of his job and the couple being forced out of Sophiatown and back to Loskop because he no longer has a pass. Tlali's depiction of this injustice suggests that the control of land and the impossibility of having any freedom of movement in Soweto in the 1980s is a direct consequence of a deliberate colonial policy that shifts into the imperialistic and racist regime which has systematically taken land from black Africans, exploited their labor and thrown them away when they are no longer productive. S'bongile in 'Point of No Return' explains how colonial rulers removed 'the black spots' as white South Africans moved to gain more land, more control, and more capital. As an old woman bitterly states in 'Go in Peace Tobias, Son of Opperman':

> People who have been used and discarded; forgotten by the glittering world of gold sixteen miles away . . . We have helped to build their skyscrapers and now we are only fit for the rubbish heap. (*Soweto Stories* 75)

However, if no one is in possession of much space in these works, women and girls struggle to own their own bodies. Three of these stories record instances of women's resistance to molestation and rape in both public and private spaces. Christina Cullhed has argued that Tlali employs narrative strategies she designates 'whispering' and 'distancing' in representing 'gendered violence' in her fiction. Cullhed defines these strategies as Tlali's 'muting the criticism of the perpetrators of gendered violence' or 'dis/placing gendered violence on the margins of the community' (Cullhed 2006: 6). While it is true that the perpetrators of harassment, violence and attempted rape in Tlali's fiction remain nameless, I would argue that she does not 'mute' her portrayal of the way African patriarchy oppresses women on a daily basis. As Tlali's narrator comments on the particular difficulties for women, 'One had to be strong to face the daily hazards in the trains of Soweto' (*Soweto Stories* 35). An unnamed girl in 'Devil at a Dead End' contrives to get a second class ticket in order to sit down for the long journey to Johannesburg, only to face a near rape by a white guard when she is alone in her own compartment. Warned by an older woman, though, who has just disembarked she has the presence of mind to preserve herself at the critical moment by announcing that she has venereal disease. Other stories record instances of women sharing confessions of enduring molestation on impossibly crowded trains or being propositioned by husbands who assume the bodies of their wives' friends are theirs for the taking.

In Tlali's story 'Fud-u-u-a!' she portrays the indignities women endure travelling on trains where they not only struggle to find a spot to stand where they will not be crushed, but must also resist the men who take advantage of the crowded conditions and molest them. Fud-u-u-a as Tlali explains in a footnote is the chant women shout as they 'wiggle their bottoms in order to make a space for themselves' (*Soweto Stories* 27). Nkele, in this story, looks forward to meeting her friend Ntombi and thinks, 'There is nothing like the knowledge that the help of another woman is available to you when you need it, when the going gets tough, as the saying goes' (*Soweto Stories* 30-31). The cruel reality Nkele testifies to in this story unveils the circumstances where commuting women do not only have to endure the herding of the 'white dogs', the sadistic white police, but also the sexual groping of African men who take advantage of the crowded conditions to abuse them. Their travelling companion Mashadi retells her 'nasty experience on the 0-Five' where like so many other women she was groped and assaulted by male passengers. As the women listen sympathetically Tlali's narrator, Nkele, comments:

> This very sad sensitive subject, sparked off by Mashadi's dilemma, was not merely an isolated case. It was a painful harrowing experience, always related in bated breath by helpless misused and derogated bitter women of all ages. (*Soweto Stories* 35)

Again, though, women find solidarity with other women 'giving each other all the moral support women in need of help *ought* to give each other' (*Soweto Stories* 29-30). Ironically the hymn the women sing collectively on this day to demonstrate their solidarity shields the cries of Nkele as she screams 'that someone was busy massaging my thighs and backside trying to probe my private parts and nobody was paying attention' (*Soweto Stories* 41).

But it is not only women's bodies which are abused. Many males suffer the indignities of incarceration and the consequent illnesses and loss of physical power. Dimomona's husband's boss fires him because he is too weak to work after his imprisonment: 'I'll have to sign you off and you'll have to go back to the farms. You'll never be able to pedal the bicycle again' (*Soweto Stories* 64). Although Tlali records the oppression of men as well as women in *Soweto Stories*, she does not ignore the ways in which women suffer from the twin scourges of apartheid and African patriarchy. In 'M'ma Lithoto' a young mother, Paballo, is forced out on the street with her son Zwandie and her niece Mahali when she quarrels with her husband since the house they live in is solely his property. The structure of this story is a dialogue between Paballo and Mahali whom she believes she has to 'educate' on where to go so that 'one day when you cannot find happiness and success in your matters, you know where to 'turn to' (*Soweto Stories* 14). Interspersed with this dialogue are Paballo's private meditations on her own dilemma of how to resolve her tensions with her husband and in-laws, and the story concludes with Paballo's return home failing to find refuge or help from male relatives since 'all her uncles were now too ill or old to deal effectively with Musi's people' (*Soweto Stories* 23). The story ends in irony with her in-laws relief when she returns – 'Thank God they are back. Where would we get all that money to pay another fine? Another ox!' (*Soweto Stories* 26). Paballo's bitter-sweet defeat is acknowledged in Tlali's denouement where the narrator comments that four and a half months later Paballo gives birth to a baby girl her husband's family names 'Mm'a-lithoto mother of bundles' yet another of Paballo's 'bundles of joy' (*Soweto Stories* 26). And all the women in domestic situations shoulder enormous work loads because of traditional notions of men's roles. Tlali does not lament the loss of the traditional structures that ensured that women would be protected and represented by male members of their families. The society here is in transition, but her wish is to subvert both apartheid and patriarchy.

Yet what is more significant than the particular oppressions these stories graphically demonstrate through Tlali's motif of the difficulty of travel and movement, the exploitation of women's bodies, and the appropriation of land, is the vision of survival and the depiction of how women live in the interstices of an unjust political, economic system. Throughout these stories, women support each other, tell stories protect and intervene on each other's behalf, join together to act politically and envision their eventual liberation. In 'Gone Are Those Days,' a story Tlali represents as related to her by 'Aunt Lizzy, a former shebeen queen,' a family is being held in police headquarters after being arrested for holding a funeral for a relative. As Tlali describes it, 'Aunt Liz was sitting there looking haggard and worried. Yet she was trying to console me, speaking about the good old days of Sophiatown' (*Soweto Stories* 97). Lizzy's final tale is her recollection of a dream she had where a procession of shebeen queens march into the company of white officials:

But as we filed in solemnly, each one of us had our hands tucked inside our aprons. We were all ready with different kinds of detergents and poisonous disinfectants. . . .Doom, Target, Surf, Persil, Punch, Rattex, Fumitabs, all of them ... All of us cooks took turns to empty the poisons into the big pots which were ready – full of gravies and soups. It was a well-planned conspiracy. (*Soweto Stories* 100)

Although as, Lauretta Ngcobo comments in her introduction to *Soweto Stories*, Tlali focuses on the 'wounds sustained in the collapse of our societies' she also records the gains made through solidarity and describes brief, triumphant moments (Ngcobo xvii).

Lamenting the ways in which post-colonial and post-modern theories cannot accommodate the literature of 'feminists of color' Carol Boyce Davies argues that these subjects have been 'speaking outside the post-colonial':

The women who are absent or have disappeared from the formulations of post-coloniality are doing something totally different. They participate as pieces in a growing collage of uprising textualities. Their works exist more in the realm of the 'elsewhere' of diasporic imaginings than the precisely locatable. Much of it is therefore oriented to articulating presences and histories across a variety of boundaries imposed by colonizers, but also by the man, the elders and other authority figures in their various societies. (Davies 1994: 88)

Davies' metaphor of 'a collage of uprising textualities' is useful in considering Tlali's writing because it accounts for her political agenda in narrating apartheid and connects her with feminists of colour globally writing texts which resist their cultures and articulate their presences and their histories. Placed along side of the *testimonios* of Latin American women, the autobiographies and autobiographical fiction of other South African writers like Lauretta Ngcobo and Sindiwe Magona, or Tsi Tsi Dangarembga in Zimbabwe and Bessie Head in Botswana, earlier slave narratives from the United States and prison narratives from women all over the world, Tlali's writing asserts the presence of black women experiencing apartheid in Soweto in the 1980's and during the colonial years. Like many other women writing in oppressive circumstances, she contributes to the project Davies sees as so essential not only in resisting injustice, but also in operating outside 'the conventions and constructions of dominance' (Davies 89). This 'elsewhere' Davies identifies offers a space where the visions of feminists of colour globally can be seen individually, but also in relation to each other, hence constituting a body of work which she sees as signifying 'resistance, reassertion, renewal and rethinking' (Davies 108). Davies' analysis parallels Caren Kaplan's conception of 'transnational feminism' in the sense that they both see the importance of finding 'intersections' and common ground with other feminists as a means of creating an alternative context for women's resistance literature or 'uprising textualities' as Davies puts it. Seen in this broader context, then, Tlali's *apartheid* writing is not just the anomaly of a single black African woman telling Soweto's stories, but one voice among many all over the world 'resisting' injustice and insisting on that 'renewal' that will empower the victims of this particular oppression.

So many aspects of her situation as a writer problematize approaches to Tlali's work: her migrations to America, the Netherlands, and elsewhere in the international community; the fact that her works were first censored and then banned shortly after publication; the phenomenon of having an international readership for works which detailed the particularities of apartheid in South Africa; the pressures which define her feminism because of the larger political agenda she addresses; and, not least, her myriad voices and modes as she shifts from dense realist prose to first person journalistic accounts witnessing arrests, incarcerations and the everyday brutality blacks endured living in South Africa in the 1970s and 1980s. In other words, the conditions of writing and publishing contemporary writers might assume were not available to Tlali because she was black, overworked, short of resources and not encouraged as a writer.

One might wonder whether Tlali's writing about apartheid has relevance for a post-apartheid South Africa as anything more than a reminder of injustices overcome. But although the laws which restricted the freedom of black Africans are now gone, the essential economic injustices remain. As Bill Keller writes in a recent *New York Times* editorial, 'South Africa Since Mandela':

In the 18 years since coming to power the ANC government has created a substantial middle class (more in the public sector than the private) and a smaller, conspicuous cadre of black privilege. But it has not – perhaps could not have – significantly narrowed the gulf between the shack dwelling underclass and everyone else. Inequality breeds serious resentment, violent protests over undelivered services, strikes, fatalism. (*New York Times*, 16 December 2012)

It is hard, then, not to read Tlali's stories, published in the 1970s and 1980s, in terms of those 'inequalities' which are historically rooted in apartheid South Africa and which persist into the present day.

NOTES

1 *Soweto Stories* which was originally published by Pandora Press in England. (1989) was re-published as *Footprints in the Quag* by David Philip in a 1989 South African edition.

WORKS CITED

Clayton, Cherry. 'Radical Transformations: Emergent Women's Voices in South Africa.' *English in Africa* (October, 1990): 25-36.

Cullhed, Christina. *Grappling With Patriarchies: Narrative Strategies of Resistance in Miriam Tlali's Writings.* Uppsala, Sweden: Uppsala University Press, 2006.

Davies, Carole Boyce. *Black Women, Writing and Identity: Migrations of the Subject.* London: Routledge, 1994.

Daymond, Margaret. 'Inventing Gendered Traditions.' *South African Feminisms.* ed. M.J. Daymond. New York and London: Garland, 1996.

Harrow, Kenneth. *Threshholds of Change in African Literature: The Emergence of a Tradition.* London and Portsmouth, N. H.: James Curry and Heinemann, 1993.

Jolly, Rosemary. 'Interview with Miriam Tlali.' *Writing South Africa: Literature, Apartheid and Democracy, 1970-1995.* eds, Derek Attridge and Rosemary Jolly Cambridge, England: Cambridge University Press, 1998.

Kaplan, Caren. 'Resisting Autobiography: Outlaw Genres and Transnational Feminist Subjects.' *De-Colonizing the Subject: The Politics of Gender in Women's Autobiography.* eds, Sidonie Smith and Julia Watson. Minneapolis: University of Minnesota Press, 1992.

Keller, Bill. *New York Times*, 16 December, 2012.

Lenta, Margaret. 'Two Women and Their Territories: Sheila Roberts and Miriam Tlali.' *Tulsa Studies in Women's Literature.* Vol 11, No. 1 (Spring, 1992) pp. 103-111.

Lugones, Maria. 'Playfulness, World-Travelling, and Loving Perception.' *Haciendo Caras/ Making Face, Making Soul.* ed. Gloria Anzaldua. San Francisco: Aunt Lute, 1990.

Marshall, Paule. 'The Making of A Writer: From the Poets in the Kitchen.' *The Norton Anthology of African American Literature.* eds, Henry Louis Gates and Nellie Y. McKay. New York: Norton, 1997.

Mohanty, Chandra. 'Under Western Eyes: Feminist Scholarship and Colonial Discourses.' *The Post-Colonial Studies Reader.* eds, Bill Ashcroft, Gareth Griffiths and Helen Tiffin. London and New York: Routledge,1995.

Ndebele, Njabulo. *South African Literature and Culture: Rediscovery of the Ordinary.* Manchester: Manchester University Press, 1994.

Ngcobo, Lauretta. 'Introduction.' *Soweto Stories.* London: Pandora Press, 1989.

Nkosi, Lewis. 'Postmodernism and Black Writing in South Africa.' *Writing South Africa,* eds, Derek Attridge and Rosemary Jolly. Cambridge, England: Cambridge University Press, 1998.

Serote, Jake. 'Black Writers in South Africa: An Interview with Miriam Tlali, Sipho Sepamla and Mothobi Mutloase.' *Ten Years of Staffrider Magazine: 1978-1998.* eds,

Andries Oliphant and Ivan Vladislavic. Johannesburg: Ravan, 1998.

Sommer, Doris. 'Not Just A Personal Story': Women's *Testimonios* and the Plural Self' *Life/Lines: Theorizing Women's Autobiography.* eds, Bella Brodzki and Celeste Schenk. Ithaca and London: Cornell University Press, 1988.

Tlali, Miriam. *Mihloti.* Johannesburg: Skotaville Press, 1984.

—— *Muriel At Metropolitan.* New York and London: Longman, 1987.

—— *Soweto Stories.* London: Pandora Press, 1989.

Vaughan, Michael. 'Can the Writer Become the Storyteller? A Critique of the Stories of Mtutuzeli Matshoba.' *Ten Years of Staffrider Magazine: 1978-1988.* eds, Andries Oliphant and Ivan Vladislavic. Johannesburg: Ravan, 1988.

Articulations of Home & Muslim Identity in the Short Stories of Leila Aboulela

LINDSEY ZANCHETTIN

Sudanese writer and Caine Prize recipient Leila Aboulela writes prose that captures and then lingers on experiences of migration. Homesickness pervades her writing, inviting us to consider what constitutes a home and what one will do to return there, even if only through scent and sound. In Aboulela's own words: 'I write about what I find moving and disturbing. Culture-shock or how, again and again, the carpet gets pulled from under our feet.'[1] In her short stories 'The Ostrich' (1997), 'The Museum' (2000), and 'Missing Out' (2010), Aboulela makes familiar and demystifies the experiences of Muslim women as they migrate from Sudan to the UK. In fact such, she produces similar work to fellow post-nationalist writers.[2] In her short stories, she lifts the limitations on writing in and about the nation state by globalizing the African experience, while at the same time individualizing it. Aboulela's characters long for highly personalized and intimately constructed notions of home. Her stories reflect the general path on which the African short story writer is moving, reaching toward an expression of the African experience that is plural rather than singular, familiar rather than exotic and other, relevant and central rather than token and peripheral. This essay examines the ways in which Aboulela's female Muslim characters articulate their notions of faith and home as a liberating practice, and, as a result, how Aboulela participates in a new iteration of the African short story.

In 1985, Chinua Achebe collected and edited *African Short Stories* as 'an introduction into the art and the world of African fiction' (viii). By imagining the African short story as a preface to the African novel, Achebe challenges assertions that the form of the short story is somehow more African, more heavily rooted in oral tradition. Rather, he argues that 'both novel and short story in

Africa have undoubtedly drawn from a common oral heritage' (vii). With the emergence of the Caine Prize for African Writing in 2000, the African short story became more accessible to scholars across the globe. The prize sparked a surge of interest in this unique literary form and many of its winners, including Aboulela, have gone on to write extraordinary novels that treat the same topics broached in their short stories, illuminating the intersections of the African novel and short story to which Achebe was alluding back in the 1980s. The prize has also paved the way for more academic consideration of African women writers, Aboulela most certainly among them. In 2011, Caine Prize recipient and Nigerian writer Helon Habila collected and edited *The Granta Book of the African Short Story*, expressing his dismay that the African short story is often relegated to second-place consideration by scholars, the academic focus and praise almost always on the novel. The reality, as it seems it must be said today, is that the African short story offers readers a rich and ever-expanding tableau that captures concepts of home, gender issues, identity formation, power relations, articulations of sexuality, and iterations of both patriotism and expatriatism, to name just a few. In essence, like most literature, the African short story offers us a portrait of humanity and should therefore be approached with the same academic rigor as afforded the novel.

In her 1999 anthology of African women writers, Zimbabwean author Yvonne Vera proclaimed, 'A woman writer must have an imagination that is plain stubborn, that can invent new gods and banish ineffectual ones' (*Opening Spaces*, 1). Aboulela is able to banish the ineffectual myth of the oppressed Muslim woman by illuminating and personalizing her experience abroad, an experience that draws her closer to her religious practice and the place she calls home. Aboulela's stories serve as beneficent fiction, because, as Achebe argues, 'we not only see; we *suffer* alongside the hero,' closing the gap between our imaginings of those who may not be like us culturally or religiously and those who are so very like us emotionally and spiritually, these two groups often turning out to be one and the same ('The Truth of Fiction,' 111). This is Aboulela's achievement. In a reflection about her own experiences missing home, she remarks, 'At twilight I looked across the Nile and saw the ferry dock at the island of Tuti. Sky, river, green fields, men in white jellabas, women in coloured tobes and it was like a painting. I had been right to cry over this, I was right to miss this' ('Fork in the Road'). Aboulela gives her characters – and, by extension, her readers – permission to ache for a place of familiarity and comfort, even if that place exists within a space that is otherwise undesirable.

The earliest of the three stories considered here, 'The Ostrich' follows pregnant Sumra accompanying her husband Majdy back to London to continue his doctoral studies. On the plane from Khartoum to Cairo, she meets the Ostrich, a man from her past at university in Sudan. Their encounter on the plane serves as a catalyst for an extended bout of nostalgia that comprises a majority of the narrative. 'The Museum', for which Aboulela won the Caine Prize, follows Shadia's experience studying abroad in Scotland and her relationship with a Scottish man, Bryan, who accompanies her to an ill-conceived museum about Africa. 'Missing Out' borrows the characters, Majdy and Samra, from 'The Ostrich' and depicts their move to London for Majdy's studies. Samra, like the character of Sumra in 'The Ostrich,' desires to return to Khartoum where life is familiar and comfortable.

All the women featured are devout Muslims from Sudan who find more freedom to express their femininity at home than in the West and Aboulela's stories are subversive in that they challenge Western media portrayals of the Muslim woman as involuntarily chained and bonded to her religion and the men of her culture. Aboulela, following the same vein as many fellow third generation African writers, discredits Western portrayals of Africa as solely a place of poverty and corruption. For Aboulela's characters, Khartoum is a place of joyful memories, romantic encounters, and safe practice of Islam. As Sumra sardonically claims about Arab women in London, 'Oppressed, that's what people would think of them. Here they respect women, treat them as equal, we must be the same he says' ('The Ostrich', 3). But treating Sumra as 'equal' in London means Majdy forcing her to remove her tobe in company and squeezing her arms and shoulders as a false sign of affection and modernism.

One of the most notable qualities of Aboulela's characters abroad is their physical sensation of being overpowered, crushed, and consumed. Before even stepping out of the airport, Sumra feels 'dazzled by the bright lights of the terminal, made humble by the plush carpeted floors, chastened by the perfect announcements one after the other' ('The Ostrich', 2). She later experiences the confinement of her London flat where even the cleanliness of the space is daunting to her, so very different is it from life back in

Khartoum. The room in her London flat 'rises up to strangle' her and 'the window beckons' her to leave (5). This is not Sumra's first visit to London; but each time she returns with Majdy, she 'is a stranger once again, made small and insignificant by the weight of this place' (3).

In 'The Museum', Shadia is relentlessly frightened and worn down by the the cold and rain of Aberdeen. Her hair, a symbol of her freedom and ease, is ruined by the harsh Scottish weather: 'She didn't like this style, her corrugated hair, and in the mirror her eyes looked too large' (73). She has to perpetually mould and manipulate her frizzy hair, reflecting her continual struggle to feel relaxed in Aberdeen. In 'Missing Out,' Samra 'would be silent for days, control herself and not mention either the future or the past. Then, like one breaking a fast, she would speak, offer [Majdy] memories and stories, and wait for him to take them' (224). Aboulela takes the image of the silenced, imprisoned woman and projects it onto the West. In 'Writing Near the Bone', Yvonne Vera describes her experience as a young girl literally writing on her body, 'deep into the skin and under the skin where the words could not escape' (559). She claims those words which she 'had dug too deep would be pulsating still, unable to be quiet' (559).

The women in Aboulela's stories have an overwhelming desire for their words to be heard, words that reveal the intimacy of their homelands. Sumra, aches to tell Majdy about their baby trapped in the confines of their London flat; Shadia locks herself up in her dorm room until Bryan coaxes her out to reveal to him the real Africa; and Samra is silent for days until she bursts forth with memories of the romantic pleasures of Khartoum for which she wishes her husband to yearn as much as she does. The pressures to modernize and tone down the outward signs of Muslim faith push their memories and words of truth deeper into their skin. In effect, the secular freedoms of their new Western worlds silence them.

In both 'The Museum' and 'The Ostrich', Aboulela constructs scenes that take place in front of mirrors. These scenes are significant in that they serve as visual manifestations of Western prejudice against African women as well as the shaming of these women by Western culture when they exhibit nostalgia for home. They also display the guilt many Muslim women feel when expressing love for their faith in the West. The public bathroom mirror in Shadia's Aberdeen dorm had inscribed on it: 'This is the face of someone with HIV' ('The Museum', 73). That mirror and its inscription 'made her feel as if she had left her looks behind in Khartoum' (74). In Sumra's case, she is made to feel ugly and inadequate by her husband, who is, as he sees it, attempting to uphold Western standards. Majdy tells her that Londoners can 'forgive you for your ugly colour, your thick lips and rough hair, but you must think modern thoughts, be like them in the inside if you can't be from the outside' ('The Ostrich', 5). Sumra looks in the mirror and confesses, 'Allah forgive me, [I] hate the face I was born with' (5). For both Shadia and Sumra, looking in the mirror reminds them that they cannot be themselves in the UK; rather, they must mask their Muslim identities, Shadia toiling over ugly hair and Sumra taking off her tobe to please her husband and his male friends. It is mostly patriarchal pressure that brings these women to mirrors in which the reflections they see are ugly and inadequate. Aboulela (in an interview with Siraj Datoo, 2011) alludes to an empowerment behind choosing to wear the hijab and claims that Muslim women 'have to do what is best for their own individual faith'. In 'Missing Out', Majdy does not allow Samra to wear her tobe, protesting, 'No, no, not here. I do not want us to be associated with fanatics and backwardness' (226). And in 'The Ostrich', Majdy tells Sumra, 'If you cover your hair, they'll think I'm forcing you to do that. They won't believe it is what you want' (5). Aboulela crafts female Muslim characters who *do* wish to cover their hair as an outward expression of their faith, and not for political reasons, but to adequately reflect who they are inside and to feel at home. When these women are forced to veil their Muslim identities by taking off their veils and feeling repulsive in front of Western mirrors, Aboulela illuminates the absurdity and arbitrariness with which we assign value and assess oppression.

In Carole Boyce Davies's essay about African feminism, she argues that 'African feminism examines African societies for institutions which are of value to women and rejects those which work to their detriment and do not simply import Western women's agendas' ('Some Notes on African Feminism,' 563). She refers to Buchi Emecheta's comments about the possible advantages of polygamy for women as a way to point out the complexities inherent in certain African institutions. Some women, on the contrary, either because of their lack of choice in the matter or the ways in which they are oppressed based on their position in the relationship, do not benefit from polygamy. The reality is that every woman has an individual experience within institutions that are quickly labelled as oppressive to women by primarily Western standards. Aboulela demonstrates this notion with her Muslim women characters. Samra's arranged marriage to Majdy, her cousin, because 'prospective bridegrooms living abroad were in great demand', is an overt critique of the practice of arranged marriages and – on a more macro level – the sex/gender system, as Samra does not benefit from this coupling ('Missing Out', 218). This practice is both tied to Muslim tradition and Sudanese culture. Samra does, however, benefit from Muslim practice in other ways – namely when she is not gifted as a commodity. Her Muslim practice comprises the root from which she self-identifies and self-expresses. Shadia, on the other hand, is not gifted to a man, yet still feels compelled to maintain her faith while in Scotland. When Shadia realizes one morning that she had not prayed, she feels guilty and equates the experience to going 'out into the street without any clothes' ('The Museum', 74). These women hold themselves accountable for their faith and practice, because nobody else does. Simply put, they choose to remain religious once they have reached the UK, where they could easily, and are encouraged to, dismiss their Muslim identities.

Geoffrey Nash argues that Aboulela makes a 'sympathetic insider's voice […] operable within the genre of "Muslim" fiction' (*Writing Muslim Identity*, 2012: 44). He goes on to suggest that Aboulela, along with other Muslim authors, is a writer whose fiction allows 'non-Muslim readers the opportunity of engaging imaginatively with conceptual issues surrounding a still by no means well understood religious identity that is becoming ever more deeply rooted in their midst' (49). Aboulela makes the Muslim migrant experience familiar. Nash examines Aboulela's novels for Muslim women characters who practice voluntary faith abroad, teaching others about Islam. This same practice occurs in Aboulela's short stories. Samra tries to convert her non-practising Muslim husband: 'She was intent on influencing him, but he was shy of the intimacy conversations about faith and practice evoked' ('Missing Out', 220). Aboulela is not afraid of these conversations in her stories; in fact, these can be seen as necessary for changing the perception of Muslim women across the globe. Shadia has the opportunity to teach Bryan, a willing student, about Muslim and African identity, but she is too afraid. Aboulela writes, 'if she had not been small in the museum, if she had been really strong, she would have made his trip to Mecca real, not only in a book' ('The Museum', 90). Teaching non-Muslims about Islam is a difficult task to undertake, but Aboulela does in each of her stories. She is not small; she is strong. Not only does she teach Muslim practice, but she renders it familiar and apolitical, breaking down the 'us versus them' binary. Further even, she makes it a sign of strength and commitment for her Muslim women characters. Aboulela by no means attempts to sell Islam to her non-Muslim readers, but rather to demystify it, to de-exoticize it.

The female characters in Aboulela's stories are constantly homesick. Aboulela conveys the human experience of missing a space through her characters, which is not necessarily tied to Muslim identity. Kerry Vincent suggests that 'The Museum' is 'one text that could be used to begin this task of rendering the comfortably strange as strangely familiar' ('Defamiliarizing Africa,' 2008: 4). He argues that Western readers bring 'conditioned responses' to African texts (4). These responses embody the learned notion that Africa is an exotic place of strangeness. Binyavanga Wainaina provides a retort to these responses in 'How to Write about Africa', in which his tongue and cheek comment, 'treat Africa as if it were one country,' quite accurately describes how many Westerners have been conditioned to read African texts. As Vincent advocates in his essay, Aboulela does the work of deconditioning Western readers. We can also add that she does the work of deconditioning non-Muslim readers and expand Wainaina's comments about writing about Africa to include writing about Islam in limited, stereotypical ways. Aboulela claims, in response to the notion that she represents Islam in her prose, that 'no one writer can be expected to be representative and that is a good thing' (Aberdeen Interview). As Wainaina's critique implies, the experiences of being African and Muslim are numerous and rich, rather than singular and flat, expected and foreign. Aboulela even suggests that fellow Sudanese writers would find foreign the fact that she is a female author writing in English. What Aboulela also achieves in her short stories is her demonstration of the feminist theory of intersectionality. She does this through her depictions of her characters' homesickness. Because Sumra, Shadia, and Samra experience Western oppression for being Muslim *and* for being African, some of their nostalgic iterations of home are tied to their Muslim identities, yet many of them are tied to family relations, the sights and sounds of Khartoum, and quite simply to memories of when life was easier.

All three women visualize Khartoum in intimate ways during moments in which they feel othered in the UK. These romantic reminiscences are private, secret, and occur when the women are alone. They represent the truths written beneath the skin, what is integral to their identities. For Sumra, her life in Khartoum is reality; she sees her life in London as 'a hibernation' ('The Ostrich', 2). The colours in London are dull compared to those in Khartoum. Sumra spends the majority of the narrative fantasizing about a former university classmate, the Ostrich. In contrast to Sumra's experience looking in the mirror with contempt at her reflection after Majdy slaps her across the face, she remembers the Ostrich telling her how beautiful she looked in her blue tobe. He affirms for her that her Muslim identity is attractive. Sumra remembers the comforting gestures of taking on and off her tobe to straighten and fix her hair. What is most vibrant for Sumra is her memory of communal prayer, a 'harmony' she belongs to, a harmony she has yet to find in London (6). She recalls the sights, sounds, and tactile feelings of these sunset prayers: 'I will always see the grass, patches of dry yellow, the rugs of palm-fibre laid out' (5-6). She remembers the birds during prayer and can hear 'the crescendo of their praises' (6). Muslim practice is not the only experience at home Sumra longs for; she also remembers 'cinnamon tea, sweet in chipped glasses' and 'roasted watermelon seeds' (6). Sumra's descriptions of Khartoum are much more vivid than her descriptions of London, many of which render London cold and colourless. In fact, Sumra feels most free as she is remembering her time at university in Khartoum with the Ostrich; she even recalls a contest in which the Ostrich had to memorize poetry and recite it on the fly. She says of him that he was 'alienated in his own hazy world' and 'free' (7). This poetry recitation is metaphoric for Sumra's liberating bouts of nostalgia. This nostalgia is literally brought to life through the figure of the Ostrich's new wife, adorned in her new tobe and bracelets, items Sumra is forced to shed upon her arrival in London. Sumra remarks that the Ostrich's wife reminds her of a 'younger version' of herself (9). She at once feels jealous and comforted by the image of the new bride. Jealous because she desires to be seen as a beautiful Muslim woman again. Comforted because, for a brief moment, 'warm like a mother's embrace,' she can bask in familiarity (9).

The memories Sumra has of her Muslim practice in Khartoum are not alienating to non-Muslim or non-African readers. Instead, Aboulela, by writing in English, is cognizant of a global audience. She suggests the possibility of a pan-Muslim practice that can be transported around the world and connect all people of Muslim faith. Aboulela's characters need this pan-Muslim practice as much as they need love or even alimentation. In 'The Museum,' Bryan yearns to belong to this pan-Muslim community, changing his outward appearance for Shadia and encouraging her to teach him about her religion and culture. With his character, Aboulela suggests the possibility of conversion. That is not to say that her texts should be read as didactic or sermonic, but rather represent her vision for a global Islam community. Of course, Aboulela implies that conversion is not an overnight change, which is why Shadia is not patient enough to help Bryan see this. The narrative concludes: 'He didn't know it was a steep path she had no strength for. He didn't understand' (90). Shadia is the most Westernized of Aboulela's characters, yet she still feels out of place in Scotland. In her dorm room on the weekends, she sits alone and remembers what weekends were like back in Khartoum. Shadia's nostalgia for home comes as a force from within: 'No sleep for the guilty, the memories come from another continent' (83). She feels guilt about feeling naturally connected to Bryan, a man her mother would not approve of her associating with back in Khartoum. But at the same time she enjoys his company and despite her resolve to stand him up for their museum outing, she shows up. Shadia's experience of a forced, artificial nostalgia in the museum elicits genuine homesickness. The museum displays artifacts intended for an arrogant Scottish audience made to feel justified for their ancestors' colonial endeavours in Africa. As Shadia walks through the exhibits, 'she wanted to see minarets, boats fragile on the Nile, people' (87). She wanted to see home. The reduction of her home continent into a collection of Scottish memorabilia is too much for her to handle and she outright rejects Bryan and his attempts, although naïve and misinformed, to understand her home.

Samra's articulation of home in 'Missing Out' is highly roman-ticized. In an extended daydream of what life would be like with Majdy in Khartoum, Samra pictures 'an afternoon under the fan' laughing about Majdy's students, hearing their future children playing on the rooftop, preparing mint tea for the neighbour, and grabbing her tobe to rush to the side of grieving friends (222). She refuses to do any housework in London, rejecting her role as a housewife. Later, she remembers the time when the electricity in Khartoum went out and Majdy kissed her for the first time in the dark, amidst candles and the scent of jasmine. For Samra, Khartoum means noises and smells and people and love. For her,

London is void of all of that. Majdy resents Samra's homesickness and becomes 'bored by her nostalgia' (226). Majdy reads Samra as 'stuck in the past,' but she is really stuck in herself (226). As he notices, she 'was meant for brilliant sunsets and thin cotton dresses,' and 'her small teeth were made to strip the hard husk of sugar cane' (226). Samra does not belong in London, forced to pray alone five times a day, with Majdy sitting in the same room thinking prayer is a distraction and waste of time. Unable to locate a pan-Muslim community in London, Samra goes back to Sudan, determined to appease her homesickness. When she leaves, Majdy feels lost, his days no longer structured by Samra's prayers. In the end, it is the strong Muslim woman who Majdy comes to appreciate, rather than the passive Westernized version of herself. Again we see the empowering capabilities of the Muslim faith for the women in Aboulela's stories.

The complexities of identity and expression that Aboulela produces in her prose are not simply remedied by her characters returning home, though. By going back to Sudan, Samra abandons a possible chance at love in order to be free from the constraints of secular culture. We do get the sense, however, that Majdy just might not survive in London without Samra by his side and will perhaps follow her back to Khartoum. Egyptian feminist Nawal El Saadawi criticized Arab literature for only allowing its female characters limited roles; either that of the loved and respected mother or that of the sexual wife perennially seeking to please her husband. In 1980, she argued, 'Arab literature is threaded throughout with innumerable examples of these two opposing and contradictory categories of women' ('The Heroine in Arab Literature,' 524). She replicates Simone de Beauvoir's concept of the myth of the woman by arguing that men are both afraid of and strongly, yet only sexually desire a feminine woman. By participating in the feminist work of problematizing socially constructed binaries, Aboulela contributes to the creation of a new genre of Arab literature that envisions complex female characters whose identities are not relegated to one category or role. This genre did not exist when El Saadawi was writing her critique, proof of the immense change in Muslim African fiction over the years. Aboulela's characters reject these roles outright. Sumra hides her pregnancy from her husband, Shadia entertains a romantic liaison with a Scottish man, and Samra sits among dirty dishes, her husband complicit in her renouncement of housewifery. These women all embody the role of the Muslim woman committed to her religious faith rather than cultural – either home or abroad – expectations of her. Aboulela's stories cause us to think that the Arab heroine has been liberated from her reductionist role of the 1970s and 1980s. Her unwavering commitment to Islam has liberated her.

Citing cultural theory, Geoffrey Nash argues that 'identity is not a fixed sign, and it is invariably constructed with the Other in mind' (8). This notion suggests that one's experiences are inevitably and uniquely different from another's and that is what gives them value. The fact that Aboulela's characters practice Islam amidst a secular backdrop heightens this sense of uniqueness. And each of their experiences is likewise distinct; Samra moves back to Sudan, while Shadia and Sumra stay in the UK, both occupying different places in British society. The post 9/11 phenomenon of conflating religion and ideology when writing about Islam is nothing less than exhibiting the same misconceptions, no matter how good the intentions are, that Bryan brings with him to the African museum in Aberdeen. As scholars, we must begin to question this conflation. Stories like those of Aboulela give us the permission and evidence with which to adequately do so. Likewise, there seems to be an overall discomfort with addressing 'the problem of Islam' in criticism. If we focus too much on characters' Muslim identities, we are reductionist and gazing. Some tell us to look past the Islamic features of a story and instead discuss its other aspects. I am not so sure how much Aboulela would agree with this kind of advice. Her female characters are intensely religious, following Islamic doctrine in all aspects of their lives, and feeling an extreme sense of dislocation from self when forced to suppress their religious practices away from home. Aboulela claims she is 'motivated by putting Islam into fiction, creating worlds where cause and effect follow Islamic logic and writing sympathetically about people who have faith' (Aberdeen Interview). Her characters are special *because* they are Muslim, not *in spite* of it.

Helon Habila writes, 'Africa's strength is not, contrary to what most people like to think, in its homogeneity, but in its diversity of cultures and languages and religions and skin colours' (*The Granta Book* 2011: xiv). Aboulela's stories champion these differences and challenge the stereotypes of Africa described in Wainaina's essay. Aboulela's stories attempt to define what it means to be Muslim in a secular world, what it means to be away from home, and what it means to make sense of these sometimes painful experiences.

In an ever increasing global climate, Aboulela's fiction is not only relevant, but beneficent. Habila chose stories for the Granta collection, Aboulela's 'Missing Out' included among them, based on whether or not the story 'illuminate[s] the preoccupations and concerns, literary and social, of the times in which it was written' (xiv). Expanding the narrow roles afforded to Muslim women in prose and talking back to Western notions of Islam as oppressive towards women and Africa as a continent of exotic others who sleep among majestic wildlife, Aboulela is a seminal voice of her time and place, without which we may not adequately understand the nuanced perspectives of Muslim Sudanese women.

NOTES

1   This statement appears on Aboulela's website, Leila-aboulela.com.
2   'Post-nationalist' is a term Helon Habila uses to describe the current generation of African writers.

WORKS CITED

Aboulela, Leila. Fork in the Road', *Granta* 111 (Summer 2010).
—— 'Missing Out'. In *The Granta Book of the African Short Story*: 215-231.
—— 'The Museum'. In *Opening Spaces*: 70-90.
—— 'The Ostrich'. Eugene, Oregon: Intangible Publications, 1997.
Achebe, Chinua, ed. *African Short Stories*. Johannesburg: Heinemann, 1985.
—— 'The Truth of Fiction'. In Olaniyan and Quayson (eds) *African Literature*: 107-114.
Datoo, Siraj. Interview with Leila Aboulela. *SirajDatoo.com*. January 2011.
Davies, Carole Boyce. 'Some Notes on African Feminism.' In Olaniyan and Quayson (eds) *African Literature*: 561-569.
El Saadawi, Nawal. 'The Heroine in Arab Literature.' In Olaniyan and Quayson (eds) *African Literature*: 520-525.
Habila, Helon, ed. *The Granta Book of the African Short Story*. London: Granta, 2011.
Nash, Geoffrey. *Writing Muslim Identity*. London: Continuum, 2012.
Olaniyan, Tejumola and Ato Quayson, eds. *African Literature: An Anthology of Criticism and Theory*. Oxford: Blackwell Publishing, 2007.
University of Aberdeen faculty. Interview with Leila Aboulela. *abdn.ac.uk.* 2007.
Vera, Yvonne, ed. *Opening Spaces*. Oxford: Heinemann, 1999.
—— 'Writing Near the Bone'. In Olaniyan and Quayson (eds) *African Literature*: 558-560.
Vincent, Kerry. 'Defamiliarizing Africa in Leila Aboulela's "The Museum"', *AfroEuropa* 2.3 (2008): 1-12.
Wainaina, Binyavanga. 'How to Write about Africa', *Granta* 92 (Spring 2005).

Ugandan Women in Contest with Reality

Mary K. Okurutu's
A Woman's Voice & the Women's Future

INIOBONG I. UKO

When on 9 October 2006, Ban Ki-moon, the eighth Secretary-General of the United Nations, launched an in depth study at the General Assembly on all forms of violence against women, it came from the awareness that African women were still suffering violence at all levels of their lives and operations. He declared 'Break the silence. When you witness violence against women and girls, do not sit back. Act.' (www.enndviolence.un.org). As a follow-up to the above initiative, in 2008 the United Nations Secretary-General launched the *UNiTE to End Violence against Women* campaign, which constitutes a call 'on governments, civil societies, women's organizations, young people, the private sector, the media and the entire United Nations system to join forces in addressing the global pandemic of violence against women and girls…' ('About UNiTE' www.endviolence.un.org). Generally, violence against women is one of the most shameful forms of human rights violation. Gender-based violence not only violates human rights, but also hampers productivity, reduces human capital and undermines economic growth. It is estimated that up to 70 per cent of women experience violence in their lifetime. The horrible act occurs everywhere – at home, at work, in the streets and it happens both in peacetime and wartime ('Violence against Women' www.makeeverywomancount.org). In cognizance of, and concern about this reality, Ban Ki-moon declares:

> We strongly condemn all forms of violence against women in Africa. Whether domestic violence or rape and killings in some parts of the continent [Africa] in conflict … There is one universal truth applicable to all countries, cultures and communities: violence against women is never acceptable, never excusable, never tolerable. ('Violence against Women' www.makeeverywomancount)

Violence against women manifests in diverse forms which include forced/early marriage, sexual harassment, female genital mutilation, forced pregnancy, trafficking in women, prostitution, intimidation at work and in educational institutions, denial of formal education, forced abortion, marital rape, use of rape as war weapon in conflict zones, and others.

Realizing the endangered status of African women, the Protocol to the African Charter on Human and Peoples' Rights on the rights of women in Africa, commonly described as The Maputo Protocol was adopted in Mozambique on 11 July 2003. It became effective in November 2005 after 15 of the 53 African Union Member States ratified it. The Maputo Protocol emerged from the realization that women's rights in Africa were often marginalized especially in the context of human rights, and thus the need for an international binding instrument addressing and protecting women's rights. The Protocol requires African governments to eliminate all forms of discrimination and violence against women in Africa, and to promote equality between men and women. Member states are obliged to integrate a gender perspective in their policy decisions, legislation, development plans and activities, and to ensure the overall well being of women. Uganda is among the 46 states that have signed the Protocol, and also among the 28 states that have ratified the Protocol as at July 2010. This implies that Uganda as a country should incorporate the rights enshrined in the Protocol into its domestic law system, and educate women about the Protocol so that they can fully enjoy the rights ('Africa: Maputo Protocol' www. makeeverywomancount.org).

An assessment of the profile of Uganda and the rights issues of its women is essential at this point to highlight its challenges over the years, and its potential as an African state. Uganda is in East Africa, landlocked by Kenya, Sudan, the Democratic Republic of Congo, Rwanda, and Tanzania. It is about 236, 040 square kilometres and is populated by about 31 million people ('Uganda Country Profile' www.culturalsurvival.org/Unganda-Country-Profile).

In pre-colonial Uganda, women enjoyed reasonable power and rights. They wielded authority in the judicial process and religious activities, even as they were very active in child-care and agriculture. They were recognized as bonafide and credible members of the family and were entitled to inheritance and land ownership. However, during the colonial period, the culture that emerged favoured and recognized men and utilized their services in the administrative, legal, religious and medical processes, while women were regarded as weak, and condemned to the domestic chores, subsistence cultivation and nurturing roles. The trend inevitably imposed on the men a sense of superiority over the women, and a corresponding attitude of dominance over, and subjugation of the woman. There is only about a 20 per cent female representation in appointments in government, as well as unequal remuneration for men and women for work of equal value. These are violations of:

1 The International Labour Organization Convention No. 100 of 1951 on equal remuneration for men and women for work of equal value, which Uganda ratified in 2003; and

2 Convention III of 1958 which promotes equality of opportunity and treatment in employment and occupation as a means to eliminate all forms of discrimination (www.ilo.org).

In Uganda, women face a wide range of challenges including discrimination in legal, social and economic matters, as well as a greater risk of HIV/AIDS infection. (asafeworldforwomen.org/womensrights). In job recruitment, priority is always given to males regardless of qualifications. Women are stigmatized and regarded as baby- producers who must go on maternity leave and cause a loss to the system. Many women are abused sexually by men before being employed. In fact, some are patronized and made to settle on low paying jobs, thus being inferior to their male counterparts. Men are generally offered educational and training opportunities over women. At retrenchment, women are always considered first. When forced out of the formal sector, they resort to the informal sector where their rights are further at risk.

Female genital mutilation is still a common practice among the Sebei people of Uganda. This has caused the victims to contract several diseases; and has resulted in the death of many others. Due to large-scale poverty among many families and communities, young girls can be forced into marriage with rich and often far older men. While the daughter is not consulted, the parents, mostly the fathers, look forward to the daughter's bride wealth as a factor that will elevate the economic status of the family.

Women are generally denied inheritance rights. Only the male children inherit and benefit from the family property, and this has caused many girls to truncate their education because of lack of financial support. This reality makes women perpetually inferior to men, and dependent on them, thus justifying the attribution of misfortunes on women.

Several myths and beliefs exist in the society that portray women as carriers or symbols of ill luck. Women are often blamed for infertility, family misfortune, defiance among the children, etc. Many religious beliefs present women as evil and as the properties of men. These notions often condition the women to desire and actually have no say in matters concerning them, and to remain at the mercy of the men. Being properties of men, they are made to stay home and care for the needs of the men. Thus, education is not considered at all for women. The woman's mediocre status is defined from childhood. She has no rights over her reproductive capabilities and when she has more children than she can cater for, her poverty is perpetuated and her vulnerability enhanced. In consequence, female children are forced to marry early, and the debilitating cycle continues (www.iheu.org/node/2439). In fact, in the 1980s women in rural areas of Buganda were expected to kneel when speaking to men. Also women are taught from childhood to be subordinate to men and accede to the wishes of their fathers, brothers, husbands as well as other men.

In post-independence and contemporary Uganda, several initiatives have sought the improved status of women in Uganda. During the first decade of independence, the Ugandan Council of Women pressed for legal reforms that would grant all women the right to own property and retain custody of their children if their marriage ended (www.en.wikipedia.org/wiki/women-in-Uganda). Women are active in the National Resistance Army and President Yoweri Museveni appointed Joan Kakwenzire, to a six-member commission to document abuses by the military. The government also decreed that one woman would represent each district on the National Resistance Council. The government-operated Uganda Commercial Bank has launched a rural credit plan to make farm loans more easily available to women.

In 1987, Museveni appointed Joyce Mpanga Minister for Women and Development. Mpanga pursued the raise in women's wages, increase in women's credit potentialities, more employment opportunities for women, and improved conditions of living for women in general. In 1989, the Ugandan government appointed two female ministers and three deputy ministers in the ruling National Resistance Movement (NRM) cabinet. Women in the civil service and professions formed an organization, Action for Development, to assist women, especially those in war-torn areas, especially the devastated Luwero region in central Uganda (www.en.wikipedia.org/wiki/Women-in-Uganda). In 1976, the Ugandan Association of Women Lawyers was founded which established a legal-aid clinic in 1988 to defend women who suffered loss of property or child custody due to separation, divorce or widowhood. The association also established common legal grounds for divorce for both men and women, common criminal codes for both men and women and assisted women and children who were AIDS victims, and created nationwide education programmes to enlighten women on their legal and other rights.

In recent years, women's efforts and contributions have been recognized in government, commerce, politics, the private sector and in religion, etc. In 2005, 15 women were honoured in a first of its kind Award ceremony dedicated to women. The recipients included the Deputy Chief Justice, the Gender Minister, the Education Minister, professors, Reverend Sisters, educationists and the first female medical doctor in Uganda, Prof. Josephine Namboze. They were publicly commended as having significantly contributed to the shaping of the Uganda society. (www.newvision.co.ug/D/8/13/463515). A Ugandan woman, Winnic Byanyima, the first and only female flight engineer in Uganda as well as former guerrilla fighter member of parliament and politician, was selected Woman of the Year 2005 by the AfroAmerican Network in its Most Influential Blacks of the 21st Century (www.ugpulse.com).

Dr Specioza Wandira Kazibwe is a medical doctor and politician. She was elected Vice-President of Uganda and she served from 1994 to 2003. She was the first woman in Africa to hold that position. From 1991 to 1994, she was the minister for Gender and Community Development (www.ugpulse.com). This appraisal reveals that the Ugandan woman has continued to gain visibility in politics, and must sustain that to make an impact in government, the professions, commerce, religious activities, and others. However, there seems to be a wide gap between the formulation of policies and the implementation. Many of the programmes targeting women should highly ameliorate the conditions of women in contemporary society, but the will, which would provide the resources for implementation, is often lacking, or may be in such short supply that the vision is hardly or never realized. This may contribute to the large percentage of illiterate and poor women in Uganda. According to the report of African Women's Economic Policy Network (AWEPON) entitled 'Women Worst hit by Chronic Poverty in Uganda':

> Women are the most illiterate. They are the most involved in un-gainful employment or work where you don't get paid. They are the ones bearing the brunt of bringing up children and ensuring they go to school. They are the poorest. They are women. Over 7 million of 26 million population is chronically poor, with women forming the bulk. Overall, 27% of the chronically poor households in rural areas are headed by women with the percentage rising to 40 in urban setting (www.awepon.net).

The report describes chronic poverty as 'poverty where individuals, households or regions are trapped in multidimensional poverty for several years or a lifetime, and where poverty is linked with intergenerational transmission'. The 'usually poor' are those who occasionally move out of poverty, the 'churning' poor who regularly move in and out of poverty and the 'occasionally' poor who are usually not poor but fall into poverty ('Women Worst Hit by Chronic Poverty' www.worldpulse.com).

The realities described above compel many families to force girl children into early marriages, while others who have been denied education and have no access to skills, resort to prostitution. This accounts for a perpetuation of the deplorable and debilitating cycle. Many of these issues are portrayed in the short stories by the Ugandan woman that this study focuses on. The stories in the collection titled *A Woman's Voice*, remove the façade that presents the Ugandan woman as liberated; the stories make a mockery of the various policies and initiatives in modern Uganda that aim to lift the woman from the dungeon of drudgery, suffering, poverty, unequal treatment, harassment and abuse.

The issues in *A Woman's Voice* highlighted in the stories selected for this study examine diverse concerns that plague womanhood in contemporary Uganda. The authors are all Ugandan and are familiar with the challenges that women continue to face in the society. The theme of poverty features directly or indirectly in the stories. In Lillian Tind Yebwa's 'Looking for my Mother', the underlying factor responsible for the complexity in the life of the fifteen-year-old Rebecca is poverty, as she recalls:

> At that time I had no choice. I had been pushed to the limits … I was fifteen. My mother had taken me upcountry to stay with my aunt while going to school there. My mother always said that she did not want me growing up in the slum area where young people normally easily learnt bad behavior. Little did she know that she had taken me to the leopard's lair. My aunt's husband, who was old enough to be my grandfather and who was a respectable member of society, had other ideas. Every time my auntie was not in the house, he would force me to have sex with him … He used to threaten me each time, saying that if I told anybody about what was happening he would kill me. (14)

Unfortunately, and as expected, Rebecca becomes pregnant, and informs him, but 'that day he almost killed me. He held a knife to my neck and said if I tarnished his name, he would not hesitate to use it' (14). Determined not to have her future destroyed by the unwanted baby, she delivers him and dumps him into the neighbor's pit latrine!

Poverty also causes the tragedy recorded in 'The Fate of an Expensive Wedding' by Margaret Ntakarimaze. As Mzee Kyondo realizes that Joshua is interested in marrying Mutume, his daughter, he demands that Joshua pays two million shillings and ten cows as bride wealth. An attempt by Mutume's mother, Merab, to plead with her husband to be reasonable, earns her a severe battering from him. He declares:

> Since when did a woman start deciding for her husband? Your role is to look after the children and when they grow up, like Mutume has now, we the men discuss bride wealth to be paid without your interference. Do you mind going back to your grinding stone … (95)

Mzee Kyondo's insistent demand of high bride wealth from Joshua causes Mutume to protest by running away from home. On return, her father beats her thoroughly and she is later found dead.

Poverty and its devastating impact on the woman constitute the thrust of Goretti Kyomuhendo's 'Hidden Identity'. Richard Kalenzi's mother explains:

> I broke down when I saw my mother's emaciated body lying in bed. My elder sister told me that my father had beaten her severely and it seemed she had had internal bleeding and had no proper treatment … The following day, she died… My father did not appear for [the] burial … (87)

Evidently, poverty seems to push the men into violent attitudes and wife battering, thus, making the women perpetual victims of the conditions they did not cause, and cannot help. The culture is structured in a way that men blame the women and punish them too for the misfortunes of the family. Ayeta Anne Wangusa's 'A Sacrifice for Maayi' also explores the excruciating poverty that forces Maayi's parents to demand of her husband to pay the bride price after many years of living together: 'My parents are demanding that if your father does not pay the bride price, I'll have to go back to their home' (45). Consequently, Maliza has to get married off so that her bride price may be used by her father to pay her mother's bride price. It therefore becomes apparent that poverty has complicated implications in both families and society.

The issue of forced/child marriage along with the related concern with the bride price is portrayed by the authors of some of the stories. Maliza in 'A Sacrifice for Maayi' is forced into marriage at the age of thirteen to a man she has never known: '... she could not let down her mother even if she dreaded the whole idea of marrying a man she had not set her eyes on. She walked to her father's house, knelt down before him and said, 'I understand everything now. You can receive the cows' (45). The same issue is the concern of Ntakarimaze in 'The Fate of an Expensive Wedding' in which Mutume misses marrying Joshua and also loses her life because of her father's outrageous demands fot bride wealth from Joshua.

As vital to human life as matters of sex and sexual relationships are, they are hardly discussed in Ugandan society. In fact, they are often regarded as obscene and must not be discussed in public or among the youth. Young people are not given any sex education; they seem to generally grope along and experiment on ideas. Lack of sex education is the cause of Joanitta's unplanned pregnancy and subsequent dropout from school in Hope Keshubi's story, 'Joanitta's Nightmare'. Joanitta meets with Jackson 'during the inter-school drama festival where they both played the lead characters in their respective school dramas. They had put in a lot of effort and they played their roles so well that when they were declared best actor and best actress, the audience gave them a wild clapping of hands...' (28). The excitement of stardom draws Joanitta and Jackson together, an experience that ends with a pregnancy, which both causes her school to take her home to her parents, and also begins a strange and painful phase of her life. In her naiveté,

Joanitta knows nothing about pregnancy or abortion as well as their consequences. Thus, the events that eventually unfold reveal to her the complexities of life which she was hitherto oblivious. Joanitta does not recall having been told anything by anybody about sex, and her innocence is obvious when she asks her school headmistress: 'Is it possible to get pregnant the first time one has sex?' (34) That is Joanitta's case. She expects the understanding of her mother, but is apprehensive of her father's reactions to her pregnancy and drop-out from school. As she feared, her father

> …grabbed her and threw her onto the ground, face upwards and placed a sharp end of his spear shaft on her belly. 'If you don't want me to use this spear to rip your stomach open and remove this unwanted bastard, name the man responsible so that I can demonstrate the effective use of my spear on him!' But threaten as he did, Joanitta could not dare tell them who was responsible for her pregnancy. She loved him so much that she did not want to involve him in this family warfare. (36)

Joanitta's father blames the mother for Joanitta's pregnancy:

> 'It is all your fault that she has gone and got herself pregnant!' he roared at her.
> 'Baba, you know very well that I do not tell my girls to become pregnant,' she said in defence.
> 'Yes, but you should have taught her how not to get pregnant,' he said heatedly. 'Anyway, I should have known when I married you that such things would happen. After all, didn't five of your seven sisters get pregnant before marriage?' (36)

The exchange above convinces Joanitta's mother that to escape the father's use of his fists on both of them, she must send Joanitta out of the house and save the family from shame. That night, as he goes to drink, he promises Joanitta and her mother that on his return he must be told the the name of the man responsible, 'if they were not prepared to do it on their own, he was going to beat it out of them' (37). Thus, as he leaves home, Joanitta's mother smuggles her out of the village to her distant cousin's home with a plea that she should look after Joanitta until her time comes.

Joanitta serves as a slave in her new home. She wakes the earliest, tends the goats, cleans around, goes to the well for water, cooks breakfast for the family, washes the pans and dishes, goes to the farm to work, obtain items for meals, makes lunch and dinner for the family, bathes the children and washes up everything before retiring. She is ill-prepared for the baby's arrival; the delivery is very difficult and she nearly loses her life, but she survives it all, and has a lovely baby girl. After five months, Joanitta decides to leave her aunty's house because she and her baby are being regarded and treated as unwanted burdens on the family. She neither tells anybody nor returns to her parents.

In Hilda Twongyeirwe's 'Becoming a Woman', the young girl knows nothing about menstruation until she experiences it and is unable to understand it, or tell anyone about it, or manage it. In her amazement, she goes to the toilet, looks at herself and examines her body; she feels no pain, but there is blood:

> I must be sick. Very sick. Something must have hurt me from deep inside... from the amount of blood on the knicker, and the fresh blood still coming, I imagined there was a huge wound! ... I wished it was a nose bleed because with that, I could easily show anybody and get help. (47)

Her mother eventually gives her small pieces of white cloth, and instructs her on how to use them. She advises her that

> every woman is supposed to see this ... This has happened as a sign that you will bear children in future ... When you become a woman, you stop playing with boys ... If you ever play with them, you will become pregnant. You will not see this blood again for nine months, after which you will produce a child. Young women who are not yet married are not supposed to produce and when they do it, it is a curse to them and a big shame to their families ... You must, therefore, stop playing with boys and men. It must only be your husband – the man you'll get married to who will touch you and give you beautiful daughters and sons ... you must try to hide this blood as much as possible. (50-51)

The euphemisms in which the advice above is encased makes the young girl afraid that she is pregnant when few months afterwards, she sees no more blood. She tells her friend that she is pregnant, but does not know who has made her pregnant because she has played all sorts of games with many boys: climbing trees, wrestling, football, throwing buttons, etc. She does not relate 'playing with boys' with 'sleeping with boys' which her friend talks about. Her ignorance is apparent as her more mature friend tells her that she is not pregnant; it is normal for the periods to break for months after the first month.

The implications of concealing information on sex education include ignorance. isolation from friends, loss of virginity, unwanted and unplanned pregnancy, truncated education, rejection from family and society, suffering and damaged psyche. On the other hand, to conceal information on sex education has caused many young girls to seek knowledge on their own, and engage in sex as something they were made to miss. This is demonstrated by the young girls who sneak from school to attend a party with big men. They arrive at an unfamiliar location, and do not know that the drinks offered are spiked, making them vulnerable. Except for Irene, the other six girls sleep with the men. Irene is unwilling and succeeds because she claims to the Reverened who tries to seduce her that she has AIDS. 'Behind Closed Doors' also demonstrates the lack of moral rectitude that pervades the society. Big men commonly corrupt young girls. This is also depicted in Tindyebwa's 'Looking for my Mother' in which the fifteen-year-old Rebecca is consistently abused sexually by her aunty's husband, who is a respectable member of the society.

Domestic violence usually reflects the frustrations of the men, the helplessness of the women victims, and the silent endorsement of the practice by society. Richard Kalenzi's mother in Kyomuhendo's 'Hidden Identity' dies as a result of the severe beating she suffers from her husband. In Ntakarimaze's 'The Fate of an Expensive Wedding', Mutume dies as a result of her father's beatings 'tonight, I am going to teach you that I am not to be angered' (96). While he beats her, his son tries unsuccessfully to dissuade him, and without a word, Mutume's mother brings a mat and mother and son keep vigil at Mutume's door all night long. By morning, Mutume is found dead.

Migisca Anne, Mugurusi's wife in Philo Nabweru's 'Where is She?' faces the misery of living with and being battered by a man she defied her whole family to marry three years before. She misses the deep passion that they enjoyed initially from her husband. Since the birth of their first and only child, Mugurusi has become so violent and brutal towards Anne that she is compelled to contemplate killing him and/or committing suicide. Underlying his beastly attitude towards his wife is his deep jealousy of their baby, and for no reason, as Nabweru describes it:

> He got hold of her long hair with both hands and shook her until her teeth chattered. He pulled it so hard you could see the veins in her face standing out. He went on screaming at her like he was demented. The woman kept muttering something inaudible as if she were going to develop an epileptic fit.

He administered several slaps to her upturned face and released her as suddenly as he had grabbed her. She landed heavily right on top of the mess of the broken dish. (75)

These forms of gruesome treatment seem to harden Anne and she begins to think of ways to help herself and their baby. Unconsciously, she also develops violent tendencies. As Mugurusi holds her to himself,

> she was desperate … Her hand gripped … the bottle of … wine which she brought crushing on Mugurusi's head. Too stunned to react, Mugurusi simply stared. Anne pulled a drawer open and snatched a bread knife. She advanced towards her dazed husband … She moved fast … Mugurusi stood rooted … dumbfounded; mesmerized by the demoniac light in her eyes. (80)

Mugurusi is shocked by Anne's dare-devil action. She does the unthinkable, and that opens her husband's eyes; he realizes how much he has wronged her. He pleads: 'please, Anne, put away the knife. I will never, ever mistreat you again. I love you so much! Please forgive me. I have been such a fool to be jealous of our child!' (81)

⁓

Generally, the selected stories in *A Woman's Voice* indicate that modern Ugandan women have significant roles to perform to save themselves from poor and oppressive treatment and to make the society women-friendly. The stories highlight the fact that what generated sadness and pain for women in previous generations should not still be happening to contemporary Ugandan women. The issues constitute the challenges in modern society that Ugandan women are still battling with.

To contest with reality, the contemporary Ugandan woman is fighting in obvious and subtle ways to surmount the structures and practices that plagued her foremothers and perpetuated their suppression in a society in which they are bonafide members. The modern woman has to deploy education and effectual networking with bodies and groups within Uganda and beyond to ensure the enlightenment of young girls and the society at large. The issue of female sexuality has to be given prominent attention, and not regarded as taboo, so that girls will realize what they need to know and be conscious of intra- and inter-gender relationships.

Female economic empowerment is a vital tool for modern

women to control the elements around them; around the home and beyond. Women must be seen and recognized as credible contributors to the well-being of the family and/or society. In fact, it is within this context that women should feel the impact of their fellow women, however few they may be, who are in the mainstream of governance, politics, commerce, etc. Women in modern Uganda should strive to ingrain the values of the declaration by the United Nations Secretary General on his vision to end violence against women, and also make good, active and workable among women the Women's Rights Protocol of 2003.

WORKS CITED

Primary Source
Okurut, Mary K. ed. *A Woman's Voice: An Anthology of Short Stories by Ugandan Women.* Kampala: FEMRITE Publications Ltd., 1998.

Secondary Sources
'About UNiTE'www.endviolence.un.org. Web. Accessed 08/11/12
'Africa: Maputo Protocol.' www.makeeverywomancount.org. Web. Accessed 28/11/12
www.asafeworldforwomen.org/womens-rights. Web. Accessed 08/11/12
www.awepon.net. Web. Accessed 15/02/13
'Chronic Poverty in Uganda: The Policy Challenges'. Oct 2005. Web. Accessed 09/11/12
www.en.wikipedia.org/wiki/Women-in-Uganda. Web. Accessed 09/11/12
www.iheu.org/node/2439. Web. Accessed 09/11/12
www.ilo.org. Web. Accessed 15/02/13.
www.newvision.co.ug/D/8/13/463515. Web. Accessed 09/11/12
'Uganda Country Profile'. www.culturalsurvival.org/Uganda-Country-Profile. Web. Accessed 28/10/12.
www.ugpulse.com. Web Accessed 09/11/12
'Violence Against Women' www.makeeverywomancount.org. Web. Accessed 28/10/12
'Women Worst Hit by Chronic Poverty in Uganda'. Web. Accessed 09/11/12

Snapshots of the Botswana Nation

Bessie Head's *The Collector of Treasures & Other Botswana Village Tales* as a National Project

LOUISA UCHUM EGBUNIKE

My work was always tentative because it was always so completely new (…) it brought all kinds of people, both literate and semi-literate, together, and it did not really qualify who was who – everyone had a place in my world. (Head 1977, 45)

Bessie Head's collection of short stories, *The Collector of Treasures*, signalled a shift in her writing which became, in her own words, 'more social and outward-looking' (Head 2007: 102). Head has described her earlier works as 'stating personal choices' expressed through the construction of '[m]anipulated characters [who] talk anxiously for the author'. The anxieties that Head alludes to are well documented in her biographical and epistolary writings; a product of an interracial relationship born into a prominent white family in apartheid South Africa, as well as the breakdown of her marriage and her life in exile in Botswana. She initially wrote literature as a cathartic expression of her troubles. Her characterization stemmed from an inward-looking anguish. The process of writing *The Collector of Treasures* was distinct from her previous writings as the stories were 'undoubtedly written over a longer period than her novels' (Ibrahim 1996: 171). The collection came to represent a 'resumé of 13 years of living entirely in village life' (Beard 1986: 45) rather than a specific chapter in Head's life. The movement into a more 'outward-looking' literature signified that 'the stories were written after she had found a home in Botswana' (Ibrahim 1996: 171). The multipositionality of the stories in *The Collector of Treasures*, presents characters that are representational of the different segments of society. Head's employment of the short story, episodic by its very nature, presents, as Craig Mackenzie suggests, 'a composite portrait of a total world' as 'it builds up the complete picture by dealing piecemeal with fragments of the whole' (MacKenzie 1989a: 146). In this essay I argue that in relaying the collective experiences of the people of Botswana, the short stories in the collection offer both critique and celebration of their society and environment. In this way, *The Collector of Treasures* may be read as a national text.

The evocation of the national and the rural in the collection's full title, *The Collector of Treasures and other Botswana Village Tales*, is further developed in, for example, the incorporation of the storyteller figure and his respective listeners. In 'Heaven is not Closed' Head uses the character Modise to fulfil the role of the storyteller so that the reader is presented with a nested story narrated by his fictional voice. 'Heaven is not Closed', one of the three short stories that will be examined here, relates the tensions between the imperialist Christian missionaries and Setswana custom, and the impact that these tensions have on the story's protagonists. 'Heaven is not Closed' serves as a localized account of a national concern, with an interface of regional vis-à-vis national, paralleled by Head's allusions to the oral tradition in the writing of a national text. In complicating the binaries between the local and national and the oral and written, the stories encompass the various dialogues which take place within postcolonial Botswana. The communion between the oral and the written narrative informed Head's canon, most apparently in the writing of *The Collector of Treasures,* and *Serowe: Village of the Rain Wind.* These texts formed part of Head's national project of chronicling the people's narratives and histories, achieved partly through conducting a series of interviews in Serowe. The interviews prove essential to the composition of *The Collector of Treasures* as eight of the thirteen stories draw inspiration directly from them (MacKenzie 1989b: 19). This semi-biographical collection of short stories contributes to Head's on-going engagement with a nation that she describes as 'the most unique and distinguished country in the whole of Africa' (Head 2007: 89). In spite of her protracted exilic status in Botswana, Bessie Head's canon is largely dedicated to exploring this nation she reveres. The interviews serve as a mode of engagement for Head with her adopted home, enabling her to enter the worlds of her interviewees and through her short stories, represent snapshots of life which are rooted in lived experiences. Head's fictionalization of the narratives of her interviewees supplies the reader with a collective of voices which speak from different perspectives, bound together by Head who acts as the proverbial collector of treasures.

The Collector of Treasures can be located in a tradition of Southern African women's writings which enter nationalist discourses through a predominant engagement with the rural woman.[1] The women in these short stories push social boundaries, challenging the heightened patriarchy of the postcolony whilst continuing to nurture their families and the wider community. Kwadwo Osei-Nyame has suggested that Bessie Head's rendering of Botswana, 'projected subversive female heroines within society as part of her revolutionary project of political non-conformism. Her ideological project interrogates normative but dominant modes of existence for women' (Osei-Nyame Jnr 2002: 103). The centrality of subversive women in Head's stories undermines the hegemony of male power which was concretized through both colonialism and the missionary influence. In placing women at the forefront of many of her narratives, Head's women challenge social norms and destabilize male institutions of power. They are the daughters, mothers and grandmothers from differing social, economic and religious backgrounds, who suppress norms and carve out spaces within the nation. Often single mothers, women are the central figures within the individual family units which Head juxtaposes with the lack of space afforded women in playing a central role at a national level. This recurring motif forms a fundamental concern for Head, as her writings engage with the histories that culminated in this social norm whilst representing the women who are reshaping the present.

The title story, 'The Collector of Treasures' encapsulates the subversiveness of women in the most striking way; through the act of matricide. The story centres on the troubled marriage of Dikeledi and her husband Garesego. Garesego neglects his wife and children, choosing instead to satisfy his 'taste for womanising and drink' (92). Garesego's unfaithfulness extends beyond mere negligence as the story depicts his attempts to exasperate his long suffering wife. When Dikeledi approaches him to contribute towards their son's school fees, Garesego displays a self-satisfied malice towards his wife as he publicly repeats his unfounded accusation that Dikeledi had taken a lover, and then 'worked up the sensation a little further' by announcing 'that he would pay the school fees of his concubine, who was also to enter secondary school, but not the school fees of his own child' (100). The spectacle enjoyed by Garesego, is contextualized as common in the 'kind of men [who] were [in] the bottom rung of government. They secretly hungered to be President with all eyes on them' (100). This brief, but revealing critique centres on a commonplace narcissistic male aspiration for power which is set against the protracted disempowerment of women, so that if Dikeledi were to tell her husband 'don't you dare put foot in the yard I don't want to see you, he would ignore it' as 'Black women didn't have that kind of power' (101). In racially charged Southern Africa, Head reminds us that the restrictions placed on Dikeledi are compounded by the combination of her race and gender. Then, in an act of further provocation, Garesego announces his return to the marital home, presenting the real prospect of the destruction of the happy life Dikeledi has so painstakingly constructed in his absence. Dikeledi ends her husband's life, significantly through castrating him. Having assumed the power denied to black women in her society, Dikeledi challenges phallocentric power in the postcolonial nation, concurrently contesting Garesego's treatment of women as disposable by disposing of his male organ.

In prison, the warden informs Dikeledi that there are 'four other women here for the same crime' (88), and so she finds herself within a commune of women who have murdered their husbands in similar fashion. The prison, located in the nation's capital Gaborone, presents a site of convergence, drawing inmates from various regions in Botswana. The narrative of abuse divulged by fellow inmate Kebonya and the inference of abuse in the unspoken narratives of the other female inmates, reiterate the breakdown of man-woman relations, locating it as a national issue which is seemingly going unaddressed. The act of murder exemplifies the lack of viable options afforded women in society to challenge abusive marriages, leading to matricide 'becoming the fashion these days' (88). The independent actions taken by these women, who are from different communities, depict a nationwide female resistance to an oppressive male hegemony which manifests in a violent eruption of reclamation of power. When asked 'Do you feel any sorrow for your crime?' Dikeledi replies quite frankly and honestly 'Not really' (89). In a paradoxical sense, the Dikeledi we see in prison has been liberated from the social confines of life as a subordinate wife to Garesego. Despite her physical confinement, she has found solace among women who share in a similar experience, forging instant bonds between them. These friendships that Dikeledi establishes qualify her as 'the collector of such treasures' (91).

The emphasis placed on the unequal power distribution in 'The Collector of Treasures' references the 'errors' of the ancestors in providing men with a 'superior position in the tribe'. This imbalance is compounded by the introduction of Victorian ideology during the colonial era in which women became further disempowered and 'the period of migratory mining labour to South Africa' catalyzed the breakdown of the family unit. During this period the man, having left his family behind, was further afflicted as he 'became "the boy" of the white man and a machine-tool of the South African mines' (92). After the emasculating and racially oppressive experiences as a migrant worker under 'white domination' in the 'choking, throttling, death-like' world of South Africa, (Beard 1986: 4) men like Garesego were then catapulted into a stark change of status in post-independence Botswana as the new government introduced a 'localization programme' and 'salaries sky-rocketed'. The multiple changes to the social order had left men as 'broken wreck[s]' and 'in an effort to flee his own inner emptiness, he spun away from himself in a dizzy kind of death dance of wild destruction and dissipation' (92). In Head's lengthy historical contextualization of the origins of this manifestation of the 'modern' man, she seeks the source in the words of Chinua Achebe, where the rain began to beat them (Achebe 1973), rather than focussing on the apportion of blame. Head's discerning treatment of the socio-historical changes that have taken place serves to account for the existence of single parent households headed by mothers, which she champions in this collection, whilst still providing a sympathetic explanation of the impact of colonization and migration on the black male experience. Within this narrative, the breakdown of the family unit is explored through socio-economic changes on a national and international scale. Head demonstrates the reach of emerging capitalist financial systems within the Southern African region. The struggles of Dikeledi, a rural woman from Botswana, can thus be located in the transnational pull of industry from South Africa.

Garesego's antithesis is offered in Paul Thebolo. Paul described by Dikeledi as a 'gift of a husband' (94), is a caring and thoughtful husband and a valuable member of the community, and his wife Kenalepe becomes a close friend of Dikeledi. The Thebolo family, who significantly move to Dikeledi's village of Pulengin the year of independence, come to denote the reassembling of the family unit, the betterment of the woman's position both within her marriage and within society and the possibilities that the independent nation holds. The mutual respect and affection between Paul and Kenalepe is accounted for by the construct of Paul as 'another kind of man in the society with the power to create himself anew' (93). This regenerative man, although depicted as being in the minority, contributes to an alternative construction of the household that contrasts with that of the abusive home or the prison. Through this nuanced portrait of rural life, Head demonstrates that it is not solely the urban centres through which to observe the impact of colonialism and the development of the nation as communities in rural Botswana display the legacies of a predominantly male emigration and the subsequent social reorganisation. As Head repeatedly references in her collection, it is the rural women who remain to nurture the next generation in the absence of the men. Head demonstrates how the lives of rural women are influenced and impacted by the changing economies of the surrounding states, so that their lives are located within both national and transnational politics and economics.

The emerging independent nation provides the backdrop to the story 'Life', for instance, as it documents the introduction of borders between Botswana and South Africa in 1963 in anticipation of Botswana's independence in 1966. Marking a new era in the nation's history, the establishment of Botswana as a sovereign nation through the creation of new frontiers is set against the nation's changing socio-cultural landscape. Prior to independence, Botswanan nationals who had settled in South Africa were obliged to return home as the story 'Life' depicts. The story introduces 'bits and bits of a foreign culture and city habits' (37) into a village that was 'ever alert to receive new ideas that would freshen up the ordinariness and everydayness of village life' (38). The village, as Head describes it, is receptive to change, but as the story progresses we learn that the changes must not deviate too far from the society's normative framework.

Life's return to her natal village from Johannesburg comes to signify the expanding influence and impact of the urban and the modern 'in a mainly rural country' (37). Whilst Life is initially well received by her community, social attitudes towards her change when she introduces prostitution to the rural society. In Life's subversion of rural gendered norms, 'the din and riot of a Johannesburg township was duplicated, on a minor scale in the central part of the village' (40). Life's residence at the heart of the village suggests that her influence disturbs the core of this society through her importation of liberal urban norms into a conservative rural setting. In Johannesburg, Life's occupations centre on her body; 'She had been a singer, beauty queen, advertising model, and prostitute'; and 'Life has had the sort of varied career that a city like Johannesburg offered a lot of black women' (39). Locating the black woman in a modernity in which the black female body is subject to the predatory instincts of the male gaze or for male consumption, the racial and gendered framing of Life's career illustrates the restricted world of the black woman in apartheid South Africa, albeit a world that Life attempts to replicate in Botswana.

The commodification of the black female body identifies the black woman as a product within the capitalist economy of urban South Africa. Despite the fact that 'the traffic of people to and fro between the two countries had been a steady flow for years and years' (37), urban South Africa and rural Botswana are constructed as having diverging norms. Even the more risqué 'beer-brewing women' who 'were drunk every day and could be seen staggering around the village, usually with a wide-eyed, illegitimate baby hitched on to their hips were themselves 'subject to the respectable order of village life' (39). Life remains a diametric figure as she could be seen to represent a racially conditioned capitalist modernity, whilst concurrently she uses her body to destabilize the patriarchal norms of Botswana society with the freedom over body and self that she exhibits.

Life's philosophy of 'live fast, die young, and have a good looking corpse', echoes a line delivered by John Derek in the 1949 American film *Knock on Any Door*. The reach of American popular culture is perceptible in its incorporation into Life's approach to life. Her proclamation of the desire to die young broke 'all the social taboos', departing from the ideals of her society which celebrates longevity, so that the beer-brewing women who were her companions made sure that they 'never followed her to those dizzy heights' (40). This ominous attraction to death is sealed when 'one evening death walked quietly into the bar' (41). The relationship with Lesego that ensued results in Life's own prophesy of a premature death. The murder of Life signals the collision of two conflicting worlds, illustrating what Martin Trump has described as 'a failure on both sides: first of the young woman to make the adjustment to village life and also of the community to offer her any meaningful alternative to the city pleasures and values with which she has grown up' (Trump 1988: 43). Read in light of the imposition of national borders, the acceptance of Life's lifestyle in South Africa and its ultimate rejection in Botswana demonstrate the different attitudes and expectations of each nation on its citizens even though 'everything had been mingled up in the old colonial days' (37). The disconnect between Life and her community leads to a tragic outcome. Life's murder at the hands of the man she married is indicative of social anxieties surrounding female sexual autonomy fuelled by monetary gain and demonstrates the suppression of challenges to the patriarchal structure.

In 'Life', as in 'The Collector of Treasures', the employment of the family unit as a motif for the nation, serves to explore changes to gender relations and the influence of urbanization and modernity on a rural society. In 'Heaven is not Closed' Head returns to the family in order to survey the changing religious landscape of Botswana. In this way home life is politicized as Head draws struggles taking place across the country into the domestic realm, so that the family is presented as a microcosm of the nation. The interface between Christianity and traditional religion is explored through the marriage of Galethebege and Ralokae in 'Heaven is not Closed'. The peaceful union between Galethebege, a Christian and Ralokae, a traditionalist, testifies to the capacity of each religion to complement the other. However, the story also points out the divisive influence of the colonial mission. This manifests through the representation of the missionaries who are shown to lack an understanding and a respect for their congregations, who they view as no more than a 'vague black blur' whom they 'did not particularly like' (10). As one of the multiple references to the racialized dynamics of colonialism, heightened in the Southern African experience, the missionaries' assumption of a position of superiority can be located in a history of unequal exchange between Europe and Africa.

The spirit of resistance to colonial and neo-colonial influences is embodied by Ralokae who recognizes that:

> The God might be alright, (…) but there was something wrong with the people who had brought the word of the Gospel to the land. Their love was enslaving black people and he could not stand it. (…) That was why he rejected all things foreign. (10)

Ralokae articulates a decolonizing narrative for the nation as he diagnoses Christianity as indicative of a mode of oppressing the people, leading him to reject its authority. Ralokae retains his religious and cultural heritage but also shows his ability to distinguish the good in Christianity from its destructive implementation. The reference to enslavement echoes the history of the forced removal of peoples from Africa who were transported to the Americas to become the property of slave owners. Referencing the slave-master dynamic, Head locates the mode of engagement in a history of subjugation, and recognizes the perpetuation of these dynamics in this contemporary manifestation. In identifying the dynamics that are being established between the missionaries and their congregation, the mode through which to subvert them is devised. The title of the short story, 'Heaven is not Closed', is indicative of the contestation of the interpretation of the Christian doctrine provided by the missionaries who assert that 'heaven is closed to the unbeliever...' (11). This proclamation serves to pacify the congregation into a submission through which the fear of hell becomes a constant deterrent from practising Setswana customs, culture and religion in favour of adopting the Christian dogma. Foreshadowed in the title of this short story, Ralokae and his community deconstruct the teachings of the missionaries, thus challenging their assertion of power both in this life and the next.

As a cultural nationalist, Ralokae grounds himself in his socio-religious heritage which provides him with a perspective of the missionaries that is distinct from his wife's, as 'it was beyond her to reason that the missionary was representative of both God and something evil'. Whilst Galethebege does not recognize the malice displayed, she is aware of the 'harshness of the missionary's attitude' (11) when he unequivocally rejects a Setswana customary marriage. Galethebege subverts the power asserted by the missionary in choosing to marry Ralokae under Setswana and choosing to remain a Christian, thereby setting her own rules of engagement. Galethebege comes to represent a form of Christianity that is in communion with Setswana belief systems, distinct from the intolerant form of Christianity coming from the missionaries. She becomes a figure of cohesion, embodied in her respect and engagement with both faiths. In doing so, Head reminds us of the unity that exists amongst the people, signified by their ability to embrace difference. Galethebege becomes figurative of a nation that has been able to absorb external influences whilst maintaining a clear notion of self.

The equilibrium achieved by Galethebege is challenged through the church's excommunication of her as a result of her Setswana customary marriage. As a figure of unity, the ramifications of Galethebege's expulsion from the church reverberate into her community. The church's inflexibility is critiqued and 'a number of people, including all the relatives who officiated at the wedding ceremony, then decided that if heaven was closed to Galethebege and Ralokae it might as well be closed to them too, so they no longer attended church' (12). The support for this couple from many members of the community demonstrates the unity that is often sought at the national level. The irrationality of the church's actions and declarations instigates community action, which is demonstrative of a collective consciousness and a collective destiny. Ralokae continues to articulate the importance of retaining cultural identity in the midst of change, but he also comes to symbolise a power base that is located in older narratives of the community as he is identified as a 'representative of an ancient stream of holiness that people had lived with before any white man had set foot in the land, and only needed a small protest to stir up loyalty for the old customs' (11). The unity, which is often associated with the communal mode of living in the rural environment as opposed to the individualism of the urban environment, provides a model for the nation, as an exemplar of the value of culture and heritage and the importance of community.

Head's women, in recasting their societies, are faced with the prospect of exile. Huma Ibrahim notes the comparative exilic experiences of Life and Galethebege, linking them to the 'coming of colonialism and the erosion it caused the family', so that:

> Life was twice exiled geographically while Galethebege was twice exiled spiritually and emotionally. The anxiety that this exile caused in the lives of these two women cannot be underestimated because they both paid dearly for it, even though Galethebege was able to muster more resistance against the dilemma that plagued her throughout her life. (Ibrahim 1996, 192)

Huma Ibrahim's analogy can be extended to incorporate Dikeledi, who faces a life in exile from her children and community in a jail in Gaborone. Her husband, a product of the imperialist capitalist system of colonialism, is the reason for her exile. Dikeledi much like Life and Galethebege are faced with the loss that is associated with a life in exile. Postcolonial Botswanan society, as represented by Bessie Head, has been shaped by differing patriarchal traditions, as women begin to re-imagine the nation they are confronted with, and the personal sacrifices they are compelled to make. Yet, the recurrent motif in the collection is the community's intervention in support of this recasting. While Dikeledi finds herself a community of women that strengthen each other, Galethebege is supported by her community that condemn the church and Life. The community disapprove of her lifestyle, but still defend her right to live; angry at Lesego, they reprimand him, 'it's a serious crime to take a human life' (45). It is through this sense of shared values and unity that Bessie Head's discourse on nationhood emerges.

The multiple perspectives in characterization expressed in this collection are facilitated by the very nature of the short story. The capacity to read each story independently of each other or to read the collection holistically replicates the varying ways in which to engage with the nation – as an entity in its own right or through its constituting regions. The three stories I have focused on are exemplary of the varying challenges that faced Botswana in and around the time of independence. The connection between the author's consciousness and the text's ideological perspectives is visible in the case of *The Collector of Treasures* partly because the author draws inspiration from history and real-life experiences for many of her stories. The researching and writing of these stories and the personal connection that Head herself sought to establish with the Bostwanan people helped her forge lasting links with the nation. The emotional investment that she placed in Botswana led her to state in clearly nationalistic and patriotic terms that:

> I don't think I'll leave Botswana, not when so much of my life and thought have gone into it (….) I have an ambition about this country. I said to myself: The best and most enduring love is that of rejection. (…) I'm going to bloody well adopt this country as my own, by force. (Head 1991: 58)

While I have focussed on three stories from *The Collector of Treasures*, the entire collection can be read as an affirmation of Head's position within Botswana society, and especially her concern with a discourse of nation-ness as exemplified in the integration of her creative writing with the people's stories – or stories of the nation. The separate stories with their specific characters present Head's imagining of her community, bound together by both the borders of the nation as well as the pages of her book.

NOTE

1 Other writers of this tradition include Yvonne Vera and Tsitsi Dangarembga.

WORKS CITED

Achebe, Chinua, 'The Role of a Writer in a New Nation', in *African Writers on African Writing*, ed. G. D. Killam. London: Heinemann, 1973.

Beard, Linda Susan, 'Bessie Head in Gaborone, Botswana: An Interview', *Sage*, 3 (1986), 44–47.

Head, Bessie, *A Gesture of Belonging: Letters from Bessie Head, 1965-1979*, ed. Randolph Vigne. London: Heinemann, 1991.

—— *A Woman Alone: Autobiographical Writings.* ed. Craig MacKenzie. Oxford: Heinemann, 2007.

—— *The Collector of Treasures, and Other Botswana Village Tales.* London: Heinemann, 1977.

Ibrahim, Huma, *Bessie Head: Subversive Identities in Exile.* Charlottesville: University Press of Virginia, 1996.

MacKenzie, Craig, 'Bessie Head's *The Collector of Treasures*: Modern Story-telling in a Traditional Botswanan Village'. *World Literature Written in English*, 29 (1989a), 139–148.

—— 'Short Fiction in the Making: The Case of Bessie Head'. *English in Africa*, 16 (1989b), 17–28.

Osei-Nyame Jnr, Kwadwo, 'Writing Between 'Self' and 'Nation': Nationalism, (Wo)man-hood and Modernity in Bessie Head's *The Collector of Treasures and Other Botswana Village Tales*'. *Journal of the Short Story in English*, 39 (2002), 91–107.

Trump, Martin, 'Black South African Short Fiction in English Since 1976'. *Research in African Literatures*, 19 (1988), 34–64.

Widowhood – Institutionalized Dead Weight to Personal Identity & Dignity

A Reading of Ifeoma Okoye's *The Trial & Other Stories*

REGINA OKAFOR

Much research has been done on the status of African women under the ideologies of feminism, motherism, womanism and accomodationism with the sole aim of correcting the devaluation of women by the early male writers such as Chinua Achebe, Ngugi wa Thiong'o, et al., who represented women as disparaged. Even early female writers including Flora Nwapa and Buchi Emecheta did not salvage their devalued situation because their heroines were crushed at the end.

At the close of the twentieth century and the start of the twenty-first century, however, some female African scholars, seeing the need for a radical elevation of African women's status, set out to correct their devalued image. As fellow women who understand their predicament they objectively portray their woeful experiences in the traditional culture. Emenyonu puts it succinctly that 'African women scholars too, were no longer satisfied to have somebody else define for them the aesthetics of female writing, or patronizingly describe for them the dynamics and intrinsic realities of being a woman in the African socio-cultural and political environment' (Emenyonu 2004: xii). These female intellectual writers redressing the injustice and subjugation of African women highlight their unique qualities to prove, according to Yvonne Vera, that 'women are what the men are not' (1991: 1). In support of the intellectual female writers who support the cause of African women, Beyala has argued that 'The African woman faces three types of battle. First, she has to struggle because she is a woman. Next, she has to assert herself as a black woman. Finally, she has to struggle for social integration. She is without doubt, the human being in the world with the greatest problems. And at the same time, she carries a lot of burden' (Beyala 2004: 70). Her 'dead weight' is that of social integration as a human being in a patriarchal society.

There is a popular Igbo saying, 'Di bum mmanwanyi' which translates to 'The husband is the beauty of the wife'. This could be interpreted to mean that no matter how pretty a woman might appear to be, her beauty is not appreciated if she is not married. And if married, she is only counted as fulfilled by making children for her husband's posterity. It is worthy of note that in this culture, a woman is considered to be married to all the members of her husband's family; they have a say in the choice of their brother's wife. And woe betide the wife if her husband's relatives do not approve of the marriage. In this case, they will make life miserable for her by finding faults with whatever she does.

We can understand why the early feminist writers like Flora Nwapa in *Efuru and* Buchi Emecheta in *The Joys of Motherhood* deal with the themes of marriage and motherhood in their novels. Ifeoma Okoye explores the same themes in *Behind the Clouds*. We witness in these novels the anxiety of the heroine to get married, and the stress, agony, and humiliation she is subjected to if the marriage is not blessed with children. The women contend with the humiliating anguish, even though the cause of the childlessness could sometimes be traced to the husband, as is the case in *Behind the Clouds*. However, after the stressful experiences of marriage, wifehood and motherhood, African widows are confronted with yet another barrier: a 'dead weight' to their personal identity and dignity.

Our study of 'Widowhood, institutionalized dead weight to personal identity and dignity' shows that a widow experiences worse scenarios of subjugation than she has suffered in marriage because when the husband was alive, his presence sometimes protected her from the meanness and attacks of the family-in-law. Now she is vulnerable and suffers the excruciating physical, emotional and psychological burden that ruthlessly strips her of all self esteem and dignity. Rather than sympathize with the widow, when a man dies, his people accuse the agonizing wife of killing her husband.

In her eleven short stories Ifeoma Okoye encapsulates the various traumatic experiences and tribulations of a widow: assaults, false accusations, exploitation and more. The ordeal of a widow is reminiscent of the proverbial saying of giving a dog a bad name in order to hang it. In many African cultures, a woman is systematically given a bad name to justify the injustices meted out to her. This injustice is evidenced by the denial of the widow's rights to the inheritance of her husband's property.

In 'Soul Healers' the widow, Somadi, accused by her husband's relatives of murdering her husband, is denied custody and visits by her two children after being subjected to the humiliating and dehumanizing traditional rites and rituals: 'When we arrived at the village for burial, my husband's brothers and sisters, his uncles, aunts, nieces, nephews and cousins, all jeered at me and spat at me and called me a murderer. To punish me, they took my children away from me … and stopped me from seeing my own children. They warned my children's teachers never to allow me to visit the children at school. … and my husband's relatives had planned to kill me' (13). Somadi escapes death from her husband's relatives; thanks to her own nuclear family who promptly take her away from the village before the funeral. Ironically, she does not witness her husband's funeral.

Somadi's husband was very possessive and overbearing. He never allowed his wife to work so that he could be in total control of her to maintain his prerogatives and authority as a man and head of the family. But Somadi desires freedom to work, acquire experience and attain fulfilment in life for self esteem as she says: '… work didn't mean earning money only. It also meant freedom, empowerment, self-fulfillment and self-esteem. It meant meeting people, gathering experience, building character and learning to live' (12). Her husband, in his pride, remained adamant even when he lost his job. Somadi defied his order, went to Lagos with her kids, Ada and KC, to take up the job.

Somadi is a faithful, loving, caring wife and mother, evidenced by her prompt arrival at the village to mourn her husband. She loves her children and wants to assume the responsibility of raising them herself. She flouts the restriction order and goes to take her kids from their school thereby making a mockery of the traditional regressive order that separates children from their mother. Her intelligence, resourcefulness and courage are commendable. Ada and KC will make her happy as they provide emotional healing from her emotional stress. Her children are really her 'soul healers' as the title of the story suggests. Though victorious, Somadi knows that the battle over the custody of her children might continue, but she will fight tooth and nail to keep her children as 'a mother hen guards her chicks from the ravenous kite'. Through this victory, Somadi has gained her self-esteem, dignity and emotional healing.

University graduate, Anayo, in 'The Trial' is good-natured, caring, respectful and nice provided her integrity and self-esteem are not compromised. Accused by her brother-in-law, Ezeji of killing Zimuzo, her husband, Anayo is summoned before the *umu-okpu*, the daughters of the husband's lineage to explain why she killed their brother. The *umu-okpu* group has a reputation for ruthlessness and rigidity in applying the traditional law. Their decision is irrevocable. Anayo being innocent cannot stake her self-esteem. Though pregnant with Zimuzo's baby, she is not allowed to sit down during the interrogation. But she holds back the tears from her eyes and fearlessly refutes the false allegation: '"That's not true," she shouted, trembling with anger, "I did not! Ezeji is wicked"' (46).

Ezeji sees his brother's demise as an opportunity to punish Anayo because he never wanted his brother to marry her for obvious reasons: her education and wisdom. He feared that she would be assertive and controlling. And when Anayo didn't get pregnant two years after their marriage, Ezeji pressurized Zimuzo to marry another wife. These facts reinforce Anayo's boldness as she defends herself because she knows that her life is at stake. A university lecturer who teaches women's studies and Oluchi, another graduate, both present at the interrogation could not utter a word in Anayo's defence or in condemnation of Ezeji. Oluchi justifies her silence by supporting tradition: 'It is not easy to challenge tradition.' Ironically, women who should bond with each other to fight the tradition now collaborate with it against their fellow woman. However, Anayo was not cowed by the daughters' intimidation; she walked out victorious.

The second phase of the trial is more decisive. In attendance are all the males in her husband's family, the oldest man in their kindred, Eletty and Anayo's mother to witness the humiliating verdict and probably Anayo's death. But she refuses to go through this stage because of the stories of juju associated with this ritual which she strongly believes is not empirical. She is also scared of the fate of the baby in her womb as an excuse not to go through the rituals. Although these reasons are legitimate, the men, especially Ezeji will not accept them.

Anayo's mother, Mama Ebo, wants her to go through the trial to avoid the consequences it might have on their family:

'Ostracize you, condemn you as a husband killer? … No man will marry a girl whose sister murdered her husband for fear of his own life. Even your brothers, no woman will marry them. … I'll be known as the mother of a husband killer. No, Anayo, you must go to the trial'. (51)

But Anayo remains resolute. As Ezeji washes the hands of the dead husband, Anayo sees him dip his finger and the poison into the bowl of water and asks Anayo to drink. But she insists on Ezeji taking a sip of the water first before she can drink it: 'Take a sip to prove your innocence and I will drink the rest' (53). Ezeji refuses. If Anayo drinks the poisoned water, she will fall dead and Ezeji will rejoice that tradition has vindicated Zimuzo. He will automatically inherit his brother's property.

His intention to kill Anayo is evident in his refusal to drink the water. Ozo dismisses the case and acquits Anayo. 'You're free to go, our wife. The accusation against you is dropped. Go and get ready for the burial of your husband' (54). Ironically, Ezeji who accuses Anayo of murder turns out to be the real murderer. Anayo has earned victory, self-esteem and dignity through her indomitable stance. She knows that the battle over her husband's property has not ended, however, as Ezeji threatens: 'You're not going to inherit the property of the man you have murdered. I'll see to it that this time around nothing can save you' (54-5).

'Between Women' focuses on Ebuka, an orphan from a very poor family and a victim of child marriage. At the age of twenty-two, she is already a widow with a daughter, Amara. Ebuka's dead weight is not from her husband's relatives but from Mrs Edet, her employer, who pays her a very meagre salary for caring for her children and doing all the domestic work. Mrs Edet is also very erratic and often flies into an excessive rage of anger which she vents on Ebuka especially on the days her husband beats her. She is abusive, selfish, controlling and wicked to Ebuka. Despite the overload of work, Ebuka is docile, submissive, hard-working and kind to Mrs Edet's children although Ebuka is not allowed to visit her own five-year-old. She works seven days a week without any break or leave. Nobody is allowed to visit her and she visits nobody. She has not seen her daughter in two years. Dorcas' visit to inform Ebuka of her daughter's illness is a turning point in Ebuka's life.

Mrs Edet's abuse ends when she does not allow Ebuka to visit her sick daughter. For once, the employee jettisons the cloak of docility and submissiveness and bravely puts on that of defiance, courage, determination and walks out on Mrs Edet and her claustrophobic house to nurse her sick child. She will hopefully find a better employer that will help her obtain good education, earn a good income and have a dignified job. Ifeoma Okoye stigmatizes the abuse of underprivileged and extols the importance of family.

In 'A Strange Disease', Enu, a widow and mother of three sons has already suffered the dehumanizing experiences of the traditional rites, but her husband's relatives including his brother Onumba still claim ownership of her husband's farmlands that Enu secures for her three sons. Onumba desires desperately to have Enu as his third wife. He visits her every night and must eat the delicious bitter leaf soup with fufu. Onumba is possessive, autocratic and selfish, evidenced in the way he talks to Enu: 'That foo-foo is taking you ages to cook. I hope you have enough of it to fill these valleys in my body. … I hope there's enough dry fish in that soup' (28). He is also proud, covetous and reputed for his virility, but cannot adequately provide for his two wives.

Enu knows that he wants to marry her for his own selfish reasons: Enu is industrious and on marriage her late husband's property and three sons will automatically pass to him. But Enu does not want to be subjected to the dehumanizing traditional rites a second time if Onumba dies. Though she is usually outspoken Enu does not have the courage to refuse him openly: the humiliation of her refusal would not go unpunished. In her wisdom, she finds a smart way of turning down his request without making Onumba feel spited. She pretends to be suffering from a serious and incurable disease that could be transmittable.

Enu cleverly spots her lower part of the body with 'white out' or 'correction fluid', strips naked before Onumba and shows him the white spots. Beset with the fear of contacting the strange disease, Onumba flees from Enu's house never to return either for the 'onugbu soup' or for marriage. Enu is free from Onumba's incessant harassment and nightly visits. Through her commendable wisdom and manipulation she secures the inheritance for her three sons and solves the problem of marriage to her brother-in-law. She peacefully enjoys her freedom, dignity and independence.

Mercy's problem in 'The New Business Woman' is job-related. Widowed and a full-time housewife with two children, she is concerned with salvaging and securing her husband's business as a motor parts dealer, but she has no expertise in the job. Odo, her husband's apprentice and his friend refuse to work with or under a woman. She inherits only a Peugeot 505 from her husband and the bank will not give her a loan without any collateral. As her friend Ezeulu explains in her desperation: 'It's going to be difficult for you to get a bank loan. You have no property and you're a woman' (64).

Ezeulu, an established and successful motor parts dealer, provides a turning point in her life by helping her on account of her ambition and determination: 'You're determined to succeed ... I'll be a very happy man if my two daughters grow up to be as self-confident and as enterprising as you. I'll help you succeed' (65). Ezeulu loans her his apprentice, Innocent, to teach her the business. Mercy is now happy to be a new business woman. The authorial voice affirms through her success that with determination and hard work, a woman can do any type of job she desires to do to attain self fulfillment. Mercy can independently raise her children.

Ebele is a victim of double circumstances in 'The Voiceless Victim'. She is from a poor family and is also a victim of child marriage into a poor family. She became a widow at the age of eighteen with two children and no brothers-in-law, education or skills. Without any education or skills, she is left with two options: prostitution and begging. Though undignified, she prefers to beg in the streets. A NITEL official is moved with compassion for Ebele's youth when she witnesses the quarrel between her and another beggar. The official advises her to find a job. This lady acts as a catalyst for change in Ebele's life because she inspires Ebele to aspire. Her timidity, facelessness and lack of self confidence result from the unfortunate circumstances of her background. Now her innate ambition, courage and determination that were dormant are awoken by the NITEL official's advice. Ebele walks into the official's office with courage, and with respectful insistence asks for any type of job. Moved with pity for Ebele's unfortunate life story, she gives her a job. She will also help her acquire the desired education that will empower her to attain self actualization and give her children adequate education. The official's compassion and help are laudable. Ifeoma Okoye's message here is for women to help each other to rise from poor situations.

In 'From Wife to Concubine', Arit's oppression and abuse start before her marriage because her husband's relatives, especially her brother-in-law, Paul, are not supportive of their union, since she is from a different ethnic group. The permanent scars on her body from the injuries sustained will always testify to their opposition. As a widow, she has suffered the humiliating traditional rites and rituals including having the hair shaved from her head. She paid all the burial expenses, but was denied participation in the planning of her husband's funeral. Paul is jealous and wants Arit's personal block of flats.

She fights relentlessly with all her resources to keep her envied property. Prior to Fred's death, he and Paul had written to her uncle, Bassey to put the property in Fred's name because they purported that it would be shameful for a man to live in a house built by his wife. But Arit's uncle refused. Traditionally any woman who is not legally married can never inherit her husband's property. Paul steals Arit's marriage certificate and then lies to everyone that she was merely his brother's concubine, not his wife: 'You are not married to Fred. You can't inherit his property, neither can your children. You were just his concubine, and concubines don't inherit properties under our customary laws' (70). Paul's blackmail backfires because Arit uses privileged information she has about Paul's murder of his cousin Samuel, at this opportune time to make him return her marriage certificate, and he will never again covet Arit's property or call her a concubine.

The theme of second marriage is explored in 'The Second Chance'. Ogoli has two children when her husband is killed and she desires to remarry and fill the vacuum created by her husband's death. Her courage to tell her uncle-in-law about her intention to remarry in a culture where a widow should not talk about remarrying outside the family is commendable. The old man explains that tradition forbids her from taking her children with her to her new husband because they bear their late father's name, Anachunam. But Ogoli refuses to uphold that cultural value. She defies the law and takes her two children to her new husband, Guery who is also a widower with three children.

Guery has a good job. He marries Ogoli who becomes the mother of the five children, and he becomes their father. The new family lives in Ibadan, a neutral city away from the inhibitive traditional environment of the provinces. The children will ever enjoy the new parental love, care and protection. Ifeoma Okoye recommends a second marriage to the couple that will adopt and raise the children from their first marriages. The children will choose which name they like to answer to, when they are grown.

Greed and the sale of daughters as merchandize are addressed in 'Daughter for Sale'. Mata is widowed with four children who she has been labouring tirelessly to raise. The two boys die leaving her with two daughters. The only male survivor in the family, Mata's greedy, wicked and insatiable brother-in-law, Uko, marries away Mata's first daughter at a very exorbitant bride price without informing Mata, the mother. Mata is very ambitious, industrious and bold. Her dream of becoming a seamstress was shattered when her father forced her into marriage to fund his drinking. At a very young age she showed her courage and bravery by expressing her dislike for her early marriage to her mother, who, as a woman, had not been consulted.

Now mature through subjugation, exploitation and abuse, Mata determines never to let Uko 'sell' her second daughter as a commodity as he had the first one, and as her own father had sold her. Mata has had enough of the insult and extortion; she will stop at nothing to prevent the renowned debtor's greed. This time, she threatens to kill Uko who, beset with fear, escapes into his house, bolts the door as Mata insults and threatens him: 'Now listen and listen carefully, Uko. I am going to disrupt the bargaining this evening. I'm going to chase everybody away with an axe. And let me tell you this. Anyone who tries to stop me will be a dead person' (87). She makes sure her daughter's suitor gives only a token fee as the bride price.

Mata has defied the traditional culture by involving herself in the marriage of her daughter. Uko quickly sends a delegation of elders to Mata to inform her that he will comply. He cannot disappoint the elders who also have a stake in the marriage: kegs of palm wine, gifts of money and tobacco. Mata's effrontery, determination, and bravery have won her victory, respect and dignity both for herself and her daughter who is not sold like a commodity. The authorial voice discourages high bride price and encourages mothers to be involved in their daughters' marriages.

In 'Waiting for a Son', Okoye makes a mockery of the importance attached to a male child in the traditional society. Egodi spent ten years in vain waiting for a son who never wrote, sent money or return for the funeral of his father. Now the anxious mother travels to Britain in search of the son. After a six-hour wait in vain at Heathrow Airport, she learns that the son has travelled with his white wife and two children to France on holidays. All the family's meagre resources were put into the son's education in Britain so that he would succeed in life and take care of the family. The son's neglect of the mother proves that he has no filial attachment to her. His abandonment negates the cultural importance attached to male children and their inheritance of the family property.

The title of the story without possessive adjective shows that there has never been any bond between mother and son. Now Egodi is consoled that her daughters are there to do for her what the son cannot do:

As if in a trance she saw her daughters, deprived, despised and degraded, standing in front of her, pleading for her love and appreciation. From their subsistence farming and petty trading, they have built her a house, sent their brother to Britain, buried their father, and paid their fare to London in search of a son who had forgotten his roots. (82)

The author proves in this story that daughters can take better care of their parents than the sons. They should therefore have a share in the family property.

In 'The Power of a Plate of Rice' Mr Aziza, principal of the school withholds Mrs Cheta Adu's salary for skipping classes without permission. Teachers are not paid regularly; the last salary received was in October last year, and it is now the end of January. Mrs Cheta Adu can only get her salary at the end of February. She is a widow with two children living with her mother-in-law, also a widow. Mrs Adu spent money lavishly on her husband's funeral and now borrows money which she cannot repay. Her several office visits to Mr Aziza to pay her salary are fruitless.

Mr Aziza is overwhelmingly dictatorial. Aziza in Igbo language literally means broom for sweeping, and in his lordly arrogance, he is ever ready to sweep his employees off their posts if they are delinquent. Though hardworking, he is corrupt and has won the members of the government to his side by giving their unqualified children admission to his school. Consequently, all the employees like Mrs Adu who complain to the government will surely lose their case.

Mrs Cheta Adu thinks that the effective way of making Mr. Aziza pay her salary is to follow him to his house. She invites herself to his table and eats the meal set for him. Mad with rage, he orders her out of his house, but she insists on being paid before she will leave. Mr Aziza has no choice but to comply. Mrs Adu's persistence, audacity and boldness have earned her salary. Ifeoma Okoye criticizes an expensive funeral ceremony and the government for late payment of teachers' salaries.

The author has effectively revealed in these short stories various ways the widows are subjugated and deprived of their rights. These widows were initially very enduring, accommodating, resilient, but languishing in silence under the dead weight of tradition. Their burdens vary from traditional rites and rituals including shaving of hair and sitting on the floor throughout the funeral ceremony, to false accusation of the murder of their husbands (Anayo, Somadi), blackmail through stealing their marriage certificate to make them look like concubines instead of wives (Arit), forcing them to marry a brother-in-law (Enu) and marrying away their nieces without informing the girl's mother (Mata). The main reason for this meanness or wicked act is to deny the widows their husbands' inheritance and keep them in perpetual subjugation and misery. Coming from poor families and without any education or skills, some of the widows take to prostitution or begging to sustain their families. Others like Udoka suffer humiliation and abuse from another woman, her employer, thus showing women as both victims and collaborators. Adversely, Ebele victim of child marriage is helped by another woman, the NITEL official who, acting as a catalyst changed Ebele's life for good.

Okoye has successfully endowed these widows with unique individuality which they exhibit at an opportune moment to fight for their rights. The resilient widows have overnight turned into raging indomitable iconoclasts against the culture of oppression. Their words become venom and weapons that men fear more than real weapons. The new womanist stance encouraged by Ifeoma Okoye is to defy the institutionalized status quo against progress and move on with victory to autonomy and dignity.

This stance is recommended by Okoye to all women who are subjugated. They should individually fight the enemy with boldness and determination like Mercy who proves to the sexists that no work is exclusive to men alone. As the customary law does not protect African women, all oppressed women should, without exception, fight individually and/or jointly until victory is won. Women should bond together in solidarity and speak with one voice to make an impact through various women organizations because 'unity is strength'.

Ifeoma Okoye exhibits courage through writing to expose the secret burden in the lives of widows. She empathizes with and encourages the widows through a new way of life to freedom, autonomy and dignity. She extols a future African society free of oppression and abuse where man and woman will have a fair and equal treatment and live harmoniously as human beings. Men, women and widows are all human beings; therefore, they should cohabit peacefully as they pursue their respective goals in life. Her recommendations are reminiscent of the peaceful Kingdom that the prophet Isaiah preaches in the Holy Bible: 'Wolves and sheep will live together in peace and leopards will lie down with young goats. Calves and lion cubs will feed together' (Isaiah 11:6). Through symbolism, imagery, idioms and characterization Okoye has given her work an African outlook and provided an insight into the excruciating mental and psychological experiences of African widows.

WORKS CITED

Beyala, Calixthe. Quoted by Tunde Fatunde in 'Calixthe Beyala Rebels Against Female Oppression'. Ed. Ernest N. Emenyonu, *African Literature Today 24*. Oxford: James Currey; Trenton: Africa World Press, 2004: 70.

Emenyonu, Ernest, N. 'Editorial Article'. *New Women's Writing: A Phenomenal Rise. African Literature Today, 24*. Oxford: James Currey; Trenton: Africa World Press, 2004: xii.

Good News Bible with Deuterocanonical Books/Apocrypha. The Bible Societies: Collins, 1979: 677.

Okoye, Ifeoma. *The Trial and Other Stories*. Lagos: African Heritage Press, 2005.

___ 'The Power of a Plate of Rice'. *Opening Spaces. An Anthology of Contemporary African Women's Writing*. Ed. Yvonne Vera. London: Heinemann, 1999: 91.

___ 'Waiting for a Son'. *Short Stories by 16 Nigerian Women*. Ed. Toyin Adewale-Gabriel. California: Ismael Reed Publishing Company, 2005: 81.

Vera, Yvonne. Preface to *Opening Spaces. An Anthology of Contemporary African Women's Writing*. op.cit.: 1.

Feminist Censure of Marriage in Islamic Societies

A Thematic Analysis of Alifa Rifaat's Short Stories

> Freedom
> My freedom
> I shall carve the words in the earth
> chisel their sounds
> over every door in the Levant...
> below the slope at every street
> corner inside the prison
> within the torture chamber
> (*Fadwa Touqan cited in Mikhai 2013*)

Formal literary writing began far later for women than men. In England for instance, Fitzmaurice et al. (1997) assert that it is virtually impossible to name a woman writer prior to Jane Austen even though women were writing as early as the time of Chaucer (1). They argue that until the seventeenth century, women writers were viewed as 'odd' adding that 'the enormous commercial and artistic success of Aphra Behn's plays on the London stage of the 1670s and 1680s marked the end of the time where only men were literary luminaries' (1).

The suppression of female expression has been a global phenomenon. In Africa, the formal education of women and their ability to express themselves in writing began even later. Many female writers on the continent in the 1980s and 1990s had very little or no education. Writing on the continent was the preserve of the masculine gender at the time for the simple reason that females were then deterred from attaining a formal education (Bertons 2001: 94). Hence though they told stories under the moonlight and by the kitchen fire; that was as far as it went.

Irrespective of this situation, through female writers like Rifaat who wrote in their native languages, the denigrating issues pertinent to women were put on the literary globe. Voices as projected by Alifat Rifaat and other Arab feminists such as Nawal El Sadaawi, Fatima Mernissi and Leila Ahmed invariably gave birth to the idea of feminist criticism in Arab literature. Theirs is an attempt to 'question the static nature of Islamic ideology that resists critical inquiry and a certain openness to change especially in terms of gender' (Mehta, 2010:11).

Portrayals of women in Arabic literature, in the words of Mikhai (2013) serve as a barometer by which we can measure the status and role of Arab women in society. Mikhai believes that though some may argue that literature and real life are two different matters, Arabic letters gives an idea about the conditions of women in Arab societies. As such, the value of literature in understanding and bringing about change, regeneration, and transformation within the very fabric of these societies is not to be underestimated (1).

Perhaps one of the most prominent theories known for ensuring that the relevance of literature in societal transformation is not taken for granted is the feminist literary theory. Feminist literary theory, since Simon de Beauvoir's *The Second Sex,* has advocated female rights and privileges through literary criticism. Bertons (2001) posits that this theory uses socio-cultural and historical circumstances as a factor in presenting literature to the world. Haslanger et al. (2010) describe feminism as 'both an intellectual commitment and a political movement that seeks justice for women and the end of sexism in all forms' (1).

In this paper, the focus is on the way 'patriarchy' is manipulated by Rifaat's Egyptian society as a sexist orientation. It is also on how the oppression of women is perpetuated through male-dominated religious structures and social arrangements. Patriarchy, Santillan (1998) avers, almost by definition also exhibits androcentrism, meaning male centeredness. Coupled with patriarchy, andro-centrism assumes that male norms operate throughout all social institutions and become the standard to which all persons adhere (Santillan 1998). The situation of Arab women as depicted in literature, is analysed in this paper from the feminist perspective with issues of patriarchy and androcentricm highlighted. Attention is paid to Rifaat as a female writer. Based on her works selected as the primary texts, the psychodynamics of female creativity; linguistics and the problem of female language and the trajectory of the individual or collective literary career; literary history, is discussed. By interrogating the sort of roles female characters play, with the themes they are associated with, implicit presuppositions from the reader's perspective and how literary representations of women repeat familiar cultural stereotypes, Rifaat's message to her readers as she expediently presents her stories about marriage in relation to the woman's rights and societal values is analyzed. The repetition could be a projection of feminine conditioning to subjectivity or an ironic or otherwise sarcastic depiction of masculine conscious annihilation of femininity. Rifaat's women to a great extent use what I call the 'kowtow strategy' as their way of expressing their own physical and psychological suffering in order to denounce the practice of vocal imprisonment in their confined spaces. This strategy is where a woman submits to the wantonness of a man to all extremes as a way of bringing out his worst. It is a non-assertive approach to protesting rights abuse where the reader is given enough room to make a personal judgement. From this perspective, Rifaat's women are discussed, in terms of human rights, sex and gender roles.

Socio-economically, the word 'feminine' itself is a cultural construction of a gender role that has been assigned to countless generations of women of varying ethnicities and religions. The Islamic world in Egypt is no exception to the cultures that have records of socio-historical and cultural biases towards women. Orabueze, a literary critic, describes Egypt, the setting of Rifaat's short stories, as an Arab society where the powerful used the subterfuge of religion to economically exploit the citizens. In this society, an Islamic woman is under the protection and rule of her husband if she is married, or of her oldest brother if she is single or widowed. She often has little or no control over finances or major decisions. In the words of Ezrahi, 'The most arbitrary powers in history hide under the claim of some impersonal logic – God, the laws of nature and, the laws of the market – and they always provoke a backlash when morally intolerable discrepancies become obvious' (Ezrahi cited in Orabueze, 2010: 127). 'Fewer women are educated in the Arab world than in other cultures. The percentage of women working in sectors other than agriculture is probably the smallest in the world and the laws regarding marriage and related matters most unequal' (Stowasser 1994: 5). Indeed such cultural and religious norms become hindrances to the freedom and development of the female life. They provide the blatant excuse for Rifaat's women's total submission to what I dare to call 'silent Killing'; a situation where a woman, hypnotized by the threatened consequences of breaking a taboo in Africa, resolves to quietly suffer 'till death do us part'. This condition is fueled by the combined repressive forces of 'religion' and 'tradition' whose effect Mernissi (1999) reiterates without mincing words:

> Not only have the sacred texts always been manipulated, but manipulation of them is a structural characteristic of the practice of power in Muslim societies since all power from the seventh century, was only legitimated by religion, political forces and economic interests pushed for the fabrication of false traditions. (8)

Alifa Rifaat is strategic in navigating a society that frowns on the vociferous female. Perhaps for this reason, though she laments the limits placed on women in Egyptian society in *Distant View of a Minaret*, she never queries Islam's ultimate legitimacy. Every story contains elements of Islamic faith as her loyalty to religion. Muslims believe there is one God, and that whatever occurs in a person's life happens through the will of Allah. Muslims are guided by the Five Pillars of Faith: the acknowledgement of Allah as the one true deity; the performance of prayer rituals at least five times a day; the giving of alms; refraining from eating, drinking, smoking and sex from dawn until dusk during the month of Ramadan; and making at least one pilgrimage to Mecca (in modern-day Saudi Arabia) during one's lifetime. These guidelines, as well as other elements of Islam, saturate Rifaat's stories and put them resolutely in the Islamic convention. She further tenders a set of narratives that is also a nuanced depiction of the hegemony embedded in patriarchal privileges which compromise women's emotional relationship with husbands and lovers. Three of her narratives are the primary texts for the discussions in this paper; *Distant View of a Minaret, Baddriyah and Her Husband,* and *The Long Night of Winter.*

Born in the 1930s, an era of uncontested patriarchy, and conditioned by politics, religion and an entire atmosphere of 'locked in the kitchen', Cohen-Mor (2012:1) asserts that Alifa Rifaat spent her entire life in Egypt. In the confines of her Islamic world, she grew up in the traditions and culture of Islam. When her ambition for higher education and a career in the arts was thwarted by her parents arranging for her to be married, she submitted since religion and state decreed this for women of her time. With the early death of her husband came some sense of an unknown freedom meshed with the anxieties of single parenthood. Irrespective of this, she raised three children alone. Years of marital, religious and political dictates of confinement that ensured the denial of formal education, meant that Rifaat, a Muslim woman, could read only Arabic. For this reason, her exposure to literature was limited to works written in or translated into Arabic, the Qur'an and the Hadith (a book of sayings of the Islamic prophet, Mohammed). It also meant she had no college education. However, she did receive some education at the British Institute in Cairo (1946–49). She continued reading works of Arab fiction and religious works, till she eventually began writing in 1955, (information from Wikipedia, the free encyclopedia). Because Alifa Rifaat had very little travelling experiences in her life, many of her stories are set in the local environs of Egypt and without influence from the West. Consequently, as an alternative to taking the conservative feminist approach of writing about how women's lives should change, she rather criticizes men for not fulfilling their roles within the Islamic tradition. She does not question the role of women according to the faith of Islam but rather depicts the hardships imposed on women because of men's inadequacies. Her collection of short stories, *Distant View of a Minaret (1983)*, is dominated by the recurring ideas of sexual frustration, pervasive cultural pressures, and death (Cohen-Mor 2012). Rifaat exhibits a sense of raw emotion and authenticity in her writing. This has been missed since her death in Egypt in 1996. However, her attempt to set the stage for Arab feminist criticism is surely more than accomplished with her masterpiece, *Distant View of a Minaret* (1983).

Distant View of a Minaret is a collection of fifteen short stories that gives readers a glimpse of what it means to be a woman in orthodox Muslim society in Egypt. The stories are not interconnected, but together they form a picturesque portrayal of the Arab woman's world. The compilation openly yet subtly depicts the raucous socio-cultural implications of the intersection of religion, marriage and tradition. This trio, notorious for their exceptional ability to disempower women in the Arab world, forms the core of the problems in all the stories in the collection. Consequently, in many of the stories, the female characters refuse to interrogate or fight against those social structures which marginalize them. They neither overtly nor subversively oppose the patriarchal tyrannies that suppress their happiness. They are passive and unable to fight back. Their actions and inactions set the stage for a critical enquiry into Rifaat's way of exploring the relationship between power and its assertion in the binaries of man/woman and husband/wife relationships as depicted in the highly patriarchal Arab world in three of the short stories in the collection: 'The Long Night of Winter', 'Badriyya and Her Husband' and 'Distant View of a Minaret'.

The first story, 'Distant View of a Minaret', concerns a woman and her husband having sex. The wife thinks about her lack of sexual fulfillment – her husband always snores as soon as he climaxes. She has told him her desires but he ignores her and makes her feel embarrassed for trying to prolong their sexual intercourse so that she too, might reach orgasm. The wife, hearing the call for the daily afternoon prayer, gets up and washes according to Islamic laws while the husband stays in bed to nap. After prayers the woman gazes out of the window of their apartment, thinking that she once had the view of the entire city of Cairo. According to her, the city has developed over the years, and now the view is limited to that of a single minaret (tower of a mosque). She had wished to have a house with a garden in the suburbs, but because of her husband's job, they got an apartment in the city. She didn't mind much because of the wonderful view, but now it is all gone.

Zennouba awakes at midnight in 'The Long Night of Winter', to learn that her husband is not in bed. She starts to think back in her life, especially of her loss of freedom since puberty. In order to keep their land in the family, she is married to her cousin Hagg. Sex with Hagg is unpleasant and soon he begins sleeping with the servant girl. When she asks him for a divorce, Hagg reveals that Zennouba's own father did the same, hence the pointlessness in granting her a divorce. This is Hagg's way of reminding his wife that she sold her freedom to make a decision concerning her own life with the option to marry. Zennouba's adoration and reverence for her father is tainted at this news. She wonders if all women are doomed to the same fate.

'Badriyya and her Husband' is another story of disappointment. After being incarcerated for stealing a couple of hollow tyres, Badriyya's husband, Omar, is released. Even then, he does not come home straight away to his wife who has waited in loneliness for him. Badriyya sees her husband walking down the street with a group of men celebrating his release from prison. Badriyya's mother once comments that he was a fool for stealing a couple of worthless tyres showing her clear disapproval of Badriyya's choice of husband. Finally Omar comes home late and drunk. He is glad that his mother-in-law has gone to bed so that he doesn't have to endure her spiteful remarks.

These three stories fictionalize some of the bizarre marriage situations that frustrate women. In many instances women have had to endure marriages instead of enjoying them. A wife loves to be put before friends but this is not what the husbands do. Omar, Badriyya's husband is a case in point. His wife and home are the last things on his mind so he comes home very late and drunk with no attention for the woman who stood her grounds against the family proposal of divorce; waiting all this while for the man she loves. Thus the sense of disappointment and the feeling of dejection is evident when

> As Omar passed, Badriyya hoped he would turn and notice her at the window. But the group passed and went on down the lane until they turned off and disappeared. (29)

The reason Rifaat gives for Omar's neglect of his wife – avoiding his mother-in-law – is perhaps the writer's way of criticizing family monopolization of the marriages of their relatives; a situation which puts unnecessary pressure on the couple and for which people like Badriyya, their daughters especially, pay for.

The scenario in Badriyya's story is similar to that of Zennouda in 'The Long Night of Winter'. In Zennouda's tale, she also has a long wait after realizing in the middle of the night that her husband has sneaked out of bed and into the room of her house help. Just as Badriyya's mother keeps Omar away from home, this house help keeps Zennouda's husband out. Rifaat criticizes women who facilitate the unhappiness of other women. Perhaps, like a typical feminist, Rifaat prefers women to look after each other instead of stabbing themselves in the back. The art of criticizing women as a feminist is what could be described as 'feminine introspection'. There is all the indication in Badriyya's story that a mother is supposed to guide her daughter through the journey of marriage and that without a mother's blessing a daughter may never find happiness in the marriage.

On the other hand, must Badriyya's mother be blamed entirely for the unhappy marriage of her daughter? Could Badriyya's unhappiness be attributed to Badriyya's mother's loathing of Omar when she even says: *The boy is not just a criminal but a fool as well.* Is Rifaat's wild language her own way of reprimanding the unnecessary interference of some mothers in their daughter's marriages? (30) Could we not attribute the woes of the couple to the circumstances that led to their marriage? Do these circumstances justify Badriyya partly blaming herself? She had blindly fallen in love and she begins to recall her romance with Omar. Omar followed her into a movie theatre and sat beside her. He asked her out the next week and talked of plans to open his own café (33). Which woman would not find a man like that promising? Thus without a second thought Badriyya felt that Omar, like the hero in the movies, would liberate her from her lonely life. Men certainly know their kind. Badriyya's uncle is able to read in-between the lines and warns her niece that Omar is 'all talk'. A month after the marriage Omar is arrested. Badriyya's uncle and mother do everything they could to get her to divorce Omar. It took Badriyya forever to appreciate the worthlessness of her husband and to disentangle herself from what Rifaat describes as 'sudden and romantic' and unsuccessful. Even then the tentacles of subjectivity embedded in her psyche and ruling her entire world taunted her as she walked back, asking herself how it would be possible for her to find the strength not to open the door to him (38).

Nonetheless, a feminist re-reading of this text makes it difficult to blame Badriyya entirely just as her mother and the rest of the family could not be held entirely responsible for her failed marriage. The shroud of flattery and deception that made her accept Omar as a husband, calling him 'my man' (30) is the very one that made her believe that Omar has actually changed. This shroud is what Badriyya's mother referred to when she said 'Love is blind' (34). The morning after Omar returns from prison, Badriyya comes home to find him with her mother laughing and playing cards. Badriyya thinks that she has never seen her mother in such a fine disposition. Her disbelief in what she sees and her belief in Omar's new leaf is merged especially when her mother confirms that Omar was a nice fellow after all. Omar tells them about the people he met in prison, in particular a contractor/vendor who has promised to help him. Omar is to meet this vendor that evening to the disappointment of his wife who is planning a festive dinner. Rifaat defends Badriyya by making her mother fall prey to Omar's schemes. By this the blame is squarely placed at Omar's door making him the epitome of male tricksters who aim to take undue advantage of women, shower them with gifts and promises and the pretence of change. Omar and Zennouba's husband are portrayed with the same characteristics. The latter also gives his wife presents to shut her up and further pretends to have changed when the servant girl whom he has been having secret sexual bustles with is sent away.

'Sex', a taboo word in Africa, serves as the marital whip in all the stories. Both Zennouba and Badriyya experience bizarre marital and sexual frustrations and there is no mention of their children. Omar stays out late and comes home tired, drunk and drugged while Hagg Hamdam stays out of his matrimonial bed altogether. It is for such reasons that Rifaat criticizes men who do not fulfil their roles within the Islamic tradition; taking care of their family and procreating. In Badriyya's case, Omar scouts for a location to establish his café at night. They have not had sex for a long time and when she complains, Omar replies that there is plenty of time for that in the future. This is what is called breach of marital contract in Islam. When Badriyya's mother asks when she can expect a grandchild, Omar spits a lie that implies that Badriyya never wants to have sex. When the issue of sex comes up, Badriyya is upset and begins to think that she is unattractive to Omar and that is why he seeks sexual satisfaction outside his nuptial home. With the deserted wife beginning to feel inadequate, we get the sense that whenever husbands start looking elsewhere there is the tendency for wives to begin blaming themselves and lose self esteem. In 'The Long Night of Winter', sex with Hagg is unpleasant for Zennouba though she does not complain. Still, she soon finds her husband in another woman's bed. Even when she asks for divorce so that she has the chance of finding happiness elsewhere, Hagg refuses her. Zennouba wants to quit her marriage but she is trapped while Badriyya has the opportunity to leave but chooses to stay perhaps with the hope that the situation might change. The two wives discussed here represent the marital situation and options available to many women in Islam.

There is yet another scenario in the third of Rifaat's stories selected for this discussion. The wife in 'Distant View of a Minaret', whose name we are not told tells a similar marital tale. Like Zennouba but unlike Badriyya, this wife has some sex with her husband. The problem with her marriage is that she enjoys having sex with her husband but not fully. Whenever she complains or attempts to urge her husband on so she can reach full orgasm as he does, she receives a hail of insults in return.. In the end, like the others, she is also deprived of sexual satisfaction. She prefers to occupy her mind with domestic issues, her true gender responsibility. Thus:

> She was suddenly aroused from her thoughts by his more urgent movements. She turned to him and watched him struggling in the world he occupied on his own. His eyes were tightly closed, his lips drawn down in an ugly contortion, and the veins in his neck stood out. She felt his hand on her leg, seizing it above the knee and thrusting it sideways as his movements became more frenzied. She stared up at her foot that now pointed towards the spider web and noted her toenails needed cutting. (2)

Rifaat seeks to reiterate that deprivation of any form in a legal marriage is a cardinal offence. Both husband and wife must therefore have a fair share of everything due to couples in marriage. This is the form of equality and equity that feminism advocates.

The deprivation of sexual satisfaction in marriage emerges as a critical feminist issue in Arab literature. It amounts to the tyranny of masculinity. Rifaat's depiction of her Muslim husbands is not complimentary. In all three stories the monstrosity of husbands is painted. They are presented as disgusting and animal-like when having sex. This is to the extent that Rifaat describes the face of the husband in 'Distant View of a Minaret' as with 'ugly contortions' (2). In 'The Long Night of Winter', the husband has 'evil-smelling breath' and repugnant 'rough hands'. The husbands are depicted as selfish infidels and often as con artists associating their wives with madness and sorcery when they attempt to ask for what is due to them (2). We find out that these wives are not the first to go through such experiences when Badriyya's husband makes reference to her father's attitude. Zennouba's mother's response, 'all men are the same' (57), indicates that she too has suffered a similar fate in her marriage.

In the face of all the grappling, Rifaat seems to suggest that perhaps when women find themselves in such uncomfortable marriage situations, they must muster the courage to speak up and also make bold decisions in their own favour, rather than subjecting themselves to the unbearable situation in the hope of a better someday, or sometimes even out of fear of breaching a cultural or religious norm. The inability of the women discussed to speak up and stand up is attributed to timidity and naivety but not ignorance. Their attitude suggests that in marriage, women are likely to work at pleasing their men to keep them rather than vice versa. The lesson, obviously, is that marriage is a collaboration of two and women deserve better treatment and respect: that is what feminism advocates. It nonetheless takes a particular interest in the importance of love in marriage. Most of the marriages in Rifaat's short stories are unhappy ones with regard to the women. Many of the husbands show unfaithfulness and their wives are emotionally and sexually unsatisfied. We are made to wonder whether all these marriages hit a similar runway because they are arranged. The couples seem not to have ever been in love. The two things we can learn from Rifaat's stories are that marriages should not be arranged, and that husbands must satisfy their wives in all areas. Arranged marriages often ignore the desires of the woman. A case in point is Zennouba's experience of 'a night of violence and pain' on her first night of marriage. Such sheer absence of love in a legal marriage is what feminism is unaligned with (Daniels-Ofosu, 2013). The call therefore is to provide women with a forum to air their grievances, coupled with an opportunity for Badriyya and Zennouba and women like them to seek redress; another key feminist objective. The situation in many Arab societies is one in which many women pay dearly for just a bit of appreciation, freedom and justice. Some of the women who are not actually widows lead lonely lives resembling those of widows. In 'Badriyya and Her Husband', Badriyya is married to a selfish infidel and has not even had sex with him. In 'The Long Night of Winter,' Zennouba must constantly deal with her husband's affairs with the servant girls and in the 'Distant View of a Minaret' a wife is called a murderer for asking to reach orgasm. Each of these wives must find the strength to endure a dejected life. This is a deviation especially when 'In Islamic law women have male guardians; woman's testimony is worth half that of a man; women are considered to have less reason than men' (Beck and Keddie 1978, 25-6). The absence and therefore urgent need for equality and justice for women in Islam is vividly fictionalized in Rifaat's *Distant View of a Minaret*.

In conclusion, Alifa Rifaat subtly yet consciously foregrounds the female subjugation lodged in her Egyptian world. This is a world metaphorically shared by many women in Islam today. It is a world that depicts a tense atmosphere whenever religion and the culture of marriage intersect. It is also a world in which, in many cases, women and children are at the receiving end of the clash. In Alifa Rifaat's short stories discussed so far, women, and for that matter wives, have fallen prey to their husbands. Wives have had to endure discomfort because either religion or culture has bid them so; a religion that allows men to have as many as four wives and a culture that calls it a taboo for a woman to be single (unmarried, widowed or divorced). Irrespective of the gloomy picture of marriage painted in these stories, the lessons to be learnt are inconspicuous. Rifaat makes it clear that sexual intercourse should be enjoyed by both partners in any legitimate marriage. To her, 'enjoyment' does not refer only to physicality; the act of sex should be one of consideration, leading to a stronger bond. The husband and wife in 'Distant View of a Minaret' must connect on a sexual level. Obviously, it is interesting to note that Rifaat is an orthodox Muslim. Her writing reflects the ideology of gender equity and equality that was preached by Mohammed. She skillfully presents a point of view that is often ignored by mainstream media in Africa especially and the Muslim world as well.

In *Distant View of a Minaret*, all thirteen of Alifa Rifaat's short stories were initially written in Arabic. In 1983 when these were published, Rifaat was described as the female writer who most convincingly expresses what it means to be a woman living in a traditional Muslim society. Many of her stories touch on sex and death in a subtle defiance. Her directness in treating sexual themes and women's thinking about them has been regarded as unusual for her time by many critics. In all the stories, the emotions behind the author's writing are quietly and deeply religious, particularly in the face of neglect on the part of her women and the wantonness of the men. Though it is difficult for a reader to agree to some of the decisions by her characters such as their resignation to their fate, it makes sense to also admire the sensibility with which Rifaat describes these characters and their lot. For instance, for what reason would a wife in the act of having sex with a legitimate husband assume that the husband is occupying a world of his own, utterly different from hers, a world from which she had been excluded? This is Rifaat's ingenuous way of depicting the sadness, alienation and a sense of worthlessness felt by a wife even as she echoes the nature of greed, selfishness of a husband and the carelessness with which they fall foul of the religious contract of marriage.

REFERENCES

Beck, L. & Keddie, N. (1978). 'Women in the Muslim World'. USA: HUP.

Bertons, H. (2001) *Literary Theory: The Basics*. USA: Routledge.

Cohen-Mor, D. (retrieved May, 2012) 'Anthology of Short Stories' http://readinpleasure. wordpress. com/tag/alifa-rifaat/

Daniels-Ofosu, J. (2013) 'The Feminist Voice in Contemporary Ghanaian Female Fiction: A Textual Analysis of Amma Darko's *Faceless* and *Not Without Flowers*'. *Research on Humanities and Social Sciences*. Madison Ave: International Institute for Social Science, Technology & Education.

Fitzmaurice, J., Roberts, J.A., Barash, C.L., Cunnar, E.R., and Gutierrez, N.A. (1997) *Major Women Writers of Seventeenth-Century England*, Michigan: University of Michigan Press.

Haslanger, S., Tuana, N., and O'Connor, P., (2011) 'Topics in Feminism,' *The Standard Encyclopedia of Philosophy* (Winter 2012 edition) CA: Stanford University. http:// plato.stanford.edu/archives/win2012/entries/feminism-topics/

Mehta, J. B. (2010) 'Excavating the Divine Feminine: Nawal El Saadawi's Creative Dissidence and Religious Contentions' in Emenyonu, E. N. (Ed.) *Emerging Perspectives on Nawal El Saadawi*. Trenton: Africa World Press.

Mernissi, F. (1999). The Veil and the Male Elite. NY: Addison-Wesley Publishing Company.

Mikhai M. (retrieved: 2013) 'The Role of Women in Arabic Literature' http://www. library.cornell.edu/colldev/mideast/awomnlit.htm

Orabueze, F. O. (2010), 'Womanhood as a Metaphor for Sexual Slavery in Nawal El Saadawi's *Woman at Point Zero*' in Emenyonu, E. N. (Ed.) *Emerging Perspectives on Nawal El Saadawi*. Trenton: Africa World Press.

Rifaat, A. (1987) *Distant View of a Minaret*. Portsmouth, NH: Heinemann.

___ 'Badriyya and her Husband' in *Distant View of a Minaret*. Portsmouth, NH: Heinemann.

___ 'The Long Night of Winter' in *Distant View of a Minaret*. Portsmouth, NH: Heinemann.

Santillan, J. (1998) Patriarchal System: The Exclusion of Women in Medical Case Studies, USA: University of California at Davis.

Stowasser, F. B. (1994). 'Women in the Qu'ran, Traditions, and Interpretations'. NY: OUP.

Zohrab, P. D. (2002). 'Sex, Lies & Feminism' Lower Hutt, N.Z.: New Zealand Equality Education Foundation.

Diaspora Identities in Short Fiction by Chimamanda Ngozi Adichie & Sefi Atta

ROSE A. SACKEYFIO

The African short story has come of age in the twenty-first century through the creative artistry of younger generation African women writers such as Chimamanda Ngozi Adichie and Sefi Atta. As leading women writers of both novels and short fiction, their literature chronicles a new reality of social change and modernity that transforms the lives of African women within a global arena. Since the turn of the century, their fiction mirrors the lives of contemporary African women who grapple with challenges of migration and displacement, and the impact of globalization. Chimamanda Ngozi Adichie's short story collection *The Thing Around Your Neck* (2009) and *News from Home* (2010) by Sefi Atta reflect the evolution of the African short story in subject and theme. A noteworthy feature of leading stories in both collections is the emergence of African diaspora identities that are ambiguous and disjointed.

In the postmodern era, African women's identities are changing and they must overcome new social and economic forces in addition to familiar barriers like patriarchy and traditional norms and customs. Globalization has thrust African women beyond the boundaries of the motherland into a world where they must renegotiate their existence in an alien western environment. This essay examines the exploration of diaspora identities of African women in selected short fiction by Chimamanda Ngozi Adichie and Sefi Atta. Diaspora experiences take centre stage through connecting themes of hybridity, clash of cultures and alienation.

Chimamanda Ngozi Adichie and Sefi Atta are young writers in a new literary age who are taking the lead in the exploration of new frontiers for women as they tell 'herstories' in their works. The perspectives from which they write are shaped by their lives as diaspora Africans who straddle both worlds. Tanure Ojaide confirms that what the younger generation writes about is different. Older or first generation authors write about the motherland in ways that are nostalgic and grounded in the African cultural landscape (2008: 44).

With reference to female writers, literary godmothers such as Ama Ata Aidoo, Flora Nwapa, and Buchi Emecheta wrote against colonization and culturally defined roles of subjugation for females in society. As pioneer writers, their works were fuelled by feminist energies as a way of writing back to the absence of strong women figures in male authored texts. In their fiction, they paved the way for the current generation of talented female writers and gave voice to feminist expression in novels set in Africa.

However, some of their fiction did introduce subjects and themes about African women who traverse geographical boundaries. Buchi Emecheta published her autobiographical novel *In the Ditch* (1972), about her life in London as a single parent. Ama Ata Aidoo's *Our Sister Killjoy* (1977), is about a Ghanaian woman who travels to Germany and *Changes; A Love Story* (1991), profiles three female protagonists, one of whom lives in London for a period. In 2012 Aidoo released *Diplomatic Pounds*, a collection of contemporary short stories that focus on the diaspora experiences of Ghanaian women. The dark side of globalization for African women is examined in Chika Unigwe's *Black Sisters Street* (2008) and *Trafficked* (2009) by Akachi Adimora Ezeigbo. In both works, African women are lured into the international sex industry in Europe. In all of the works, women's identities take on new dimensions in western environments that command interrogation of the African 'self'. Chimamanda Ngozi Adichie and Sefi Atta express, in their short story collections, a connecting thread to these earlier works through incongruent cultural realities that fragment women's identities in modern society.

~

Chimamanda Ngozi Adichie's literary works command attention in both Africa and the Western world by earning prestigious awards of enormous distinction. *Purple Hibiscus* (2003) was awarded the Commonwealth Prize for Best First Book in 2005. In 2006, her second novel, *Half of a Yellow Sun* was released, for which she won the Orange Broadband Prize for fiction in 2007 and she was awarded the MacArthur Foundation (Genius) Fellowship in 2008 in addition to the O'Henry Prize for the short story, *The American Embassy*. Her third novel *Americanah* was published in 2013 to great acclaim and her short stories have been published in many important literary magazines and journals such as *The New Yorker, Granta,* the *Financial Times* and *Zoetrope* and her work has been translated into thirty languages. Her career has developed mainly in America where she attended college and graduate school.

Adichie's remarkable talent firmly establishes her reputation as a master of her craft and her contribution to writing has not only expanded the female gaze in literature but has also given credibility to youthful energies and insight that bridge the gap between African writers of different eras.

Her recognition and acceptance by western audiences is clearly shaped by her visibility and marketing opportunities in America and her works have charted a new course in the evolution of the African short story. Adichie's short fiction is a window into lived experiences of contemporary African women expressed in fresh and compelling prose. Onukaogu and Onyerionwu have noted a marked sense of 'a biographic link between Adichie and her fiction of the diasporic inclination, especially since many of her characters are young female characters in their prime' (2010: 239).

The Thing Around Your Neck is a collection of twelve stories. Several of them read like modern dilemma tales revealing the way African women's identities are transformed by unfamiliar environments, tensions and contradictions within new spaces. In the story *Imitation*, the first in the collection, Adichie portrays the unhappy life of a young and wealthy Nigerian wife living in Philadelphia. Nkem learns that her husband, who resides in Nigeria has not only taken a mistress, but has moved her into their home in Lagos. The story is told in the third person and skilfully unravels Nkem's inner battle to rediscover her womanhood as she attempts to alter her appearance.

Adichie artfully weaves the theme of hybridity into the story through the strong symbolism of the Benin mask and Nok terracotta that her husband brought from Nigeria on his yearly visits. The art works are imitations but their beauty and cultural significance are lost outside the historical context of Nigeria. The symbolism parallels Nkem's worthless existence in America as she attempts to copy the appearance of her husband's mistress in Nigeria. Her inner conflict deepens through voiceless submission and vacuous perceptions of herself, her life and her empty marriage. Nkem recalls that 'when she first came to America she had been proudly excited because she had married into the coveted league, 'The Rich Nigerian Men Who sent their wives to America to Have their Babies league' (Adichie 2009: 26). Though she is materially comfortable in her American dream role as the wife of a 'Big Man', in reality her life is fragmented and disconnected from her culture. She begins to contemplate her lonely existence when a Nigerian woman she meets at a wedding tells her that, 'our men like to keep us here … they visit for business and vacations, they leave us and the children with big houses and cars, they get us house girls from Nigeria who we don't have to pay outrageous wages and they say business is better in Nigeria and all that' (28).

She is torn between two worlds because despite these new revelations, a part of her celebrates her questionable existence in America as she thinks that:

> she really belonged to this country now, this country of curiosities and crudities, this country where you could drive at night, and not fear armed robbers, where restaurants served one person food for three (37).

She admits to herself that… 'America has grown on her, snaked its roots under her skin' (37).

Nkem describes her neighbours as 'pale-haired and lean' but she liked them and their lives, 'Lives Obiora often called plastic' (24). It is as if they are imitations of real people. And although she does miss home and her friends, she has never seriously considered moving back to Lagos.

In a pivotal scene in the story, her husband brings an original piece of artwork from Nigeria that dates back to the eleventh century. As she reflects upon the historical significance of the carving, her consciousness begins to stir, and although she has remained unquestioning and shallow in her thinking, she awakens to reclaim her Nigerian identity. The story ends on an upbeat note as she announces to her husband that she and her children will return home after all. The idea that she has been stretched out of shape emotionally in a foreign environment is a modern day parable of diaspora conflict. Adichie allows the possibility of individuals recovering what they have lost or pushed aside in the rush to acquire the trappings of western life. Imitation is a realistic and vivid rendering of the pitfalls of acculturation.

The Thing Around Your Neck is the title of the collection as well as the most compelling story. It illuminates the life of another young woman from Nigeria who is searching for something elusive in America. She has won the American visa lottery and arrives at the home of her uncle in Maine. Akunna experiences culture shock throughout almost the entire story and the third person narrator recalls an endless array of stereotypical encounters and abrasive experiences that confront her on a daily basis.

The clash of cultures trope is dramatized through accounts of pointed questions, condescending remarks, and ridiculous assumptions by people in her New England environment. Adichie's artistry interweaves a binary construction of stereotypes that is laced throughout her disquieting existence. The negative comments by the people around her are juxtaposed alongside her own unrealistic expectations and ideas about life in America. The opening lines of the story jolt the reader's senses because Akunna thought that 'everybody in America had a car and a gun' (115). Before she departs Nigeria both she and her family expect her to get rich quick and 'send handbags, and shoes and perfumes and clothes' (115). Her family expects that within months she will acquire a big house and a car.

Akunna's uncomfortable experiences begin at the community college she attends but they are heightened when she strikes out on her own after leaving the sheltered home of her uncle. She ends up in Connecticut after rejecting his sexual advances which pushes her into a world of crushing loneliness. Her new environment is incomprehensible as she is asked 'where she learned to speak English', whether people in Africa had real houses, and questions about her hair. She faces a barrage of questions that are based upon what her uncle describes as 'a mixture of ignorance and arrogance' (116). The story provides insight into the impact of failed expectations and disappointment that many African and other immigrants face when reality sets in.

Akunna retreats further into a solitary existence as a waitress in a restaurant. Her hopes for a college education are dashed as she enters a period of adversity and disconnection from her family back in Nigeria. Her inability to send them anticipated gifts prevents her from writing to them although she sends them money. She wants to write but is overwhelmed by the enormity of her situation. She continues a downward spiral emotionally and does not tell her family where she is. Akunna thinks to herself that she felt 'invisible....at night something would wrap itself around your neck, something that very nearly choked you before you fell asleep' (119). These thoughts convey the tension at the heart of the story that engulfs the young protagonist. The' thing around her neck ' begins to loosen when she meets a white male and begins an unexpected and uncertain romantic interlude.

This relationship is another of the story's ironies that depicts a hybridized existence. On the one hand, it offers Akunna emotional validation of her humanity through the sincere affection of her lover. However, she is unable to accept and return the sentiment through a lasting bond of friendship. The clash of cultures is never more apparent than in the contrasting world views, ethnic and cultural differences between her and the unnamed boyfriend. He came from a wealthy background of privilege and culturally diverse experiences including travel to Africa. Her loneliness and isolation loosen her emotions as she begins to share her life and experiences with her friend. Her relationship has ushered in a new life of emotional release that is thrown against the backdrop of stares and pointed comments from both blacks and whites that they encounter as an interracial couple.

Finally, she writes home and includes her address but is shocked and emotionally devastated to learn of her father's death five months ago. Her friend not only comforts her but offers to buy her a ticket and accompany her to Nigeria. She refuses, and when he asks whether she will return, her response suggests that she will but the reader is unsure. The ending is a sad one as Akunna wonders what she had been doing on the day her father died. 'The Thing Around Your Neck' is a poignant account of an alienating existence despite the possibility for love in the future.

In 'The Arrangers of Marriage', the paradoxical features of life in America create unhappiness and conflict for Chinaza Okafor. Her aunt and uncle have arranged her marriage to a doctor in America that turns into a disaster. Her expectations for happiness and security are ruined by the contradictions and confused identity of her Nigerian husband. Adichie highlights cultural dissonance in this story of an empty and unsatisfying marriage that has no future. Chinaza is expected to be a grateful and dutiful wife who will embrace a false identity that is modeled by her husband. As the story evolves, the layers of contradiction begin to surface. In coping with the immigrant experience, her husband Ofodile Emeka has renamed himself Dave, and rejects his Nigerian identity as a route to success in America.

He pressures Chinaza to do the same by assuming a new name, Agatha Bell, and by adopting new behaviours such as speaking only English, and cooking American food. He is critical of immigrants who maintain their ethnic identities and when he and Chinaza are shopping he tells her, 'Look at the people who shop here; they are the ones who immigrate and continue to act as though they are back in their countries' (175). He constantly corrects her speech and reminds her of the importance of blending into the mainstream. Chinaza doesn't quite know what to make of all this but thinks to herself that, 'I felt as though I were in a different physical world on another planet… The people who pushed against us, even the blacks wore the mark of foreignness, otherness, on their faces' (176). The world around her is a blur of inscrutable differences that her mind is unable to fathom. The sights, sounds, tastes and strange behaviours assault her sensibilities as her husband commands her to assume a new persona that will erase her Nigerian identity.

Adichie's use of irony is further illustrated when Chinaza meets Nia, an African-American neighbour who has visited Africa and who has an African name. She wonders how 'she, a black American had chosen an African name while my husband made me change mine to an English one' (180). Tension is heightened when she learns her husband has had a previous arranged marriage in order to acquire a green card. This betrays the fallacious nature of her marriage, and sharpens her feelings of otherness. The only thing that grounds her is the new friendship with Nia. Her husband admits his happiness when he saw Chinaza's picture because her fair-skinned complexion would help their children to fare better in America. For Chinaza this is the last straw that causes her to pack her bags and go to Nia's apartment. She learns from her friend how she can eventually become financially independent. Nia offers support and advice and promises to help her find a job:

> You can wait to get your papers and then leave …You can apply for benefits while you get your shit together, and then you'll get a job and find a place and support yourself and start afresh. This is the U.S. of fucking A., for God's sake. (186)

Adichie ends the story on a hopeful note. Chinaza can chart a future for herself. The story holds merit through its aesthetic appeal as well as the elements of feminist realism to which Adichie is committed (Onukaogu and Onyerionwu 2010: 195).

'Arranged Marriage' illustrates that despite the disheartening features of the immigrant experience in America, western society may provide a woman with routes of resilience and survival. Feminist consciousness is an underlying theme as women characters forge ahead and take charge of their destiny. The story evokes parallels with Buchi Emecheta's autobiographical novel *In the Ditch,* set in London, where Adah leaves her husband but survives on her own in a housing development with other women. The setting is reminiscent of urban American 'ghettos', but Adah eventually climbs 'out of the ditch' of poverty. 'Arranged Marriage' amplifies the idea that women can become self-determined and draw strength from sisterly support

Adichie's 'Tomorrow is Too Far' is a gripping tale of remorse that traverses national boundaries of Nigeria and America. In contrast to other diaspora tales, the action takes place in the spatio-temporal locus of time and distance instead of a specific western setting. The unnamed young woman recalls the accidental death of her brother, eighteen years earlier and, unlike 'The Thing Around Your Neck' and 'The Arrangers of Marriage', the story is unveiled through a series of flashbacks in the mind of the female narrator. 'Tomorrow is Too Far' centralizes themes of cross-cultural conflict and gender bias that tear apart a family already disconnected by geography and ethnic differences.

The children of an African-American woman and a Nigerian man are married and live in America. The siblings spend summers in Nigeria with their grandmother whom the female narrator has learned to resent. Adichie interprets the preference and privilege that is frequently showered on male children that are heirs to the family name in Igbo society. As an adult looking back on her childhood, she recounts her pain and bitterness as a girl growing up who was emotionally neglected by her grandmother. She was intelligent and skilled at so many tasks but is always passed over by her grandmother in favour of her brother Nonso.

Her parents have had a troubled marriage that ends in divorce and the unresolved tensions between African-American and Nigerian culture are a framework for the dark undertones of the story. The cultural dichotomy caused by centuries of acculturation to western life by African descendants is a sad but predictable legacy of the Atlantic slave trade. It surfaces as a sub-theme in the work because the young woman's African-American mother does not like her Nigerian mother-in-law, and neither does the female child at the centre of the tale. The grandmother represents traditional African culture, and her character is somewhat reminiscent of Papa Nuukwu in *Purple Hibiscus*. The female narrator harbours a terrible secret about her brother's accidental death.

When her grandmother dies in Nigeria, the young woman returns and confronts the real cause of her brother's death. Speaking in the second person, she remembers when she was ten years old, the summer that 'you knew that something had to happen to Nonso, so that you could survive. Even at ten you knew that some people can take up too much space by simply being, that by existing, some people can stifle others' (Adichie 2009: 195). She suggests that Nonso climb a tree, and then yells. 'A snake! 'This frightens him, causing his fall from the tree. He dies instantly from hitting his head on a rock. To make matters worse, she lies to her mother by telling her that Grandmama had asked Nonso to climb the tree to show her how much of a man he was. Her mother, shouts on the phone to her father that... 'Your mother is responsible! She panicked him and made him fall! She could have done something but instead she stood there like the stupid fetish African woman that she is and let him die!' (194).

All this rushes into her consciousness as she holds back from telling her cousin about 'the pain in your chest, and the emptiness in your ears and the roiling air after his phone call, about the doors flung open, about the flattened things that popped out ' (197). The story ends with her crying under the tree and the reader is left to ponder her future. Her splintered family life and fragmented existence between two worlds is the catalyst that surfaces the buried secret. The story vividly conveys the interplay of time and distance in the healing process.

∾

Sefi Atta is one of the brightest stars in the constellation of contemporary African women writers. She is a prolific writer of stories, novels and drama. Her works include three novels: *Everything Good Will Come* (2005), *Swallow* (2010) and *A Bit of Difference* (2012), and a short story collection, *News from Home* (2010). Her stage plays include: *An Ordinary Legacy* (2012), *The Naming Ceremony* (2012), *Hagel auf Zamfara* (2011), *The Cost of Living* (2011) and *The Engagement* (2005). She has won numerous awards and some of them include The Noma Award (2009), The Wole Soyinka Prize for Literature in Africa (2006), The Penn International Award (2005), The BBC African Performance Prize (2003), and the (2002) MacMillan Writers Prize for Africa. Her works have been translated into several languages, and merit critical acclaim internationally. Like Chimamanda Ngozi Adichie, her artistic vision is among the clearest coming from African writers and her literature discloses the lives of African women in the contemporary landscape of social transformation and flux. Her writing deftly explores such themes as coming of age, the feminist impulse, political activism, sisterhood, patriarchy and cultural norms and expectations for African women.

Her recent novels and short fiction are altering the African short story through the inclusion of themes that narrate the impact of globalization on women's identities in the twenty-first century. An important, but unnerving theme resulting from international economic and cultural interdependence is the female body as text motif that informs Sefi Atta's novel *Swallow* and a dark themed story called 'Last Trip' from the collection, *News from Home*. Of the eleven stories in the collection, 'Last Trip' stands out through its emblematic portrayal of a Nigerian single parent who becomes a 'drug mule' for thirteen years to support her son who is mentally challenged.

As the story opens she is bargaining for more money from Kazeem, a dangerous man whom the reader learns has 'hired killers to dispose of difficult couriers who have double-crossed him ' (Atta 2010:140). The drug-filled balloons she is carrying are worth over a thousand times more than the amount Kazeem pays her. The reader does not know her real name and her alias, Simbiyat Adisa symbolizes her false identity. Although much of the story is set in Lagos, the young woman's role as a drug smuggler denotes a fluid geographical identity as the reader travels with her across national boundaries to London. The story is distasteful as it unveils the seamy underworld of the drug trade in Lagos. It is laced with graphic descriptions of drug addiction, the trade itself and the human degradation of swallowing illegal substances in balloons and expelling them when reaching one's destination abroad. As she reflects on the experience, she goes over her plans upon arrival in London:

> she will take a dose of laxatives and hopefully pass the balloons before her contacts arrive. She is humiliated by their expressions whenever

they have to wait for her to finish in the bathtub. She herself cannot stand the smell, or sight, as she rinses her feces off. She wonders who would smoke a substance, knowing that it has come out of a stranger's bowels, or sniff it up their noses, or inject it into their blood. (163)

The precarious nature of drug smuggling in this way displays the commodification of the female body as a text of exploitation, poverty and desperation. The story provides insight into the ways that social and economic forces offer poor uneducated African women few choices of how to survive with dignity. Unable to support herself after her husband throws them out just days after Dara is born, she 'was almost considering prostituting herself when Kazeem came along' (154). She says she will continue to work for Kazeem to keep her son in school. The precarious nature of swallowing heroin-filled balloons is described when she thinks that:

what she fears most are flight delays. An hour is nothing to worry about, two hours and her heartbeat will rise; three, and they will leave the departure gates and find their way back home. She knows couriers who have convulsed and died when balloons bust inside them. That is why she refuses to travel Nigerian Airways. British Airways flights are fairly timely. (156)

She says this is her last trip because her nerves will not hold up for another delivery, but we know her choices for survival are limited.

'News from Home' is the lead story in the collection for which it is named. It is a brilliant and captivating work that is ripped from news headlines during the mid-1990's in the Niger Delta region of Nigeria. It is a fine example of historical fiction that collates multiple themes of political activism, diaspora challenges, cultural dissonance, and feminist consciousness. It qualifies as a novella because of its broad scope, depth and complexity. Eve is a young woman who has come to America to be a live-in nanny for a professional Nigerian couple. She is a qualified nurse and secretly hopes to strike out on her own in America. The structure of the story moves back and forth in time and space as the reader glimpses the social environment of the Kalabari people of the Niger Delta. Her family and friends come alive in the story as they are cast against the horrific exploitation of the environment by multi-national oil companies. The story is moving and powerful because of the realism evoked by Sefi Atta's prose. The Americanized behaviour of the children she cares for in New Jersey displays the emptiness of their falsified western identities. The children are culturally rootless and are socialized to reject things African. Their references to Africa are stereotypical and negative: Daniel tells Eve that 'he sawed a picture of Africa. And the boy had no hair, and his belly was all swelled up, and he lived in a hut, with um, no windows, and I don't like Africa' (174). The story explores Eve's own reflection on the difference in cultures as she listens for news from home.

The feminist dimensions in the work are beautifully construed in the awakening activism of the women in her town back home. These events mirror the peaceful demonstration in the Niger Delta organized by women, who shut down a Chevron-Texaco oil terminal in 2002. The women held talks with oil company management to demand that they provide roads, water, schools and jobs to develop what is the poorest region of Nigeria where the people do not benefit from the oil. In addition, more real life events are written into the story through a retelling of the hanging of the activist, Ken Saro-Wiwa in 1995 and subsequent brutality against the Ogoni people. Eve gives a flashback account of the damage to people's health by oil pollution. While working as a nurse back home she saw people with 'strange growths, chronic respiratory illnesses, terminal diarrhea, weeping sores, inexplicable bleeding … We had too many miscarriages in our town, stillbirths, babies dying in utero, women dying in labor. People blamed the gas flare' (177).

Sefi Atta is writing to raise consciousness of political issues through her artistry. The story's effectiveness sparkles with clarity and insight into diaspora existence that is juxtaposed with Nigerian political realities that still exist today. The story illustrates that there are no easy solutions to life's surprising ironies and it ends with Eve receiving news from home about the women who successfully stage a protest. Among the women she sees is her mother, best friend, and the strong leader of the women. The ending is a hopeful one and suggests that she moves on from her role as a nanny. What is also promising is that she is grounded in her Nigerian identity, and is comfortable in her own skin. This story illustrates and confirms the author's comments in an interview with Walter Collins where she agrees that third generation Nigerian writers are less concerned with ideology and more concerned with self-discovery. Sefi Atta creates female characters in her novels and short fiction that are clearly on a journey to map out their lives in different ways (Collins 2007: 130).

The literature of Chimamanda Ngozi Adichie and Sefi Atta has charted new directions in the African short story. Their fiction heralds a contemporary perspective on women's immigrant experiences that foregrounds their insight as writers who live outside Africa. Their writing is thus didactic in purpose and scope through connections to their literary foremothers who paved the way for women to tell their own stories. Their works ironically raise more questions than they answer about women's survival, independence, and the price to be paid in the pursuit of opportunities in transnational spaces. The subjects and themes in both collections are socially relevant as a caveat for African people attempting to improve their condition in a globalized world. As Nigerian women writers, Chimamanda Ngozi Adichie and Sefi Atta are brilliant artists who share with the world their vision of the African reality through the lens of gender.

WORKS CITED

Adichie, Chimamanda, N. *The Thing Around Your Neck*. Toronto, Alfred A. Knopf, 2009

Atta, Sefi. *News from Home*. Northampton, MA, Interlink Books, 2010

Collins, Walter. 'Interview with Sefi Atta'. *English in Africa, Vol. 34, No.2* (Oct., 2007), pp.123-131

Ojaide, Tanure. 'Migration, Globalization, & Recent African Literature'. *World Literature Today*, March–April 2008

Onukaogu, Allwell A. and Onyerionwu, Ekechi. 'With Love from Paradise: Adichie's Image of the Diaspora', *Chimamanda Ngozi Adichie: The Aesthetics of Commitment and Narrative*. Ibadan, Kraft Books, 2010

—— Adichie's Strong Women', *Chimamanda Ngozi Adichie: The Aesthetics of Commitment and Narrative*. Ibadan, Kraft Books, 2010

Exposition of Apartheid South African Violence & Injustice in Alex la Guma's Short Stories

BLESSING DIALA-OGAMBA

Every oppressive system has witnessed a literature of protest that uses themes of violence, racism and conflict within the writers' ideological framework. It is the desire to change oppressive human history, to place man in a better position to understand his environment and subsequently harness his resources to boost his living condition that makes artists protest subtly or violently against factors that inhibit their quest. In South Africa, colonialism took the form of a settler colony, where land was forcibly confiscated and the owners reduced to the status of wage-earning labourers. The settlers, in order to perpetuate their authority over the Africans, devised several means of subjugating the indigenes. It is in response to this that writers like Alex la Guma, Peter Abrahams, Arthur Nortje, Dennis Brutus and others, have attacked the oppressors in their various works. This article explores the various ways in which Alex la Guma uses his short stories to expose the violence and injustice meted against the blacks in apartheid South Africa.

Leif Lorentzon in his 2007 article, 'Jazz in Drums', discusses how jazz music has integrated into African life and he also gives an idea of how short stories appeared in *Drum* from the early 1950s as 'part of an urban black Atlantic and para-colonial/Apartheid popular culture in South Africa ....' (218). Lorentzon continues the exploration by saying that,

> With *Drum* there was a place for fiction during the fifties. Prior to this there was hardly anywhere for the black South African writers to be published. The short stories in *Drum* in the fifties mark the beginning of the modern black short story in South Africa ... But like so much else it all ended before the decade was over: the last short story was Alex la Guma's 'Battle for Honor' in November 1958. (219)

Many African writers such as Bloke Modisane, Can Themba,

115

Arthur Mogale, Richard Rive, Lewis Nkosi and Ezekiel Mphahlele used *Drum* as a stepping stone for their careers as writers. 'In *Drum* it turned into an urban phenomenon, and the magazine became in the 1950s the major outlet for short stories by black writers, also black writers from West Africa and the United States appeared' (219). *Drum* was the beginning of black expression through writing in South Africa.

Born on February, 1925, in a slum area of District Six in Cape Town, La Guma lived through his childhood in very close contact with the politics of apartheid and resistance. Educated at Trafalger High School and Cape Technical College, he worked as a clerk, a book-keeper, a factory hand and a journalist. La Guma started his political career as an elected member of the Colored People's Congress because his family was active in politics. He was one of the hundred and fifty-six members of the Congress Alliance leaders charged with treason and the trial lasted for five years. The prolonged trial was intended to ruin many of the accused both financially and professionally and to clamp down on their enthusiasm for revolution. They were later acquitted and discharged. La Guma was banned from attending public meetings, rallies and publishing anything that may incite the public.

It was while in prison and under house arrest that La Guma read widely and started writing short stories and novels. He wrote eleven short stories and five novels. In spite of what he had gone through, La Guma was consistent in his struggle for total liberation of the black people through a realistic mirroring of his society. His experiences spurred him to continue writing and in an interview with Robert Serumaga in 1966 he says, 'I write... to expose the situation with a view to changing people's ideas or their acceptance of ideas so that they can move forward and take down the barriers that exist between the different people' (Duerden and Pieterse eds, 1972: 91). La Guma was persecuted and victimized for his single-minded dedication to the ideals of social justice and racial equality. His works grew directly from his experiences during the crucial decade immediately preceding his exile. This fact explains in part the functional value which he attaches to literature and the quality of engagement of his works right from his earliest short story to his last novel, *Time of the Butcherbird.*

La Guma's short stories demonstrate his interest in the various and crucial aspects of South African life, the most central among which were the continual struggle of blacks as well as coloureds against the crippling social laws of South Africa, the tensions which arise from inter-racial love, racial violence and murder, and the harrowing experiences of convicts in the South Africa's overcrowded prison cells. It is from his novels that we get his most impressively articulated appraisal of the South African situation, but the short stories indicate a sense of urgency to the readers.

The short story, just like the novel, is fiction. According to M.H. Abrams, Poe defines the short story as 'a narrative which can be read at one sitting of from half an hour to two hours, and is limited to a certain unique or single effect ...' (194). The quickest way to expose an idea about something whether positive or negative is through the short story genre. The short story is fiction that focuses on a story line with very few characters. The short story writer 'cannot afford the space for the leisurely analysis and sustained development of character, and cannot undertake to develop as dense and detailed a social milieu as does the novelist' (194). In view of this concept, Alex la Guma uses his short stories to expose the evil effect of apartheid in South Africa. In order to quickly alert the outside world, to let them know about the suffering and brutalization of the non-white South Africans during the apartheid regime, he decides to use the medium of the short story. He wrote mostly while he was in prison and some critics describe his style as journalistic. Lewis Nkosi (1981) observes that the form of South African writing is essentially journalistic, '... what we do get from South Africa ... most frequently is the journalistic fact parading outrageously as imaginative literature ...' (79). Yes, South African writings are journalistic on purpose. The situation the writers find themselves in, does not warrant embellishing their works with detailed analysis of events and development of plots, rather they prefer the medium of the short story to get important information across and maximize the limited space they have. Alex la Guma is no exception to this because he does most of his writings from prison cell. He uses this journalistic style to quickly get his message across to the outside world as a way of seeking help and justice for the non-whites. On the other hand, La Guma explains that he writes '... to expose the situation with a view of changing people's ideas or their acceptance of ideas so that they can move forward and take down the barriers that exist between the different peoples' (Heywood, 1971: 93). The barriers that he expects to be taken down are the different apartheid laws and legislation that inhibit the growth and progress of the non-whites. Lindfors (2011) observes that black South African journalists and school teachers produced some literary pieces in English and opted to 'deal with contemporary life in South Africa in a medium that was readily accessible to their public and in a language that enabled them to reach the widest possible readership' (21). They chose the short story genre due to the 'peculiar environment in which the black writer was forced to operate' (22). Lindfors further observes that 'Bloke Modisane agreed that environmental circumstances in South Africa were conducive to short story writing because they forced black writers to adopt a short term morality ... You cannot budget for six months in order to write a novel. The short story, therefore, serves an urgent, immediate, intense, concentrated form of unburdening yourself – and you must unburden yourself' (22). Bessie Head also agrees in an interview with Andrew Peek that working with *Drum Magazine* made her writing journalistic; however, the experience helped her in her writing to be able to put a lot of things down in a short time (Peek 1985: 5). As a writer, La Guma's vision was to use literature as an effective weapon in the struggle for social justice, and this is what he does in his works, using appropriate ways to expose the harsh realities in apartheid South African.

In 'Tattoo Marks and Nails' ([1962] 1967)[1], La Guma exposes the inhuman treatment meted to prison inmates through the protagonist, Ahmed the Turk, as he describes the uncomfortable situation in the cell in the following sentences, 'The heat was solid. As Ahmed the Turk remarked, you could reach out before your face, grab a handful of heat, fling it at the wall, and it would stick' (92). Ahmed the Turk is an 'alleged housebreaker, assaulter and stabber' (92) thus the imprisonment. The prison cell is so hot that people are very uncomfortable staying there. Ahmed the Turk compares the cell to the prison in Libya when he was an Italian prisoner in a war camp there. These are prisoners awaiting trial. The prisoners are deprived of their clothes anytime they are locked up. This is injustice, inhuman treatment, and oppression. It is true that someone should be punished for crimes committed. Serving a prison term is enough punishment; however, prisoners should not be dehumanized if the essence of prison is to help change the prisoner for the better. All prisoners here are put together in one cell no matter the nature of the crime committed. The hardened criminals in turn brutalize the prisoners who commit minor crimes. For example, in this prison cell, 'the Creature, so named after some fantastic and impossible monster of the films, and his gang were persecuting some poor wretch who had arrived that morning' (93). The Creature and his gang, can in this process of persecution, kill the new prisoner and the warders would not be bothered. La Guma uses the situation and the brutality in the prison to expose the violence that goes on uninterrupted by the warders. Lawrence Ries opines that when a system compels people to 'live in conditions of abjection, helplessness, wretchedness that keep them on a level of beasts rather than men, it is plainly violent' (6).

In 'At the Portagee's', the writer exposes the theme of poverty, neglect, and discrimination suffered by a man who comes into the bar requesting money from Banjo whose real name is Edward Isaacs, and his friend, whose name is not revealed. He says '.... old pal, spare a sixpence for a bite, man' (103). Banjo is mad and asks him, 'Who you bumming from? .... From who do you bum' (103). Banjo's friend tells him to leave the man alone and gives him sixpence. The man thanks him and leaves. The two friends continue making advances to the girls whose names are Hilda and Dolores, until they succeed. It is interesting and natural that in the midst of violence and poverty, people still find time for love. As the group gets together, another man in the tattered navy-blue suit comes into the café and asks the Portagee for a sixpenny fish, but the Portagee sends him out of the café telling him that there is no sixpenny fish. The man in the tattered suit leaves the café holding himself very straight, while some people in the place laugh (105). After watching him leave, Banjo tells his friends a story about a man who goes to a posh café with his own sandwiches and asks the waiter to give him water. When the waiter brings the water, the man asks him why the band is not playing. This man knows that he cannot afford the food in this posh café and goes there with his own sandwich just to listen to the band. La Guma uses these stories to show the readers the extent of abject poverty suffered in South Africa.

There is also the theme of dehumanization in 'At the Portagee's'. An example can be seen when Hilda explains that like Banjo's friend, her father is also a messenger. She says that her father 'worked forty years for the firm. Now he's head messenger. Last year they gave him a silver tray with his name on it, and 'For service-something' (106). La Guma uses stories like those told by other people to expose the inhuman treatment meted out to the blacks in South Africa by the apartheid regime. The stories are not funny; instead, they are told to set people thinking about life in apartheid South Africa.

In another story entitled 'The Gladiators', La Guma depicts the theme of violence and class consciousness where blacks are incited to fight one another. Kenny the coloured protagonist is preparing to fight as he is being promoted by Noor Abbas. The promoters are more interested in the money they will make from the fight, than in showing any emotional attachment to the fighters. As a young coloured man, Kenny is tired of fighting other blacks. He is now aware that blacks are pitched against one another in the name of money. He is initially elevating himself as belonging to a higher class because he is coloured, but is quickly corrected by his friends. Kenny tells his friends when they ask how he is feeling, 'I feel first class ... I'll muck that black bastard' (109); however, his friends remind him that '.... We all blerry black, even if we off-white or like coffee. Be a blerry sport, man' (109). The crowd is only interested in supporting the person who gives the most punch without having personal connections with any of them. The panther wins the match making the crowd excited at the blood they see, thus revealing their lack of empathy.

La Guma continues to explore the themes of violence and discrimination in another story entitled 'Blankets'. Here, the protagonist Choker has been stabbed three times, 'each time from behind. Once in the head, then between the shoulder blades and again in the right side, out in the street, by an old enemy who had once sworn to get him' (116). This time, Choker is lying on the bare floor waiting for the ambulance to go to the hospital. Meanwhile, 'somebody had thrown an old blanket over him. It smelled of sweat and having-been-slept-in unwashed and it was torn and threadbare and stained. He touched the exhausted blanket with thick, grubby fingers. The texture was rough in parts and shiny thin where it had worn away. He was used to blankets like this' (116). It is ironic that such a dirty blanket can be used in covering someone with an open wound. Choker does not care, because he is used to such treatment and being covered with dirty blankets. He decides to take his mind off his wound while taking in what is happening in his surroundings as he waits for the ambulance. Choker's attitude here shows disgust. Even when the guard allows him to pick two blankets, Choker rummages through the pile looking for a thicker one. The guard laughs at him and throws two blankets at him which are described as 'filthy and smelly and within their folds vermin waiting like irregular troops in ambush' (116). When the ambulance eventually arrives, Choker realizes that the sheet around him is as 'white as cocaine, and the blanket was thick and new and warm. He lay still, listening to the siren' (118). This scene confirms Henrick Verwoerd's policy statement in 1953 related to equal rights, which states that, 'If the native in South Africa today, in any kind of school in existence is being taught to expect that he will live his life under a policy of equal rights, he is making a big mistake. There is no place in the European community above the level of certain forms of labour' (90). Poverty, subsistence living, ghetto existence and deprivation are also effects of South African apartheid policy which make the black characters in South African literature react violently to situations.

The next story entitled 'A Matter of Taste' revolves around abject poverty. In this story, Chinaboy, the protagonist, and his friend are brewing coffee in a tin. They have empty condensed milk cans they use as tea cups. Chinaboy goes to get the cans and realizes that someone is coming out from the bush beside them. The dirty looking white stranger tells them that he has smelt the coffee and asks for some. They invite him to join them for dinner. The white boy joins them for dinner and they call him Whitey. Talking with Whitey, they eventually find out that he is looking for a way to join the train to Cape Town where he can board a ship to the United States. Whitey tells them, 'I heard there's plenty of money and plenty to eat' (121). They talk about the kinds of food seen in American picture books, and Chinaboy wishes that he could one day sit down and eat himself 'right out of a load of turkey, roast potatoes, beet-salad and angel's food trifle. With port and cigars at the end' (122), and Whitey tells him that 'it's all a matter of taste. Some people like chicken and others eat sheep heads and beans!' (122). They make jokes after eating and tell Whitey when he can come back to jump on the train without being detected. The train appears on time. 'The coal-car came up and Whitey moved out, watching the iron grip on the far end of it. Then as it drew slowly level with him, he reached out, grabbed and hung on, then got a foothold, moving away from us slowly' (124). They wave to him as the train continues. In this story, Whitey tells them a story about someone who goes to a restaurant with his own sandwiches and only orders a glass of water. When the waiter brings the water the person asks the waiter' Why ain't the band playing' (122)? The same story is told in 'At the Portagee' by Banjo and his friends, indicating that people who live in abject poverty experience the same things. That the friends are boiling water for coffee in an empty milk can, also shows the abject poverty they are in and the reason Whitey is leaving the country. It is interesting to note that in apartheid South Africa where racism is the order of the day, the poor whites interact with the blacks just as seen in the relationship Whitey had with Chinaboy and his friend.

In the last story entitled 'The Lemon Orchard', La Guma continues the theme of discrimination and dehumanization through the narrator as he tells how a man is caught and punished severely for asking for his right. 'All of the men but one wore thick clothes against the coolness of the night. The night and earth was cold and damp, and the shoes of the men sank into the soil and left exact, ridged foot prints, but they could not be seen in the dark' (125). These men are walking through an orchard at night and one of them comments, 'It's as dark as a kaffir's soul here at the back' (125). The orchard is dark and the person who has the only lantern is walking in front. The unnamed coloured man is not dressed properly for the cold. 'This man wore only trousers and a raincoat which they had allowed him to pull on over his pyjamas when they had taken him from his lodgings, and he shivered now with chill, clenching his teeth to prevent them from chattering. He had not been given time to tie his shoes and the metal-covered end of the laces clicked as he moved' (126). The man is too cold to answer when they ask him if he is cold. The leader presses the muzzle of the shotgun into his back saying, 'When a bass speaks to you, you answer him. Do you hear? .... Do you hear, hotnot? Answer me or I will shoot a hole through your spine' (127). 'This is mos a slim hotnot.... A teacher in a school for which we pay. He lives off our sweat, and he had the audacity to be cheeky and uncivilized towards a minister of our church and no hotnot will be cheeky to a white man while I live' (127). One of the men tells the leader that there is no need to shoot the colored man but the leader says, 'I will shoot whatever hotnot or kaffir I desire, and see me get into trouble over it. I demand respect from these donders. Let them answer when they're spoken to' (128). After he is beaten, the teacher moves to the city but according to the leader, 'We don't want any educated hottentots in our town' (129) and they decide to teach him a lesson insisting that 'He won't demand damages from anybody when we're done with him' (129). 'The minister of the church' must be the school principle and as a minister of a church, he is supposed to be sympathetic to the requests of the teacher and see him as human, but rather he supports the beating of the teacher. Frantz Fanon rightly observes that sometimes religion is introduced to implant foreign influence in the core of the colonized people; and when domination over the colonial countries becomes difficult, the colonialist decides to carry out a rear-guard action with regard to culture, values and techniques. The colonialist represents hostility, violence, aggressiveness but he lives well and enjoys himself at the expense of the native (50). Brutalizing the teacher is a way of silencing him, and by extension other dehumanized people, so no one can demand answers, or justification for being punished unduly.

What Alex la Guma does with the stories is to focus on the different kinds of violence, inhuman treatment, abject poverty and oppression in apartheid South Africa. He exposes how blacks and coloured people are dehumanized, tortured and silenced when they ask for their rights like this coloured teacher. The whites do not want to see educated coloured and black people in the city because they know that there may be the possibility of their being given fairer treatment than when they stay in the remote areas of the country. Being educated is the surest way to awareness. It is a way of achieving social, political, economic, and self-awareness. Education is a way to think and rethink issues, possibilities, and make appropriate decisions about life in general. The bass/police officers in apartheid South Africa know this; consequently, they try to stifle the blacks and coloureds so they do not make attempts to demand their rights.

Most of the characters in the stories are nameless and some have only first names or funny names, but no last names. Some of these names are 'Gogs, Kenny, Banjo, Turk, The Creature, Nails, Choker'. These may be the nicknames they give themselves, but it is important to note that most of the oppressed characters to not have last names. The coloured teacher in 'The Lemon Orchard', even with his level of education has no name, showing lack of identity. The characters suffer psychologically, emotionally and physically, and have no way of retaliating or even rejecting the brutality. The writers in this society suffer the same brutality, thus they stick to writing and smuggling out their works to be published elsewhere as a way of exposing the inhuman treatments meted to them. Censorship is an indispensable part of an interlocking system of repressive laws. It reduces the interest of a lot of new writers; however, those who attempt to write do so from a racial point of view because they do not know enough about other races due to segregation laws. In his autobiography, Mphahlele remarks that 'No South African journals circulating mainly among whites would touch any of my stories nor any others written by non-whites unless he tried to write like a European and adopted a European name' (Lindfors 27). The apartheid laws keep people within their racial enclaves, thus the black writer is limited in his presentation of white character and vice-versa. Ezekiel Mphahlele opines that 'as long as the white man's politics continues to impose on us a ghetto existence, so long shall the culture and therefore literature of South Africa continue to shrivel up, to sink lower and lower; and for so long shall we, in our writing continue to reflect only a minute fraction of life'(109).

Literature naturally draws its sustenance from culture, but South African literature is lacking in this area. The characters presented in South African literature are shown to be alienated from their culture because of the apartheid principles upon which the country is built. The violent experiences and horror in which the black man lives become an impediment to writing. From the point of view of Nkosi, 'It is not so much the intense suffering which makes it impossible for black writers to produce long and complex works of literary genius as it is the very absorbing violent and immediate nature of experiences which impinge upon individual life ...' (17). It is difficult for writers to deviate from their social background and feign ignorance of the dehumanizing situation in their works of art. Thus, Nkosi sees literature in South Africa as a way of exposing racial conflict and segregation while Adrian Roscoe says: 'the imaginative area of literary activity risks starvation for the sake of the basic course' (225).

Just as some other South African writers have done, Alex la Guma describes the injustice, violent activities, dehumanization and other inhuman treatments meted out to the non-whites in apartheid South Africa for the world to see, hear, and react positively to help the non-whites to put a stop to the apartheid regime. He therefore uses the opportunity of his imprisonment to start writing short stories, smuggling them out for publication to help the outside world gain experience and come to a point of realization about the atrocities the non-whites suffer in apartheid South Africa. The short stories become a ready avenue for circulating messages about the sufferings in South Africa because of their urgency. The writers are bent on painting a realistic picture within a short time, thus they adopt a style criticized as being 'journalistic' with no artistic beauty or aesthetics. Lindfors also says that:

The black writer, whether writing for *Drum* or for the liberal and radical publications, addressed readers at every level of the pyramid. He had to write about characters and situations all his readers would understand, and he had to employ a style that all would accept. His writing thus was reduced to the lowest common denominator of his readers' experiences, interests and tastes. His audience determined what and how he wrote. (28)

In a country where blacks and whites are perpetually at logger-heads with one another, the writers do not have time for artistic beauty; they should rather be encouraged and applauded for risking their lives to come up with stories that expose the inhuman treatment meted out to them. Writers like Denis Brutus, Peter Abrahams, Bessie Head and others, owe it to themselves to interpret and reflect the world around them in their writings and that is what La Guma has done in his short stories. George Lucas observes in Eagleton's *Marxism and Literary Criticism* that a writer should not only reflect his society dynamically in its complexity but also for the improvement of, survival and growth of that society. This means that literature should serve not only emotional needs, but national needs as well. There should be no limitations set as to how a writer should use his creative powers or artistry. A writer should be free to express his artistic freedom as he deems fit just as Henry James rejects conventional methods of writing fiction, and also 'rejects a priori prescriptions and rules about how to write a novel; he rejects limitations on the artist's freedom of choice in respect to subject matter and technique; he rejects traditional concepts of plot; and, climatically, he rejects Walter Beasant's formulation concerning 'the conscious moral purpose of the novel' (Kaplan and Anderson 1991: 386).

The South African writer suffered a great deal of political, economic, social and racial oppression. These conditions give room for excellent materials for rigorous literary activity. Many world renowned writers wrote under these conditions protesting unjust rule and inhuman treatment. The South African writer however, was not able to protest under normal circumstances because of 'persistent turmoil of oppressive racism he lives under' (Heywood 1971: 86). The political and economic situation in South Africa under apartheid created ready-made themes for the writers, but they are debarred from writing to reflect the exact happenings in their country. Nadine Gordimer believes that South Africans cannot expect to rid themselves of the Publications Control Board until they get rid of apartheid (Heywood 100). It is, however, important to note that the black writer was a member of the oppressed masses and had no place in South Africa during apartheid rule. He is relegated to the background like the masses. Verwoerd's policy statement in 1953 proved this when he said, 'If the native in South Africa today, in any kind of school in existence is being taught to expect that he will live his adult life under a policy of equal rights, he is making a big mistake. There is no place for him in the European community above the level of certain forms of labour' (Heywood 90). This statement is the justification for mistreating the nameless teacher in the story 'The Lemon Orchard'. The statement is also a policy that controls the apartheid system which affects blacks in general.

La Guma in his stories brings out the sordid details of inhuman treatment meted out to the non-whites in South Africa. His background as an apolitical activist enabled him to vividly expose, through different themes, the sufferings of the non-white South Africans who were dehumanized by apartheid and racism. His works portray the evil effects of South Africa, economic exploitation, racial segregation, inhuman treatment, frustration and all levels of crime and violence. These themes reoccur in his novels and short stories.

NOTE

1 Page references are to the 1967 edition.

WORKS CITED

Abrams, M.H. *A Glossary of Literary Terms.* Fort Worth: Harcourt Brace, 1993.

Duerden, Dennis and Cosmo Pieterse (eds) *African Writers Talking.* New York: Africana Publishers, 1972.

Fanon, Frantz. *The Wretched of the Earth.* Middlesex: Penguin, 1972.

Heywood, Christopher (ed.) *Perspectives on African Literature.* London: Heinemann, 1971.

Kaplan Charles and William Anderson (eds) *Criticism: Major Statements.* New York: St Martin's Press, 1991.

La Guma, Alex. *A Walk in the Night.* [Ibadan: Mbari Publications, 1962] Evanston: Northwestern University Press, 1967.

Lindfors, Bernth. *Early Black South African Writing in English.* Trenton: Africa World Press, 2011.

Lorentzon, Leif. 'Jazz in *Drum*: An Ambiguous Discourse. The Short Stories in the 1950s' in *JALA* Winter/Spring 2007.

Mphahlele, Ezekiel. *The African Image.* London: Faber and Faber, 1962.

Nkosi, Lewis. *Tasks and Masks: Themes and Styles of African Literature.* London: Longman, 1981.

Peek, Andrew. 'Interview with Bessie Head' in *New Literary Review.* No. 14, 1985.

Reis, Lawrence. *Wolf Mask: Violence in Contemporary Poetry.* New York: National University Publishers, 1977.

Roscoe, Adrian. *Uhuru's Fire: African Literature East and South.* Cambridge: Cambridge University Press, 1971.

Locating a Genre

Is Zimbabwe
a Short Story Country?

TINASHE MUSHAKAVANHU

'Short stories have long been the poor relations of Zimbabwean literature', T.O. McLoughlin once observed. Critics and commentators in the Zimbabwean literary discourse have paid scant attention to the short story and have treated it as a footnote to the novel, some kind of practice ground for the more serious business of writing novels. And yet the short story engenders vital issues that have contemporary relevance.

The development of the short story in Zimbabwe as a separate, concentrated short form of literature reveals remarkable vitality, and it holds up in a natural manner as an effective mirror to the Zimbabwean society. The intensity of the form comes from its subjective points of view, pervasive imagery, controlled tone and ellipsis, and as a matter of fact, the Zimbabwean short story presents human experience in its most distilled essence.

In Zimbabwe the history of the short story can be traced back to three representative writers: Charles Mungoshi, Dambudzo Marechera and Stanley Nyamfukudza respectively. As they published the first individual short story collections, these three writers automatically become 'the fore-bearers' of the short story genre in Zimbabwean fiction in English. Charles Mungoshi became the first black writer from Zimbabwe (then Rhodesia) to publish a short story collection, *Coming of the Dry Season*, in 1972. With Mungoshi the Zimbabwean short story in English germinated in the form of homely anecdotes drawn from colonial experiences. The Rhodesian Board subsequently banned Mungoshi's book in 1975 because one of the stories, 'The Accident', contained subtle insinuations about the political order of the day, especially in its criticisms of the Rhodesia Police force. In these stories Mungoshi employs irony and understatement in order to subvert censorship.

His subsequent collections *The Rolling Stones* (1975) and *Some Kinds of Wounds* (1980) are also powerful in their dissection of the black experience in colonial Rhodesia.

However, it took Dambudzo Marechera's first collection, *The House of Hunger* (1978) to shock the Zimbabwean readership into realizing that short fiction is a powerful medium in its own right and with its own peculiar qualities. With Marechera the narrative of the Zimbabwean short story was radically transformed. Marechera used the short story as a literary vehicle for a more individual expression of personal experience. By abandoning the widely manipulated beginning-middle-and-end plot, by refusing to judge his characters, by not striving for a climax or seeking neat narrative resolution, Marechera in a very Chekhovian way, made his stories agonizing and almost unbearably lifelike. And to some extent, it is the continued popularity and influence of Dambudzo Marechera that has resulted in the resurgence of the short story as an expressive genre in post-colonial Zimbabwe. Younger writers such as Brian Chikwava, Nhamo Mhiripiri, Ignatius Mabasa, Ruzvidzo Mupfudza and myself are considered to be Marechera apostles, either in the form or content of their writings.

Stanley Nyamfukudza's *Aftermaths* (1983) mainly deals with the mental and physical implications of independence in Zimbabwe. And with Nyamfukudza, the Zimbabwean short story widened in its range of subject matter and achieved greater depth. His follow-up collection *If God was a Woman* (1990) is mainly concerned with the condition of women in Zimbabwean society. Nyamfukudza's stories are almost essayistic in character.

Between 1980 and 1999, the amount of short fiction published was relatively small. But, this was not indicative of the levels of creativity in Zimbabwe as many young people were writing under the auspices of the Budding Writers Association of Zimbabwe (BWAZ) and Zimbabwe Women Writers (ZWW). At this time, the Zimbabwean publishers were mainly interested in individual collections, and almost always by established or better known writers – Alexander Kanengoni, David Mungoshi, Shimmer Chinodya, Barbara Nkala, Yvonne Vera. Therefore, the publishing patterns of this period are not necessarily reflective of the productive rate of Zimbabwean writers in general. Certain writers were preferred over many others for whatever reasons. However, two anthologies published in 2000 break this trend – *No More Plastic Balls* and *A Roof to Repair* – these books are produced by an entirely new generation of young writers with both the talent and technical ability to produce well crafted stories. These young writers include Nhamo Mhiripiri, Shakespeare Nyereyemhuka, Memory Chirere, Robert Muponde, Ruzvidzo Mpfudza, Clement Chihota and Joyce Tsitsi Mutiti.

Early themes in the short story are clearly represented in T.O. McLoughlin's *Sounds of Snapping Wire* (1990), the first major multi-authored collection after independence, question post-colonial society on the promises that were made before independence, comparing the hopes and dreams of the freedom fighters and their supporters to the sometimes crude and cruel facts they are now confronted with. As some of the stories were written before independence, there's repetition of themes, where writers are still focusing on the confrontation against the colonial system and its attendant values. In the late 1990s, there was a shift of focus. Urbanization with all its effects: disintegration of the family, alienation, anonymity, decay and immorality became prevailing themes in short fiction in Zimbabwe.

Whereas novels and poetry were the most convenient forms to articulate cultural nationalism and political sovereignty, the Zimbabwean short story has emerged to be what Ben Okri aptly described as 'the perfect form for the age we live in' (2000). Zimbabwean society is sick, and literature, particularly the short story, can save it. The temperament of the creative writer evolves out of a preoccupation with concrete, practical matters, and a tendency to rush and hurry, thus demanding that its literature be terse and to the point. And, since most of the young writers who are gaining prominence today work other jobs and do not depend on writing as a vocation – they only write when they have time – and this could be one major reason why the short story has been adopted as a convenient medium of fictional expression.

The Zimbabwean short story represents a reaction against the social strenuousness of the current milieu because in essence, literature is not merely a reflection of the socio-economic relation-ships of society nor an urgent message to contemporaries, but a record of subtle craftsmanship working at the focus of the most vital aspects of the writer's existence and capturing a unique, fugitive and imaginative vision.

Early writers were mainly concerned with the past, while later writers have shifted their interest and attention to the present. The reasons for the pessimistic and seemingly unpatriotic tone in much of the literature produced in the 1990s to the present day have become clear. Urbanization, alienation and disillusionment account for a highly individualistic and sceptical outlook. Theirs is a free, modern, open-minded view of society unfettered by political biases. In their short fiction, contemporary writers are trying to come to terms with the rapidly changing conditions of the post-colonial character in Zimbabwe.

The popularity of the short story in recent years is not only circumstantial but significant as well. Literary forms and styles are contextually produced and are meant to reflect the different ways in which writers respond to, organize and interpret their condition. It is generally agreed that each generation of writers respond to the central human questions of its age. And this dialectical truth is qualified by Vassily Novikov (1974) a Russian literary scholar: 'Literature develops along with life as writers try to meet the challenges of their time, tell the readers the truth about themselves, the world and the current events, and voice their concern about the future, the truth without which mankind cannot advance.' Novikov further adds that, 'every method, style, trend and genre produces its own set of devices and its own "truthfulness".'

However, in Zimbabwe there is a dearth of critical appreciation and focus on the short story genre. There is, in fact, not one single study in Zimbabwean literature that specifically examines the short story genre in detail. Pioneering critical works by leading academics like Kizito Muchemwa, George Kahari, Musaemura Zimunya, Ranga Zinyemba, Rudo Gaidzanwa, Flora Veit-Wild, Rino Zhuwarara, Robert Muponde and Ranka Primorac have overlooked the importance of the short story. These writers dwell more on thematic and historical concerns, especially the sociological and cultural relevance of literary works produced in Zimbabwe, creating what Maurice Vambe terms, 'the poverty of theory in Zimbabwean literature'.

University of Zimbabwe lecturer, Ruby Magosvongwe declared in 2008 that Zimbabwe is a short story country. Zimbabwe is indeed a short story country. The canonical trendsetters of Zimbabwean literature, escaped the throttling grip, noose and net of the Rhodesia Literature Bureau via the short story. Around 20 anthologies have been published by Zimbabwean publishers since 2000, featuring new and established writers. In the same period, there were a handful of novels published and no poetry published at all. Magosvongwe stressed the importance of the short story in Zimbabwean literature.

Her argument was essentially that every Zimbabwean writer who is prominent today started off with short stories or has had a short story collection somewhere along the way. Her list included all the greats: Dambudzo Marechera, Charles Mungoshi, Alexander Kanengoni, Stanley Nyamfukudza and Yvonne Vera.

However, it should be pointed out that the short story has not suddenly emerged as a popular literary genre simply because there are too many brilliant practitioners (no doubt there are exceptional writers I can single out such as the late Ruzvidzo Mupfudza, as well as Memory Chirere, NoViolet Bulawayo, Brian Chikwava, Christopher Mlalazi, Wonder Guchu, Nhamo Mhiripiri, and Petina Gappah). On the contrary, I will argue, the popularity of the short story in Zimbabwe seems to derive from the fact that the form has been adopted as an economical publishing strategy. For over a decade now, Zimbabwean publishers have radically shifted from single author short story collections to multi-authored ones. Under the current economic challenges, it appears to be convenient for publishers to capture various voices in one book. Besides, there is happily the move towards democratizing space through the presence of dialoguing voices. Meanwhile, writers are offered the opportunity to practise and experiment with form. One realizes that there is now a fast growing community of local short-story writers.

Anthologies do not really offer a wide variety of themes; rather, they all seem to be fragments, repetitive snapshots of the Zimbabwe crisis that obtained as a result of the political mismanagement engineered by Robert Mugabe and company. As such, the Zimbabwean short story in English is a polemical documentation of the conditions of the prevailing tyranny and oppression. The story that the world tends to associate with Zimbabwe is too simplistic (a stark reminder of Chimamanda Adichie's talk on the dangers of a single story); one version being that the president of that country woke up one day and chased white people from their farms; then he started to kill his own people... and ZANU PF is bad, MDC is good. Other versions focus on how grim life is in Zimbabwe, how everyone is unemployed and starving, and so on. While that's how the media works, it should not be how literature works. If you are seeking entertainment, go to the media, if you are looking for complex coverage of life, go to literature. The short story in Zimbabwe has played a major role in depicting the historically interesting decade. The only weakness so far is that some of the collections were agenda anthologies, driven by the need to cover certain, timely themes, which means that they tend to repeat that which has been covered by CNN or the BBC, with the only difference being that in most cases the writer of the short story lived the situation, and hence related to it in a deeper sense than the BBC journalist reporting on Zimbabwe from South Africa.

This reads like the prose straight out of the independent press's critique of government activities. Perhaps in a place where the press cannot report freely, literature begins to play the role of the independent press, and as readers, we are likely to accept the journalistic details that temporarily delay the story, or we accept that the reporting is the story. This is a common thread in most of the works coming out of this period of Zimbabwean life; the voice of witness, the voice seeking what seems like a distant audience, the voice that's a cry for some intervention, the see-what-they-are-doing to us voice. It is hard to ignore; you connect with it at an emotional level, and what you may suspend isn't disbelief but art.

But, considering this huge flux of short story collections that have been overflowing from our local presses, the more interesting question would be to ask whether these writers of short fiction have contributed anything to the form? How have they been handling the form? What styles are emerging? Can we classify all the writers in these books as short story practitioners in the true sense of the form? What is the ratio of men and women in these collections? If there is an under-representation of women, is it because the short story in Zimbabwe is a 'male' genre? What vision of the world do these women contribute, and how does it compare with the vision we associate with Zimbabwean literature, a literature so deeply preoccupied with the struggles of men? How do these women relate to this predominantly male tradition, do they identify with it, adapt it to their needs, reject it, or ignore it? These questions provide new and engaging issues.

There is a culture in Zimbabwe to anthologize its authors; what we know of them is fragmentary, what we see of their potential genius are just but glimpses. Some appear in one or two anthologies and never to be heard from again? But even if one is good enough, local publishers are not interested in individual works unless one is Shimmer Chinodya or John Eppel. So is it, therefore, possible to define a writer's style or vision on the basis of two or three stories in different anthologies? The tragedy of the situation is this: instead of developing and nurturing talent, Zimbabwean publishers have been killing it? It is clearly evident that what has been emphasized is theme (message) over form (technique or craft). To some extent Zimbabwean writers have been unwittingly politicized because most of these anthologies are thematized, thus limiting narrative scope. This may also account for the reason that most of these short story collections contain almost journalistic narratives. Could it also be that these anthologies are audience targeted? Could it be that the message is meant to project the interior of a troubled country for an outside readership? Zimbabwe no doubt is a country of message writers because most of the writings derive their strength from the force of the message to the extent that the message becomes the story.

What is also apparently lacking in Zimbabwe is a viable literary magazine culture. Countries where the literary magazine has flourished such as Kenya, Nigeria, South Africa, Uganda have been dominant on the literary map of Africa. These are publications that have not only been significant literary forums for writers and readers in these respective countries but the international community at large. Useful? Literary magazines are essential and a good one testifies to the literary activity of a place. It is the memory of a particular period and the laboratory of new ideas. It represents a fairer and more balanced means of judging the richness of a national literature. Once upon a time, defunct magazines such as *Parade, Horizon, Mahogany, Transition, Nigeria Magazine* and *Moto* were favourites with young Zimbabwean short story writers. Now, there is nothing. It used to be that you could not get anywhere without first going through these magazines. These magazines were the way you cut your teeth, flexed your writerly muscles. And if you got a story published in any one of these magazines, you were a real writer. It was not easy but once you made it in, then you certainly had great potential.

The sad reality is that publishers in Zimbabwe have usurped the role and functionality that literary magazines are expected to play. They will probably argue that they are filling this gap through their primary publication of short story anthologies by multiple authors. There is a danger that they are also stifling the local literary scene by institutionalizing short fiction and making it an official, almost propagandistic model. Perhaps the uniformity of reportage in most stories is a function of the limited publication opportunities in the country; the stories become an identity not so much of the writers but of the one or two publishers selecting the stories that tell the story of Zimbabwe's lost decade. However, the full Zimbabwean story, in its complexity, has not yet been told. There is a danger of our publishers repeating the mistakes of the 1980s, pushing a uniform literature of liberation, laudatory poetry and blame-casting fiction chosen by just a few editors. Some of the works then were driven by the euphoria of independence, and this guaranteed them a spot on the national curriculum. Those works that did not fit in these modes were not promoted, but rejected and banned.

WORKS CITED

Chihota, Clement and Robert Muponde. eds. *No More Plastic Balls*. Harare: College Press, 2000.

Chirere, Memory 'The Short Story Pricks like the Doctor's Needle'. *The Herald*, 25 October 2010.

Magosvongwe, Ruby, '2008 Cover to Cover Short Story Competition Awards Ceremony Speech'

Marechera, Dambudzo. *The House of Hunger*. London: Heinemann, 1978.

McLoughlin, T.O. *Sounds of Snapping Wire*. Harare: College Press, 1990.

Mungoshi, Charles, *Coming of the Dry Season*. Nairobi: East African Publishing. 1972.

—— . *The Rolling Stones*. Nairobi: East African Publishing House. 1975.

—— . *Some Kinds of Wounds*. Gweru: Mambo Press. 1980.

Muponde, Robert and Ranka Primorac, eds. *Versions of Zimbabwe*. Harare: Weaver Press. 2004.

Mushakavanhu, Tinashe. *The Short Story Genre as a Mirror of the Times in Zimbabwe*. Midlands State University, Gweru, Zimbabwe, 2005 (unpublished BA thesis).

Novikov, Vassily. *Artistic Truth and Dialectics of Creative Work*. Moscow: Progress Publishers. 1974.

Nyamfukudza, Stanley. *The Non-Believer's Journey*. London: Heinemann. 1980.

—— *Aftermaths*. Harare: College Press. 1983.

—— *If God Was a Woman*. Harare: College Press. 1990.

Orakwue, Sarah. 'All Hail the Short and Sweet'. *News Africa*, 14 August 2000.

Vambe, Maurice in *Versions of Zimbabwe: New Approaches to Literature and Culture*. R. Muponde and R. Primorac. eds. Harare: Weaver Press, 2002.

Zhuwarara, Rino. *Introduction to Zimbabwean Literature*. Harare: College Press, 2000.

Zimunya, Musaemura. *Those Years of Drought and Hunger*. Gweru: Mambo Press, 1982.

Mohammed Dib's Short Stories on the Memory of Algeria

IMENE MOULATI

The work of the contemporary Algerian author Mohammed Dib defines the notion of colonial and postcolonial terrorism in Algeria and their impact on Algerian identity. I use the term 'terrorism' in this paper in keeping with Martha Hutchinson's definition that takes terrorism as 'acts of emotionally or physically "destructive harm"' (1978: 18). Accordingly, I classify terrorism in Algeria as coming from two different directions: the French colonial terrorism of the 1950s and the extremist terrorism of the 1990s. Both types involve 'acts of [physically] atrocious or psychologically shocking violence' (19) that are destructive to Algerian identity. Dib's short stories reflect what Dominick LaCapra describes as '"writing trauma" [that] involves processes of acting out, working over, and to some extent working through in analysing and "giving voice" to the past' (186). This article is a study of Dib's literary representation of the Algerian trauma through four short stories: 'Naema- Whereabouts Unknown,' 'The Savage Night', 'The Detour', and 'A Game of Dice'. The paper is in three parts. Part 1 gives a historical background from the French colonization of Algeria in 1830 up to the 1990s civil war. Part 2 is an analysis of Dib's vision of French colonial terrorism and its impact on Algerian identity through 'Naema–Whereabouts Unknown' and 'The Savage Night'. Part 3 examines Dib's literary perspective on extremist terrorism through 'The Detour' and 'A Game of Dice'.

For a hundred and thirty two years, France claimed Algeria as an integral part of its empire calling it 'L'Algérie Française'. Janice Gross states in *The Tragedy of Algeria* that 'the most relevant chapter of the country's story began in 1830 when France arrived as colonizer, bringing with it the duty to realize a linguistic and cultural "civilizing mission"' (2002: 3). This 'civilizing mission' exposed the barbarity of the French against Algerians. As Martha Hutchinson observes in *Revolutionary Terrorism*, because of the French occupation, 'the traditional life of Algeria was literally destroyed and replaced with an alien system from which Algerians were excluded' (2). On 8 May 1945, a group of Muslim Algerians marched, explains Alistair Horne in *A Savage War of Peace*, carrying signs which read: 'down with colonialism', 'for the liberation of the people, long live free and independent Algeria' (1977: 25). These unarmed demonstrators ran into French police who shot them indiscriminately, killing thousands of Algerian civilians. In *Massacre du 8 mai 1945 en Algérie* Farid Alilat states that 'En Algérie, officiellement le nombre de victimes de ces événements a été arrêté à 45 000 morts' (In Algeria, the official figure of this event's victims is 45 000 dead). After of this massacre, people decided to fight for their freedom, leading to the founding of the FLN: Front de Libération Nationale ('National Liberation Front'), 'a new nationalist organization determined to use violence' (Hutchinson 6). On 1 November 1954, The FLN declared a legitimate war against French colonization and announced its goal to attain independence through the restoration of a sovereign democratic Algerian state within the framework of the principles of Islam, and the preservation of all fundamental freedoms without distinction of race or religion. Determined to re-establish its power over Algeria, France launched a campaign of terror based on systematic torture and executions of Algerians. In 'Algeria: The Tortured Conscience' Chester Obuchowski states that French soldiers were brought to Algeria and ordered to 'torture, kill, ravage – but win' (1968: 15). After years of struggle, Algeria won its independence on 5 July 1962, and stories about French terrorism became an integral part of the Algerian public memory.

Thirty years after independence, Algeria was engulfed in a civil war. The conflict began in January 1991 with the cancellation of elections by the Algerian army in order to prevent the transformation of Algeria into a tyranny under the rule of the extremist FIS ('Islamic Salvation Front'). Madani Abbassi, FIS president accused the existing government of manipulating the electoral laws and called the cancellation of elections 'injustice and fraud' (Stone 1997: 169). In response, FIS declared a 'jihad' (holy war) against what it called a 'secular' government as a way to establish an Islamic Algerian state, creating 'a civil war that would inflict irreparable harm on the Algerian population' (Maerhofer 2010: 4).

This marked the beginning of the Black Decade that claimed 'over 120,000 lives between 1990 and 1998' (Gross 2002: 6) in what was widely known as the 'Algerian civil war' but what Algerians perceived as 'war *against* civilians' (Gross n5). Terrorists massacred Muslim families, explains Abdelmajid Hannoum, mostly on holy nights and 'violated the spaces defined by the sacred' (2010: 174). These terrorist attacks contradicted the principles of Islam, which states that 'if anyone killed a person not in retaliation of murder, or (and) to spread mischief in the land – it would be as if he killed all mankind' (Koran 5:32). Some Algerians, skeptical about this source of the terrorism 'began to ask if insiders within the military regime were manipulating the bloodshed in order to sabotage any attempts at dialogue with the Islamist guerrillas' (Evans and Phillips 2007: xiv). However, people were reluctant to seek the truth for, as Tzvetan Todorov explains, 'truth is harder to uncover when it's known that prison or fines are the probable result of the investigation' (2002: 9). Consequently, the memory of the Black Decade became more tormenting as it failed to provide reasonable explanations for 'one of the bloodiest conflicts in the history of postcolonial Algeria' (Maerhofer 2010: 3).

Mohammed Dib gives voice to the colonial past of Algeria through 'Naema–Whereabouts Unknown' and 'The Savage Night'. As he imagines the creation of the FLN ('National Liberation Front') freedom fighters in the first narrative and analyses the fighters' psyche in the second, Dib exposes through his short stories the destructive impact of French colonial terrorism on the Algerian psyche. In 'The Detour' and 'A Game of Dice' however, Dib writes the trauma of postcolonial Algeria where he reveals the absurd nature of extremists' terrorism. Through these short stories, Mohammed Dib reconstructs the wounded memory of Algeria.

In 'Naema–Whereabouts Unknown' Dib traces the transformation of the narrator from a caring father into an FLN freedom fighter. The story is part of the narrator's diary, which describes the achy state of his mind caused by the mysterious disappearance of his wife Naema, and explains his decision to join the FLN. Naema's disappearance represents that of thousands of Algerians in the 1950s who, as Martin Stone explains in *The Agony of Algeria*, were 'subject to punishment without referral to the court' (32). Dib depicts through the story the brutality of the French against

Algerians who were not even allowed to see their families before being imprisoned, killed, or tortured to death. Like Naema, they simply disappeared and 'no one has ever returned home from that place (prison)' ('Naema' 15). Naema's disappearance represents a psychological trauma for her family as the narrator explains: 'not to know where she is, what they have done to her, is a torment' (17). The narrator suffers a double trauma. He suffers from the inexplicable loss of his wife and from his inability to save the fading innocence of his traumatized children. Naema's children are also victims of what Cathy Caruth (1996: 3) calls a 'double wound', because they suffer from the loss of both their mother and the right to know how she disappeared.

Having 'lived three years of war' (Dib, 'Naema' 16), Rahim, Naema's eldest son, has become insensitive to violence. Though he is only seven, Rahim, whose name means 'Merciful' in Arabic, develops shocking ideas about the war. The child tells his father that the only way to stop French terror is to 'kill the lot. Keep throwing bombs' (16). Rahim's violent language, which ironically contradicts the meaning of his name, represents a damaged psyche particularly for a little boy of seven. Dib suggests that the child's violence is a result of the French colonial terrorism that he, like all Algerian kids, has experienced. For Rahim, bloodshed has become a daily event as well as 'killings, attacks, ambushes . . . there's an echo of it all in his words and thoughts' (16). It is important to note, however, that this fact does not criminalize the little boy: Rahim cannot not be blamed for his violent thinking. According to Elizabeth Dutro, trauma 'starkly alters our equilibrium' (2011: 3) and it is clear that Rahim is a victim of a deep trauma inflicted by the war. In fact, Rahim stands for the Algerian youth who have been terrorized by 'one of the most bitter and bloody wars of self determination in history' (Stone 1997: 37). Indeed, Dib suggests that through the case of Rahim that the French colonial terrorism has created a crisis in young Algerian generations. Moreover, these generations suffer trauma without any kind of psychological assistance because the older generation is deeply traumatized as well.

Dib employs the narrator's journal as a materialization of Algerian consciousness during the war of decolonization. The journal presents strong images of desolation and anger that reflect the state of people's consciousness in the 1950s. The narrator is overwhelmed with 'sadness' when his son asks him 'you mustn't dawdle, Daddy, must you, when you throw a grenade?' (Dib,

'Naema' 16). He then becomes 'upset and feel[s] guilty' as he encounters the serious gaze of his son because he cannot think of a reasonable answer since an imaginary tale 'doesn't work anymore' (16). In addition to the fact that his seven-year-old son asks questions about throwing bombs is terrifying, the narrator's feeling of helplessness towards the destructive transformation of his young son causes tremendous anger in him. Clearly, the narrator's grief, feeling of guilt and anger are expressions of his own trauma. Rahim and his father display the signs of trauma which Caruth defines as 'a wound inflicted not upon the body but upon the mind' (3). Moreover, according to Laurie Vickroy, 'trauma often involves a radical sense of disconnection and isolation' (2002: 23) that makes the victim detach himself from reality in order to escape the causes of his trauma. The narrator's journal contains moments of 'disconnection and isolation' as he says, 'I sat up and looked around; it all seemed so absurd to me . . . why these children? What were they doing there?' (Dib, 'Naema' 18). The narrator's disorientation represents his traumatized psyche that demands to distance itself from the painful reality by creating a 'sudden desire to dress and hurry out' (18) in order to avoid the painful loss of his wife, his freedom, peace and happiness.

In *Writing History, Writing Trauma*, Dominick LaCapra talks about trauma as 'absence and loss' (2001: 43) and explains the difficulty of drawing a clear line between the two. According to LaCapra 'the difference (or nonidentity) between absence and loss is often elided' (47, 48). This condition is presented in the story as Dib depicts people's perception of life during the war when 'no one can . . . imagine what life is like without continual bursts of firing and explosions' (Dib, 'Naema' 19). This image is one of the 'loss' and an 'absence' of peace: a loss for the older generation on the one hand and an absence for the younger generations on the other. However, the intensity of the trauma blurs the distinction between the two and the feeling of loss turns into a sense of absence for both generations. The perception of absence creates profound frustration and despair that transforms death into a blessing for Algerians as the narrator declares 'we are prepared to die' and 'there are times when I should like to meet my death in one of the numerous outrages committed every day' (18-19). During the war of independence, 'disappearances, deaths and funerals have become so numerous that no one counts them anymore and those of yesterday cause today to be forgotten' (17). Sacrifice has become a necessity for a peace that has been rendered absent by French colonization. The narrator confirms this fact as he describes his emotions during a French attack: 'I don't remember being afraid. I was calm and collected; just curious to know what would happen next . . . the seconds passed sluggishly' (17). The arrival of such a calm emotional state during a massacre is not a sign of courage or cruelty, but a sign of a trauma. This latter combined with the absence of freedom, justice, and peace lead to the narrator's decision to join the war as an FLN freedom fighter. The narrator's decision to finally use violence and risk dying in exchange for dignity and freedom enacts the despair of Algerians in the 1950s and their decision to sacrifice their lives for peace.

Dib's 'Naema – Whereabouts Unknown' depicts how Algerians have realized that violence was the only way left to stop the French colonial terrorism. During this war, Algerian identity was shaped by terror, despair, and hate caused by colonial violence, oppression, and humiliation. Being subject to brutal colonization for over a century, Algerians, like the narrator have realized that they 'have paid too dearly already, to hesitate or draw back' (19) or to relinquish their hope for freedom and dignity. In the end, the narrator declares that his agony has turned into a 'hunger for life, a thirst to know what will happen after, that I am ready to face the armies and police forces in the world' (19). The narrator's statement represents the devotion of FLN freedom fighters in the war against the French army. Todorov explains that in the 1950s 'torture, military violence and capital executions had as their immediate effect the transformation of the entire Algerian population into the sworn enemies of France. For each man who fell in such circumstances, ten rose to take his place' (3). 'Naema –Whereabouts Unknown' justifies the use of violence as the only solution left for Algerians to stop the terror carried out by the French army. Dib suggests that the Algerian memory has been irreversibly traumatized as 'something has got under way which is even worse than war' (19). Amidst the war, Algerians have lost all hope for a normal life. For them 'the world has lost its savor and its color' and it has become impossible 'to give it a human face' (19) again.

In 'The Savage Night' Dib depicts two young Algerian revolutionaries, a brother and sister, on their way to bomb a café in Algiers. Nedim and Beyhana who 'were, and could be nothing but children from an old Algiers family' ('The Savage' 49) represent the young FLN freedom fighters who 'wanted to create an atmosphere of violence and insecurity that would be ultimately intolerable for the French, and bring Algeria to the attention of the world' (Evans 1997: 56). The story explores the legitimatization of FLN violence and exposes the psychological damage that has been inflicted by the war on the Algerian. The story is a flashback of Beyhana, who recalls the traumatic loss of her brother during the attack, an experience that leaves her 'without recourse to psychological closure or material advancement' (Maerhofer 2010: 6). Dib portrays Beyhana as 'the perfect image of light-hearted serenity, the perfect image of feminity' (Dib, 'The Savage' 54), and a freedom fighter as well. Beyhana represents the 1950s Algerian woman who has chosen to sacrifice her beauty, feminity, and life in exchange for dignity, freedom, and peace. Nedim is, however, portrayed as a caring brother, a passionate lover, and a violent fighter at the same time whose violence is not innate but caused by the savagery of the war. 'The past' observes Richard McNally 'leaves its mark on behavior as well as on thought' (2003: 30), a fact that explains Nedim and Beyhana's act of bombing a café as a natural reaction to their traumatic past under French colonization.

On their way to bomb the café, Nedim and Beyhana 'had a smile on their faces, a smile that could have easily changed into giddy laughter' (Dib, 'The Savage' 47). Dib suggests, through his characters' 'smile' and 'giddy laughter' a struggle to ignore their distress and an attempt to find courage to bomb the café, especially considering the grave consequences of their act. Dib depicts Nedim suffering an enormous psychological pressure that is apparent in his behaviour and thoughts. As he approaches his target, Nedim is suddenly transformed into a very violent person 'charged with savagery. Sinking down into the darkest regions of madness, regions in which his resolve would nevertheless always find new strength' (50). Nedim changes suddenly and mechanically from a smiling gentle brother into 'a stranger so wrapped into his own solitude that he would forget you were even there' (52). These quick contradictory changes depict Nedim's trauma 'which create[s] a state of disorientation, agitation or even confusion' (LaCapra 46). Dib implies that, like Nedim, the Algerian youth has been devastated by the terrors of colonialism. For them, there exists only one reality: French occupation means humiliation, massacres, and 'a violent uprooting of languages and customs' (Evans 75) that have to be restored at any cost.

In a stream of consciousness, Nedim pictures his victims '*on the slaughter house* [sic]' (Dib, 'The Savage' 50) [1] and thinks: '*these passengers dummies, soon, they too, they too will be offered up to the flames, reduced to smoke* [sic]' (54). In this image, he appears obsessed with the violence of death, an attitude that contradicts his soft emotions towards his sister for whom he has deep love. For instance, Nedim shows a moving tenderness towards his sister as he thinks: '*Sweet love, I know not what favors I await from you. But for her, may the heavens lavish everything upon her!* [sic]' (51). Nedim's thinking about death and his thoughts about his beloved sister are paradoxical because they come from different sources – his two personalities: one an FLN fighter and the other a loving brother. This paradox in Nedim's identity reflects his suffering from and reaction to the terror of the war. Through his short story, Dib gives voice to an Algerian subconscious that is centred on the traumatic presence of death as he puts it in Nedim's words: '[D]eath. All this time it had been walking arm in arm with those who shared in being overly suspicious, overly hateful, overly blind to what was at stake. *Now nothing will be able to keep this particular story from starting back at the beginning and rewriting itself differently and in letters of blood* [sic]' (57). This passage also portrays Algeria's agony during the decolonization war when terror destroyed identities and filled minds with a desire for revenge and for freedom. According to Stone, 'the history or perhaps more often the mythology, of this period underpins the consciousness of every Algerian over the age of thirty and continues to shape the unconscious of the country's vast youth' (30). Young people, like Nedim, were haunted by conflicting emotions: a deep love for their identity that is symbolized by Beyhana for Nedim, and a terrifying anger at French colonialism that is represented by the horrors of the explosion.

∾

In 'The Detour', however, Dib demonstrates the impact of the extremists' politicization and manipulation of Islam on postcolonial Algeria. The story follows the detour of two young Algerians, Ben and Soraya, that led to their murder by some extremist villagers. The villagers call their victims 'saints' as they address them: 'you who have been sent to us by the will of the almighty . . . to be our protectors . . . whom we will humbly serve' (33). In other words, the murder of the protagonists, who are unaware of any reason for their death, is justified by the extremists as a necessary holy sacrifice for the good of the land and people. Ironically, this extremist belief contradicts the principles of Islam which sees killing as a capital sin: 'And whoever kills a believer intentionally, his recompense is Hell to abide therein, and the Wrath and the Curse of Allâh are upon him, and a great punishment is prepared for him' (Koran 3:93). Islam's position against killing provides an explanation for the astonishment of the victims when they hear the villagers' statement: '[P]raise the lord! . . . You have become our patron saints! The all merciful in his infinite kindness has answered our prayers' (Dib, 'The Detour' 33). Ben and Soraya do not understand the meaning of the villagers' prayer and praise because they have neither reasonable basis nor an Islamic significance. Therefore, Ben asks in disbelief: '[W]hat do you want your tribesmen to take us for? The type of saints that will resolve your problems in exchange for lighting a candle on their tomb? That would be a real joke!?' (34). Indeed, Ben's surprise and inability to make sense of the terrorists' act represents the shock and skepticism of most Algerians about the goal of terrorism during the Black Decade.

The detour that has led Ben and Soraya to their death in Dib's short story can be read as an analogy of the historical and political detour that has displaced Algeria from projects of peace and democracy in the 1960s, leading to years of destruction and bloodshed in the 1990s. The villagers in 'The Detour' are a metaphor for the extremist armed groups who have used religion as an excuse for their crimes. Ben and Soraya represent the 1990s victims who have been, as Maerhofer explains, 'oblivious to the reasoning behind their execution' (2010: 12). Throughout the narrative, Dib stresses the villagers' manipulation of the sacred to glorify their violent acts. For example, the Fellah ('farmer') makes a typical extremist statement as he tells Ben 'So you want to start a fight without even invoking name of the Almighty?' (23). Dib makes the Fellah's statement symbolic of the extremists' language that tends to relate the name of God to hate and violence contradicting the Islamic discourse that calls for tolerance and peace.

Similarly, Dib represents in 'The Detour' the clash between religion and extremist terrorism as he portrays the villagers 'lined up on the long mat, all the men of the dechra [('village')] were praying. Standing, kneeling, bowing to touch their brows to the ground, they humbled themselves before God' (34) right before they murder Ben and Soraya. This image of Islamic prayer paradoxically precedes the action of the villagers who 'humbled themselves before God' a few minutes before committing murder, considered capital sin in Islam. With this scene, Dib epitomizes the extremists' manipulation of Islam to justify terrorism during the Black Decade. Through 'The Detour', Dib exposes the misuse of Islam by extremist groups, leading to 'one of history's most savage and incomprehensible civil wars' (Gross 6). As such, in 1990s Algeria, no one was safe from extremist terrorism, moreover, people no longer knew who was doing the killings and why.

In 'A Game of Dice', Mohammed Dib also examines the nature of extremist terrorism. Through the story of two young terrorists in their first mission to kill, Dib analyses the complex killing machine that Assia Djebbar describes as 'the mad machine [which] had a mind of its own; day after day, violence, murders, repression' (86). 'A Game of Dice' begins when 'two boys . . . eighteen and twenty years old, no more' (Dib, 'A Game' 173) enter a house to kill the man who owns the house. However, The Man surprises his aggressors with gunshots. He kills one terrorist and tries to communicate with the other. The young terrorist's dialogue with The Man reveals some facts about the nature of extremist terrorism. The young terrorist justifies his decision to kill as a reaction to the inequality and poverty that characterized postcolonial Algeria. He denounces life for failing him and expresses vehement anger at Algeria and its older generation as he screams at 'The Man':

> Life should be held accountable for it all! ... life pushes us around shamelessly trampling everyone underfoot! Only death can bring pardon ... life betrayed us ... and you ... you ... a-a- ... adults ..., you, the men who ... who came before us – you too have ... Have betrayed the confidence that ...we put in you! [sic] (182-3)[2]

Clearly, this statement, as it is barely articulated, depicts the disorientation of the terrorist who represents the youth of the 1990s Algeria. This poor, unemployed, and frustrated young generation had little knowledge about religion, a fact that made them easy subjects for the extremists' manipulation. Unfortunately, for this youth with little education and deep despair, the fundamentalists' promises of change encouraged uncritical obedience, especially when people who showed opposition to their ideas were persecuted.

Extremists announced their 'divine mission' to 'purify' Algerian society of French cultural residue that 'polluted' the Islamic identity of Algeria and restore equality and happiness. Ironically, this 'divine mission' was carried out by suicidal and 'drugged acolytes – drunk with evil brews of false religion and politics, and with every stimulant available, as autopsies have repeatedly shown

– [who] had lost their bid to overthrow the Algerian state and were determined to bring down as many people with them as they could' (Marrouchi 2003: 34). In other words, extremists' terrorism can be explained as chaos-oriented suicidal acts. Through a dialogue between The Man and The Terrorist, Dib dramatizes this latter's ignorance about the reason for his attack. The Terrorist confirms his ignorance as follows:

> The Man. What wrong have I done?
> The Terrorist. You have wronged God.
> The Man. Was it God who told you that?
> The Terrorist. Not to me, sir.. to the chief. [sic]
> The Man. O God confides in the chief?
> The Terrorist. I don't know, sir. (176)

Here, the boy, who symbolizes the 1990s young terrorists in Algeria, is oblivious of the meaning of his 'mission' to kill The Man. However, he answers mechanically that murder is a punishment for a man who has 'wronged God' and that God himself told 'the chief' about this. Moreover, The Terrorist admits that he does not know if God really 'confides in the chief', nonetheless, he accepts the instruction to kill. The Terrorist's answers represent the madness of the situation that plagued Algeria in the 1990s. Dib shows that The Terrorist accepts his 'holy mission' only as a revenge for his insignificant life as he declares: 'There's nothing left in me to kill! I'm nothing but pain as far down as you can reach. I'm nothing but an open wound. I'm nothing but a dead man suffering from not being all the way dead yet' (184). Dib shaped his short story as a testimony, which, according to LaCapra, 'provide[s] something other than purely documentary knowledge' (2001: 86) when it presents a terrorist's point of view about his own acts. Through these testimonies, Dib exposes the absurdity of the religious claims by fundamentalists as he points out their ignorance and disorientation.

Dib gives voice to the agonizing past of Algeria in the 1990s as he adds a scene that, through its brutality, portrays an example of the horrors of extremist terrorism. In this scene, The Man confronts The Terrorist with the savagery of the terrorist's actions and tells him:

> You won't be spared hearing about what you people did to a young mother last Wednesday night. Right in front of her daughters, you slit her throat, even though she had just begged you to have the mercy of killing her somewhere else. Then you tore her head off, which you

threw out into the street. After performing this great feat of heroism, you turned tail and ran, and the oldest child had to go and find her mother's head to put it back on the body. (182)

This scene, explains Leila Sabbar, reproduces a real crime that was frequent in Algeria during the civil war with a long 'liste des attentats meurtriers, des massacres, egorgements, décapitations, mutilation, tortures. Une mort violente dans la souffrance et les cris' (1999: 108) ('[long] list of murderous attacks, massacres, decapitations, mutilation, torture. Violent deaths of people screaming in agony'). Dib depicts the insanity of assassinations and the psychological damage they inflicted mostly on the youth. In fact, the younger generation that experienced the Black Decade was irreversibly traumatized as Stone states: 'Algerians grew accustomed to unexplained explosions and bursts of gunfire at night; to news of yet another colleague or relative being knifed to death or gunned down while on the way to work or out shopping' (2). Through the analysis of Mohammed Dib's short stories; 'Naema–Whereabouts Unknown', 'The Savage Night', 'The Detour', and 'A Game of Dice', Algeria and Algerian identity seem to have been irreparably destroyed by terrorism. Violence became a foundation for the subsequent development of Algerian history, memory, and identity. Therefore, a colonial trauma that has never been worked through in addition to a postcolonial frustration generated an uncontainable anger that ruined people's lives in the Algeria of the present. Indeed, today's Algerian memory is burdened with hate, despair, and anger at the past, at politicians and at fundamentalists. In *The Tongue's Blood Doesn't Run Dry*, the Algerian writer Assia Djebbar states that people in Algeria learned how to live 'three days of tears and silence for assassination, for two assassinations! Then life goes on' (12). However, in reality, people have learned how only to pretend that 'life goes on' in order to preserve their sanity or what remained of it.

NOTES

1   Mohammed Dib italicizes Nedim's thoughts in 'The Savage., Night' in order to differentiate them from his spoken words.
2   Mohammed Dib expresses The Terrorist's inarticulate speech with periods that break the sentences in 'A Game of Dice'.

WORKS CITED

Caruth, Cathy. *Unclaimed Experience: Trauma, Narrative, and History.* Baltimore: The Johns Hopkins University Press, 1996.

Dib, Mohammed. 'A Game of Dice'. *The Savage Night.* Trans. C. Dickson. Lincoln, University of Nebraska: Bison Books, 2001.

—— 'The Detour'. *The Savage Night.* Trans. C. Dickson. Lincoln, University of Nebraska: Bison Books, 2001.

—— 'The Savage Night'. *The Savage Night.* Trans. C. Dickson. Lincoln, University of Nebraska: Bison Books, 2001.

—— 'Naema–Whereabouts Unknown'. *One World Literature.* ed. Spencer, A. Norman. Boston: Houghton Mifflin Company, 1993. 15-25.

Djebar, Assia. *The Tongue's Blood Does Not Run Dry.* Trans. Tegan Raleigh. New York: Seven Tories Press, 2006.

Dutro, Elizabeth. 'That's Why I Was Crying On This Book. Trauma as Testimony in Responses to Literature'. *Changing English* 15.4: 423-34. Web. 20 July 2011.

Evans, Martin and John Phillips. *Algeria: Anger of the Dispossessed.* New Haven: Yale University Press, 2007.

Evans, Martin. *The Memory of Resistance.* New York: Berg, 1997.

Farid, Alilat. 'Massacre du 8 mai 1945 en Algérie: Les archives inédites du consul britannique à Alger'. *DNA – Dernières Nouvelles d'Algérie.* 16 Septembre 2010. Web. 29 July 2011.

Gross, Janice B. 'The Tragedy of Algeria: Slimane Benaissa's Drama of Terror'. *Theatre Journal* 54.3 (2002): 369-87. Web. 29 January 2012.

Hannoum, Abdelmajid. *Violent Modernity.* Massachusetts: Harvard University Press, 2010.

Horne, Alistair. *A Savage War of Peace, Algeria 1954-1962.* London: Macmillan, 1977.

Hutchinson, Martha Crenshaw. *Revolutionary Terrorism.* California: Hoover Institution Press, 1978.

Koran. Trans. Taqi-ud-Din Alhilali, Mohammed, and Mohammed Muhsin Khan.

LaCapra, Dominick. *Writing History, Writing Trauma.* Maryland: The Johns Hopkins University Press, 2001.

Maerhofer, W. John. 'Algeria 'Revisited': Imperialism, Resistance, and The Dialectic of Violence in Mohammed Dib's 'The Savage Night' *College Literature* 37.1 (2010). Web. 2 July 2011.

Marrouchi, Mustapha. 'Introduction: Colonialism, Islamism, Terrorism' *College Literature* 30.1 (Winter 2003). Web. 5 August 2011.

McNally, J Richard. *Remembering Trauma.* Massachusetts: Harvard U P, 2003.

Nezzar, Khaled and Mohammed Maarfia. الجيش الجزائري في مواجهة التضليل ['The Algerian Army against Deception']: محاكمة باريس ['Paris Trial']. دار الفارابي [Elfarabi P]. لبنان [Lebanon], 2003.

Obuchowski, Chester W. 'Algeria: The Tortured Conscience'. *The French Review* 42.1 (October 1968): 90-103.JSTOR. Web. 18 July 2011.

Sabbar, Leila. 'Algérie, L'énigme d'une Guerre Sans Nom'. *Magazine Littéraire* 378. (1999) :106-108. Web. 29 January 2012.

Stone, Martin. *The Agony of Algeria.* New York: Columbia University Press, 1997.

Todorov, Tzvetan. 'Torture in the Algerian War'. *Salmagundi* 135.136. (2002): 15-23. SKIDMORE. Web. 20 July 2011.

Vickroy, Laurie. *Trauma and Survival in Contemporary Fiction.* Charlottesville: University of Virginia Press, 2002.

Ama Ata Aidoo's Short Stories

Empowering
the African Girl-Child

HELLEN ROSELYNE SHIGALI

Within nearly all nations today the centre is located in the dominant
social stratum, a male bourgeois minority – Hence the need to move
the centre from minority class establishments within nations to the real
creative centres among the working people in conditions of gender,
racial and religious equality.
(Ngugi wa Thiong'o, *Moving the Centre*, 1993)

The female [African] writer should be committed in three ways: as a
writer, as a woman, and as a Third World Person.
(Molara Ogundipe-Leslie, 1994)

I don't deny that we belong to a larger, non-northern world and the
dynamics that operate in a situation like that, but find my commitment
as an African, the need to be an African nationalist a little more pressing.
It seems there are things relating to our world, as African people, which
are of a more throbbing nature in an immediate sense.
(Ama Ata Aidoo, quoted in Adeola James, 1990)

Ama Ata Aidoo's collection of short stories: *The Girl Who Can and
Other Stories* (1997) is a creative work that could be justifiably
described as woman-centred in a progressive sense. In it she
foregrounds female characters, women's needs and issues. The
collection seems to have fulfilled Molara Ogundipe-Leslie's
requirements for the African female writer to be committed 'as a
writer, as a woman and as a Third World person' (1994). Aidoo
herself has added commitment as an African nationalist to the list
(ibid). A keen analysis of the stories reveals yet another criterion
which includes the common concerns basic to all women's
movements worldwide: understanding patriarchal ideology and
power, rejecting socially constructed dichotomies and dualism,
demonstrating solidarity with women, and affirming women's

148

agency (Antrobus 2004). All these levels and dimensions of commitment encapsulate obstacles to the emancipation of African women which Ogundipe-Leslie metaphorically describes as six mountains, namely: colonialism and neo-colonialism, oppressive traditional structures, African woman's backwardness, racial oppression, oppression by African man, and the African woman's own internalized oppression (Ogundipe-Leslie, 1994). Aidoo's complex, conscious or unconscious, handling of these multifaceted dimensions of women's experience and gender discourse expands the African short story in the unique ways she succeeds in representing the African girl-child and woman as a fully human, ambitious, intelligent, active and successful achiever. This is in sharp contrast to stereotypical portraits of woman as subordinate/inferior/dependent/passive/all-emotion-no-thought... In other words, Aidoo inscribes the African woman into the African short story in an elevated, reconstructed capacity and stature. I title this article as inscribing in the denotational dictionary sense of the word: 'a piece of writing written or cut on or in something, especially as a record of an achievement or in order to honour someone'. It is in this sense that Aidoo adds value to the genre. This authorial vision is augmented by an enterprising aesthetic innovation.

The defining story in the collection is about a girl-child Adjoa who from a tender age of seven is portrayed as a critical thinker. This is considered problematic for a girl. Adjoa is a reflective listener to the words and keen observer of actions of the adults around her. She analyses her own reflection logically but is forced into silence by a cultural socialization process that constructs femininity:

> I find something quite confusing in all this. That is, no one ever explains to me, why sometimes I shouldn't repeat some things I say: while at other times, some other things I say would not only be all right, but considered so funny, they would be repeated many times for so many people's enjoyment. You see how neither way of hearing me out can encourage me to express my thought too often? (28)

In this story Aidoo interrogates gender stereotypes that define masculinity and femininity starting with social constructions of the mind of each gender. Critical thinking is supposedly an inherent masculine trait which serves a productive purpose. The converse feminine construct focuses on the female body and emphasizes its reproductive function. Aidoo dispels the first myth by creating a credible thinking girl-child, who is unfortunately, yet realistically silenced in order to affirm the myth of passivity. Whereas this is a patriarchal strategy to disempower women, it is ironically perpetuated by their own gender. Adjoa's mother and grandmother have internalized the discriminatory ideology. Two extensions of the myth of natural femininity-cum-subordination are dramatized. First, a critical female mind is problematized and strategically silenced into supposed passivity. Both of these elements are man-made since patriarchy is presumed to benefit men. But the congruent internalization of the myth by women relieves men from overt perpetuation of patriarchal culture in the nurturing process. It is the older women who suppress the younger generation's development of positive self-image. Once Adjoa is silenced, the story then shifts to her long legs that are deemed unsuitable for reproduction which is the main feminine function. And the girl-child is made to take responsibility for this biological mismatch. According to Nana:

> As I keep saying, if any woman *decides* to come into this world with all her two legs, then she should select legs that have meat on them: with good calves. Because you are sure such legs would support solid hips. And a woman must have solid hips to be able to bear children. (29)

Nana blames her daughter in turn for having made the wrong choice of husband hence the wrong legged granddaughters. Adjoa interrogates the discourse on legs and even tries to discover the ideal legs in vain, because all adult females around cover their legs in wrappers. When Nana grudgingly allows Adjoa to go to school, the girl puts her thin legs to productive use and becomes an award winning athlete. Nana's attitude is transformed instantly and she herself summarizes the moral of the story thus: 'That '*saa*', thin legs can also be useful ... thin legs can also be useful ... That 'even though some legs don't have much meat on them, to carry hips ... they can run. Thin legs can run ... then who knows?...'(32-3).

The tone of this story is sarcastic. It exposes the illogical myths of male mind versus female body and the attendant constructions that constrict men and women to polarized gender traits that are misrepresented as binary sex roles. The author rewrites the girl-child into the short story as a naturally thinking active human being who transcends the cultural constrictions perpetuated by fellow women in what appears to be intra-female-gender oppression that has been translated into the 'woman her own worst enemy' epithet. Aidoo subverts this divisive truism by exposing the underlying ignorance that keeps a grandmother in bondage, her daughter in fearful confusion, and granddaughter in silent interrogation and thankfully eventual action. Adjoa reckons that action speaks louder than words: 'It's much better this way. To have acted it out to show them, although I could not have planned' (33). The practical challenge is indisputable. The girl can do and achieve much else besides reproduction. The very title of the story deconstructs all the subsequent myths derived from the supposed passivity of the female mind. Aidoo does so in subtle ways using the socially defined female space of home and nurturing role. She explores presumed simplistic women's talk but which culminates into liberative action and utterance in the denouement.

'She-Who-Would-Be-King' and 'Heavy Moments' further demonstrate Aidoo's commitment to write the girl-child into culturally prohibited spaces in hitherto unimaginable capacities such as First Female President of Africa and First Female Flying Soldier respectively. The fictional creation of the former turned prophetic in 2006, two decades sooner than Aidoo's futuristic timing 2026, when Ellen Sirleaf Johnson became first African female President elect in Liberia. Another African (old) girl Joyce Banda became President of Malawi in 2012.

'She-Who-Would-Be-King' opens with an argument between a ten-year-old girl and a twenty-year-old adult man. The girl announces her ambition to become the president of her country. The man thinks she is mad and states that 'the men of this country will never let a woman be their president' (55). The adult male who remains nameless lives to see the adolescent girl's granddaughter Afi-Yaa announced president of an imaginary Confederation of African States (CAS) half a century later on a futuristic date 25 May 2026. This historic event is symbolically attributed to a combination of African culture and European influence symbolized by the She-King's homestead 'a classical African clan courtyard, which is also a lounge in the European style' (57). Indeed, western education is a factor in her success but her ambition is in-born considering that her grandmother may not have been literate. This affirms women's capacity for ambition, achievement and leadership. The nameless male character symbolizes a patriarchal ideology that is subject to dynamism of change. In as much as women's leadership calls for celebration, there are reservations over co-opting them into an unreformed political system symbolized by man-made calamities, civil wars, diseases, drought and floods. There is no guarantee that the female president will transform African leadership which is known to be power hungry. Although Aidoo is pro-women's development, the pessimistic ending is a realistic caveat from the African writer who functions as the 'oracle of the people'. She is aware that power corrupts and a different gender installed in unreformed system of governance is vulnerable to its characteristic excesses.

'Heavy Moments' narrates the encounter of two girls who aspire to be flying solders: Akuba Baidoo and Sarah Larbi. The story begins with a dramatization of the physical challenges that women face as they move from the culturally defined space and gendered division of labour to the male-dominated public space and professions which symbolically change into male attire. Trousers appear dysfunctional for a female attending to the call of nature. Then comes the resistance, prejudice and isolation that women must surmount to achieve their ambitions. Ambition is a natural characteristic common to all people. Akuba like Afi-Yaa the first female president identifies her ambition in early childhood. She hangs onto it despite her difficult upbringing and eventually joins the Air Force Academy. This quest remains unimaginable to her grandmother until Akuba lands at an airstrip near her home village on her test flight. The story focuses on women's ambition and capacity to achieve just like men, despite all the odds: 'It had never occurred to the questioners that Akuba Baidoo and Sarah Larbi wanted from the academy what they too had gone there for. That if being a flying soldier was something to be enjoyed and lived by, then other people – including women – could want it too. They even tried to ignore the two recruits and carry on as if they were not around' (55). This authorial intrusion echoes Aidoo's statements made at the Second African Writers' Conference in Stockholm 1986. She argues that 'millions of women and girls have been, and are being prevented from realizing their full potential as human beings, whether it be the possibility of being writers and artists, doctors and other professionals, athletes or anything else outside the traditional role assigned to women' (cited in Petersen 1988: 156). Thwarting anyone's ambition is tantamount to negating her humanity. To foreground women's ambition, which as Aidoo shows is inherent and visible from childhood, is to acknowledge the aspect of their humanity that is suppressed by the many myths constructed around femininity. This positive portrait of the African woman inscribes her into the short story as an equal among equals. The author gives credit to the two female equals whose very presence in the Air-force academy destabilizes the social equilibrium and discourse:

Whereas before you could say anything you liked about women – these days, you had to watch everything: your steps, your mouth and over your shoulder.

Earlier, they had thought it wouldn't matter. But it had come to matter. Terribly. At first, an alarm sounded through the academy when first the rumours, then later hard facts had come out. Two of the very best candidates that year were women:

'Women?'
'Women.'
But – but – but
'what do they want here?'
'What do they want here?'
'What do they want here?'
Everybody asked the same question (64)

In the short story 'Choosing' Aidoo addresses the hard choices available to the female writer. It reads like a rendition of her famous article: 'To Be an African Women Writer' presented at the Second African Writers' Conference in Stockholm in 1986 and published in *Criticism and Ideology* 1988. It also echoes the questions posed by Adeola James to African female writers in the interview in, *In Their Own Voices: African Women Writers Talk* (1990): 'How does the writer cope with the multi-faceted roles of a parent, wife and writer? Are the roles of "writer" and "woman" in some ways incompatible? What advice would they offer to aspiring African women writers?' (3). The interviews in the text elicited responses to many other questions including: 'What motivates their writing, what being African and a woman mean for their individual creativity, the various constraints they encounter in trying to write and how they have managed to cope' (ibid). In 'Choosing' the female writer becomes one among 'the girls who can' whose story is inscripted into the African short story as a kind of miniature biography of the African female writer. In this case it appears to be a list of challenges and tribulations of the African female writer.

The list of tribulations begins with basic questions: Can an African woman have an ambition to write? How would she identify it? What are the options open to her? Is the ambition to write dispensable? Can she live on writing? If not, how can she survive in order to write? 'Choosing' seems to affirm Aidoo's assertion that everything to do with African women is despised:

> Therefore, we experience some sadness – though mixed with some more positive emotions – at the mere confrontation with the notion of African women and writing – certainly however, there is no denying the pathos and the wonder in being an African (and a woman) with sensibilities that are struggling ceaselessly to give expression to themselves in a language that is not just alien but was part of the colonizer weaponry – there is pathos in writing about peoples, the majority of whom will never be in a position to enjoy and judge you. And there is some wonder in not letting that or anything else stop you from writing. Indeed, it is almost a miracle, in trying and succeeding somewhat to create in an aesthetic vacuum. (Petersen 1988: 157)

The main character of 'Choosing' is one 'girl who can', uniquely named 'The Writer-Turned-Teacher. She encounters many challenges and consequently undergoes various stages of development replete with doubt, confusion and indecision. The process can be summarized in the form of brevity that only Ama Ata Aidoo can marshal! No wonder she can afford to boast that no one handles (or may be appropriately-mishandles) the English language the way she does! In short, the writer in 'choosing' moves from 'The Writer-Turned-Teacher' to 'The Writer-Turned-Teacher-and-at-the-crossroads' to 'The Writer-Turned-Teacher-Turned-Trader' before she finally seeks wise counsel from her mother. The latter advises as follows: 'It seems to me that the only way out would be to do best, what you do well' (24). To which the writer screams 'But Mother, writing does not pay ! … And will not pay however well I do it!' (25).

But the writer also admits that 'buying and selling has created more problems for me' (ibid). The writer's conversation/philosophizing with her Mother ends on an ambiguous verdict on the dilemma of the writer's calling and optional sources of livelihood. Nonetheless it has optimistic undertones:

> It is not easy to be wise about these things or make rules about them. It depends on what you are looking for. The only thing I can say is that the places we know well are very few. Those we don't know are many. If you think of how large the earth is, then you can see how small is the part of it we know well. So if we are looking for something, then it might be better to start from where we know best. Because for one thing, it is not really big. So that if what we are looking for is not there,

we would know quite soon enough, and then we will feel free to comb the rest of the big, wide world for it. (25)

For all the attendant tribulations, writing is a calling – an indispensable ambition and the 'girl who can write' is admonished to pursue it. Aidoo contends that:

> Whereas one is not saying that all women in the world could be writers if their basic needs for shelter, food, decent medical care and maximum education were met, it should still be possible to imagine how many hundreds more writers we could have. In any case, if it chanced that every single one of those millions of women actually turned out to be a writer, wouldn't it be superb? (And that's quite conceivable with African women!). (1988: 156)

Aidoo defines 'Choosing' as 'a moral from the world of work'. Here, she definitely does not connote the real world of gendered construction of labour where women's art suffers erasure. As Molara Ogundipe-Leslie and Carole Boyce Davis show in the special issue of *Research in African Literatures* on Women as Oral Artists (1994), the practice prevails even in discourses on African orature. Therefore, Aidoo's sarcastic emphasis inscribes the female writer's production into valued work. If it remains unpaid, it is the nature of the writing profession irrespective of the gender of the writer. The author's commitment to redefine work is revisited in 'Comparisons' or *Who Said a Bird Cannot Father a Crab?* The story is an indictment of gendered division of labour where women are overloaded and yet the very work they do is overlooked, trivialized and devalued despite the fact that it is the backbone of human existence. It nurtures and sustains current and future generations of workers for national development.

'Comparisons' between Nora Cobbina and her Mother versus their spouses constitute the proverbial crab fathering a bird. The story connotes the essence of oppression that women are subjected to across generations despite changing economic circumstances. The short story is an indictment of the unequal, ironical gendered division of labour where the presumed weaker sex gets the giant share of work. The overload combines what Caroline Moser describes as 'the triple role of women' namely: reproductive, productive and community managing work in *Gender Planning and Development: Theory, Practice & Training* (1993). Each of the three roles in turn comprises several work activities:

The reproductive role comprises the childbearing/rearing responsibilities and domestic tasks undertaken by women, required to guarantee the maintenance and reproduction of the labour force. It included not only biological reproduction but also the care and maintenance of the workforce (husband and working children) and the future workforce (infants and school-going children. (29)

The second role involves:

The productive work done by both women and men for payment in cash or kind. It includes both market production with an exchange value, and subsistence/home production with actual use-value, but also a potential exchange value. For women in agricultural production this includes work as independent farmers, peasants' wives and wage workers. (31)

The third role involves:

Activities undertaken primarily by women at the community level, as an extension of their reproductive role – it is voluntary unpaid work, undertaken in 'freetime'. The community politics role in contrast comprises activities undertaken by men at community level organizing at formal political level. It is usually paid work, either directly or indirectly, through wages or increases in status and power. (34)

Herein lies 'the rationale for the differential value placed on "women's work and hence" the link between gender division of labour and the subordination of women' (29).

Once again the woman's job description in Ama Ata Aidoo's 'Comparisons' reads like a rendition of Moser's analysis of women's work worldwide. For the African women in this short story work includes: all nurturing and other chores in the household, welfare duties such as visiting the sick and providing free services for festival celebrations and so on. And for the African woman in paid employment, there is additional work. Yet at the end of it all society and men like Norah's husband wonder what women do with their time. This line of thinking that women mainly sit and gossip is familiar to many cultures. All the while, the stronger sex, like Norah's husband have their concept of work to do in the household which includes being waited on much of time. Aidoo reckons that the situation for the non-African woman is not much different. Indeed, many social science studies have confirmed this observation on gendered construction of labour and its centrality to discriminatory gender relations. Colin Williams, *Examining the Nature of Domestic Labour* (1988) is very informative of this discourse. March et al. (1999) note that devaluation of women's labour delimits their participation in national development.

Aidoo's depiction of gendered division of labour and its conse-quences across generations is part of her commitment to redefining levels of commitment for the female writer. If women's work is as crucial as Moser shows, then serious commitment to nationalism begins with the theory and practice that hinders half of the nation's people, and by inference half of global population, from effective participation in development. From Norah Cobbina's daily routine it is clear that her energies are sapped by the unequal share of domestic labour she bears amidst lack of cooperation and appreciation from the household members. The latter are current and future workers. Paradoxically the work of raising the nation's generations of workers is not valued! Norah's day is ruined long before she gets to the office to tackle paid work. Inspite of the fact that she is better paid than her mother who did not have additional full time employment in the public space. And her husband's conduct remains very much like her father's. In effect economic advancement does not axiomatically affect any change in the patriarchal discriminatory ideology and practice which originates in gender division of labour. Even when the woman becomes co-bread-winner or even major bread-winner in the household like Norah, her lot in domestic labour remains the same. To be a good African woman she must bear the burden without complaint even though she is virtually in tears much of the time.

Aidoo advances the theme of women's work to international level in 'Some Global News': A short four-voice report. The story depicts the stressful experience of Yaa-yaa Mensah – an African woman attempting to work in the global space. This elite female character resigns from a teaching job at the university in order to start her own Non-Governmental Organization (NGO) that aims to serve teenage girls dubbed 'VENTURE 16'. Management of the venture takes the founder all over the world. She discovers that the African teenage problem is assumed to be universal and is consequently misinterpreted to be proof of the continent's participation in globalization: 'So if Third World countries and First World countries are facing the same problems, then can we agree with those who think the world is now a global village?' (77-8). This is used as one of the indicators of the ambiguous concept dubbed 'globalization'. However, Yaa-yaa Mensah's analysis of the concept reveals a perpetuation of racial and class discrimination akin to racist colonialism. This character notices that her global village has become a space for assimilating the underdeveloped, post-colonial Third World into a fallacious universalism that still operates on the old discriminatory racist class ideologies and attitudes. At personal level, the resultant effect of engagement in the supposedly global space and discourses connotes 'using the same terminologies and internalizing the converse implications: ... the result was a kind of galloping post-colonial lack of confidence – or loss in self-confidence' (78). Yaa-yaa Mensah's loss of self-confidence springs from a most unexpected aspect of life – the politicization of her wardrobe:

> If, some years ago, anyone had told Yaa-yaa that clothes are political, she would have laughed out aloud. Now she knows better. Everything is political and everything about clothes is political: the fabric they are made out of; the dyes on the fabrics; the cut; who does the cutting, and on and on and on. (79)

The detailed politics of clothes, that divert from Yaa-yaa's NGO's serious commitment to address developmental challenges of the African girl-child, prompt the character into deeper analysis of globalization discourses. She discovers euphemisms such as 'tropics' which camouflage 'underdeveloped – stroke – third world countries,' 'International fashion' which means dressing by northern standards courtesy of 'the fashion dictators of the Euro-American world.' All these politics added to Yaa-yaa's 'Busybusybusybusybusy ... Busybusybusybusybusy' schedule produce unprecedented stress levels in this elite African woman who ventures into the ill-defined global space on behalf of the African girl-child. But her stress level can be dismissed on the basis of some superstition and background. Aidoo easily does so humourously: 'it is reported that stress levels are exceedingly high in anyone born a twin in Southern Ghana, who finds themselves in Europe or North America on a Friday, after September First' (72).

In this story Aidoo exploits the techniques of foregrounding and deviation combined with stylistic devices of hyperbole, irony, paradox and parody to maximum effect in order to tease out redefinitions of hitherto unexamined assumptions about globalization and its implications for the African woman. Her resolution seems to be that all third world Africans – men and women – remain subject to various levels of discrimination by the northern races and dominant classes which encapsulate gender.

In this context, globalization becomes a euphemism that is best captured by Yaa-yaa's friend thus:' 'Are you saying that they are telling us we live in a global village, but only some of the people are expected to make the necessary adjustments so we can all continue to live in it?' (82).

Whereas in 'Comparisons' Aidoo examines all women's general experience under universal patriarchal division of labour, none-theless, she makes a distinction between levels of this essence of women's oppression under variants of patriarchy that incorporate racial and class discrimination. In this context the African woman becomes 'triply' oppressed by all the three discriminatory structures. Many of Aidoo's contemporaries share this perspective: Flora Nwapa, Buchi Emecheta, Bessie Head, Muthoni Likimani, Lauretta Ncgobo, Sindiwe Magona – to name a few. This is an important distinction because it delineates the convergence and divergence in Southern women's standpoint in liberation discourses. These writers scrutinize and unsettle the idea of homogeneity of women's oppression that underpins Northern-oriented women's movements that are dubbed global yet they are region-specific and exclusive. It is in this context that the African female writer takes on her responsibility as African nationalist and post-colonial person. In 'Some Global News' and 'MALE-ING NAMES IN THE SUN' Aidoo functions in these roles effectively. In the latter story she interrogates colonial practices that exacerbated the oppression of African woman, yet they have since been internalized as indicators of civilization.

In all the other stories in the collection, Aidoo lives up to her promise in the epigram above. She succeeds in inscribing the African girl-child-woman into the African short story in reconstructed portraits. The essence of her inscription was succinctly expressed by Aidoo's contemporary, the South African Lauretta Ncgobo at the Second African Writers', Conference in Stockholm in 1986. In her article, 'African Motherhood – Myth and Reality'; she advocates change in creative writing:

> We are looking for a changed portrayal of women in our books; an accurate and a just portrayal that will recognize the labour that women put into the economy of their societies, a liberating literature that not only forgives women their mistakes but condemns men who take advantage of women and does not condone men's infallibility. (Petersen 1988: 151)

For Ncgobo, changing from stereotypical portrayal implies reconstructing traditional gender roles assigned to women, and recognizing other capacities in which women serve their society:

> Women should not have to be martyrs to win respect of their societies. We are looking for a self-defining image of women who win respect in their own right because they are strong and achieve things in their lives and triumph, not only because they are men's wives or mothers of sons but because they are valued members of societies as bread winners, teachers, farmers, nurses, politicians and whatever else. These portrayals will in time focus correctly on the values that our societies should uphold and preserve. (ibid)

Ncgobo concludes that: 'in the context of our African struggles for freedom – freedom from imperialism, neo-colonialism and all oppression – it makes little sense to condone such extremes of oppression as our men are prepared to put the woman of Africa through' (ibid). Her treatise provides parameters by which male and female African writers' reconstruction of women's portraits may be evaluated at the level of authorial ideology. What makes Aidoo's reconstruction in *The Girl Who Can* much more refreshing is her aesthetic ideology. She handles language in a manner that can be described as liberative – for want of a better word. She scrutinizes society's illogical trivialization of women's work, capacity experience and progress. Her short stories transcend the generic format in terms of plot, time span, and structure as outlined by Valarie Kibera (1988). In conclusion, the value that Aidoo adds to the African short story in this collection resides in her gender responsive authorial ideology augumented by her enterprising aesthetic ideology. In my view, this level of enterprising reconstruction is best delineated in Ngugi wa Thiongo's *Moving the Centre: The Struggle for Cultural Freedoms,* hence the epigram above. It is noteworthy that *The Girl Who Can and Other Stories* is dedicated to the gender responsive Ghanaian writer Ayi Kwei Armah, among other notables, in recognition of the common endeavours of both African male and female writers as 'Oracles of the People' whose duty it is to reconstruct the damage done by and to society by negative discriminatory portrayals of women.

WORKS CITED

Aidoo, Ama Ata. *The Girl Who Can and Other Stories*. Oxford: Heinemann, 1997 (2002 Edition).

Antrobus, Peggy. *The Global Women's Movement: Origins, Issues and Strategies*. London: Zed Books, 2004.

Emecheta, Buchi. 'Feminism with a small 'f'.' *Criticism and Ideology: Second African Writers' Conference*. Kirsten Holst Petersen (ed.). Uppsala:Nordiska Afrikainstitutet, 1988 (173-85).

James, Adeola. (ed.) *In Their Own Voices: African Women Writers Talk*. London: James Currey, 1990 (1991 edition).

Kibera, Valerie. *An Anthology of East African Stories*. Harlow: Longman, 1988.

Likimani, Muthoni. *What Does A Man Want?* Nairobi: Kenya Literature Bureau, 1974 (1991 edition).

Magona, Sindiwe. *Forced to Grow*. Claremont: David Philip (AfricaSouth new Writing), 1992.

March, Candida, Ines A. Smyth and Maitrayee Mukhopadhyay. *A Guide to Gender-Analysis Frameworks*. Oxford: Oxfam Publications, 1999.

Moser, Caroline O. N. *Gender Planning and Development: Theory, Practice and Training*. London: Routledge, 1993.

Ncgobo, Lauretta. 'African Motherhood – Myth and Reality.' Petersen op.cit., 141-54.

Ogundipe-Leslie, Molara. *Re-creating Ourselves: African Women and Critical Trans-formations*. Trenton: African World Press, 1994.

Ogundipe Leslie, Molara and Carole Boyce Davies (eds). *Research in African Literatures: Special Issue – Women as Oral Artists*. 25:3, 1994.

Petersen, Kirsten Holst. ed. 'To Be an African Woman Writer – an Overview and a Detail'. *Criticism and Ideology:Second African Writer's Conference*. Uppsala: Nordiska Afrikainstitutet, 1988 (155-72).

wa Thiong'o, Ngugi. *Moving the Centre: The Struggle for Cultural Freedoms*. London: James Currey, 1993.

Williams, Colin C. *Examining the Nature of Domestic Labour*. Brookfield: Avebury, 1988.

Ama Ata Aidoo

An interview for ALT
by Maureen Eke, Vincent Odamtten & Stephanie Newell
1st December 2012, ASA Annual Conference, Philadelphia

---

* M. Eke and V. Odamtten fielded the questions, S. Newell transcribed the text of the interview

Maureen Eke: What do you see as the place of the short story in African literature?

Ama Ata Aidoo: I think the short story is unfortunately rather misrepresented. As somebody who has also worked with that other 'brief' genre, poetry, I have found that African scholars and teachers have paid attention only to the novel. This is to be lamented.

Vincent Odamtten: Sometimes people accuse me of over-reading *No Sweetness Here* (1970), but when I look at your collection there is a sense of an interrogation of the moment after independence: you use the notion of post-independence to interrogate women's lives in particular, and the society's life more generally, and you ask what it means to be independent. The stories that you selected seem to have this bond between them. What choices do you make to select particular stories for your collections? What motivates you, and what is the controlling paradigm that you use to include one short story and exclude another?

Ama Ata Aidoo: First of all, I think that any kind of attention to one's work is valuable as far as a writer is concerned. Even the most outlandish readings into my stories, my poems, my novels or my plays, are most welcome! If you don't talk about a piece of work, then you are killing it; you may not actively intend to kill it, but as I said earlier this afternoon [in the M. K. O. Abiola Lecture, 'Clapping With One Hand, Or A Fundamentally Flawed Management of Post-Colonial African Public Spaces'], we can do all we want as writers, but if people don't read us and don't talk about our work, our books are not worth much because it is the interaction that completes the work. So, for me there is nothing like over-reading. People – scholars and ordinary readers – bring to the work their own perceptions, their personal histories, their scholarship, their research, and so on and so forth. I have no problems at all even with over-reading.

As for what determines my selection of particular stories as against others: it depends. I've produced these three volumes of short stories (*No Sweetness Here* 1970; *The Girl Who Can and Other Stories* 1997; *Diplomatic Pounds and Other Stories* 2012). I was amazed at that panel in Dallas [The African Literature Association conference, 2012] to hear you all looking at these stories, placing them historically and so on, simply because I don't select my short stories based on the perspectives of a critic. At most, what I do is see how the stories relate to one another, which is probably what you've just said anyway. Mind you, these three volumes have been put together at pretty long, irregular intervals, so the stories also reflect not so much my intentions as the period in which they were produced. *No Sweetness Here* reflected the so-called immediate post-colonial and post-independence era in Ghana. These are exclusively Ghanaian stories in the sense that Ghana is where I was living and working at the time, but they are not just Ghanaian: they are rural. Even the title story, where the main action takes place in the city, is from the perspective of rural people.

Maureen Eke: In *No Sweetness Here,* and also in your new short story collection, *Diplomatic Pounds,* the question of migration is central. Both collections depict different kinds of migration: from the rural to the city and back, and even inter-continental migration. In your plays, *Anowa* (1970) and *Dilemma of a Ghost* (1965), you also deal with this issue of migration, looking at the history and the experience of black people. How do you see this issue of migration, not only in terms of the past with the movement from the village to the city, but also now that these cities have established themselves on the continent and in the nation? Do you see these issues of migration as a perennial subject that we should be looking at, especially as they occur in your stories?

Ama Ata Aidoo: I was born into a world that was already reflecting itinerancy, or migration. I had an amazing childhood. When I was a child and growing up in my father's house, my mother was always cooking for visitors – people like peddlers of exotic materials, gold ingots and stuff, plus the itinerant prophets, who in those days would come to our village and start singing from our river bank as they entered the village, announcing themselves very clearly. These days the prophets announce themselves with street microphones, but in those days it was with their voices.

For a child growing up in a Ghanaian village in the Central Region, this was a major source of curiosity and wonder about wandering. For me, migration has always been an element that I have had to deal with, and my own life has not been that sedentary. I've always travelled: from the village to go to my cousins in town, and to go to boarding school. We were on the road going home, then going back to school: this was my world.

Now things have become more sophisticated, but the basic paradigm is the same. People have always had to travel, and this is what I see. No city in the world, including the African city, is mono-ethnic. Not even uni-national. It's a mix, and, listening to you, I suspect that maybe it had always, right from the beginning of my writing career with *The Dilemma of a Ghost*, excited my imagination: migration. Why people leave home.

Maureen Eke: You raise these questions in 'Certain Winds from the South' and 'In the Cutting of a Drink' [in *No Sweetness Here*].

Vincent Odamtten: One of the fascinating things I see as we move from your earlier collections to your later ones is the widening circle that the stories encompass. Margaret Atwood said that often writers don't talk about the basic things we do, like eating, but I've noticed that in many of your stories food comes to play a part in the way the narrative moves. In *Diplomatic Pounds,* food becomes a problem. How do you think of food in your stories? To me, it occurs in a way that makes its presence known.

Ama Ata Aidoo: It's almost like a character.

Vincent Odamtten: I'm curious as to how you see food and the function of food. For instance, in 'The Stone Soup' food is at the centre of the story, but the other stories in *Diplomatic Pounds* are also concerned with food, its consumption, its circulation, etc.

Ama Ata Aidoo: I just like food! When I was younger and more energetic, I loved feeding people. It's very difficult to feed others without also eating: it's not done in any culture that you cook for people and you don't join them. That has been one aspect of my interaction with people. The lament from people like my daughter, and others who knew me at the University of Cape Coast, is that I don't cook any more. It's not just the fact that I like food, or that food is a vital element in any people's culture and in any individual's life. Since I started coming here [to the USA] many years ago, I have been interested in the clash between African ways of doing things and specifically Western ways of regarding food. This is what led me eventually into exploring some aspect of it in 'Diplomatic Pounds', the title story, and in the story set in New Orleans 'Mixed Messages'. It's not as if I told myself 'now I have to explore this'. The themes just came. My imagination had been trying to deal with these things for a very long time, and so when I sat down to write, then the ideas came, and I thought I should be as relaxed and frank about this issue as possible.

One of the things I appreciated so much about New Orleans in spite of whatever other question marks I may have about my sojourn in that city, is the food. You know, food is an aspect of many people's lives, whether they are in Barcelona or Trieste. The people of the sea are interested in cooking, because fish and sea-food are excellent to taste, but at the same time not good. We develop ways of cooking sea-food in such a way as to get rid of the scent of the sea or at least to camouflage it. That's why these things are so good to eat: I learnt that immediately from New Orleans. In 'Mixed Messages', I find myself exploring the food in New Orleans against the background of what I call the specific criminalization of obesity in Western – and gradually global – culture. Somebody who is perceived to be 'obese' – anything from 2 pounds overweight to whatever – is actually regarded as antisocial and almost criminal. This particular story was inspired a long time ago when I was in New Orleans: a friend and I were going to Weight Watchers together. I've been through all that! One day coming home, we fell into discussing where we would spend Thanksgiving and she said she wouldn't go to her family at all because, 'if I pick a piece of drumstick, everybody says I'm eating too much and in the meantime, they will have mountains of food in front of them'. It hit me so hard. This conversation happened in 1974, and it sat in my mind all these years. My imagination was obviously working with it, and then I wrote this story. Overweight or obese: the weapon for fighting it is the bathroom scales, which gave rise to the title of my collection, *Diplomatic Pounds.*

Vincent Odamtten: One of the stories in *Diplomatic Pounds* that particularly struck a young Asian-American student of mine was 'Feely Feely', where the major characters are male. On being asked why he found the narrative so engaging, he said that even though it was very much a story he could see was from Ghana and about Africans, it was as though it described his own family. What has struck me increasingly is that your stories have this effect of being able to speak to people in other cultures and other societies. *Diplomatic Pounds* seems to have a resonance for people of very different cultures and backgrounds: this is a mark of great writing, but the question I have concerns whether you are aware of this other audience, this non-African audience that is engaged in reading your work?

Ama Ata Aidoo: You critics are always trying to put these short stories into context. I was intrigued by listening to you all [in Dallas], and very pleased. To be honest, even with *Diplomatic Pounds,* I didn't have any notion of the audience while I was writing it. I write! I know at the back of my mind that my readers are any Ghanaian and any African who reads English, and any person of African descent anywhere in the world who reads English, and then the rest of the world. I never tell myself that I'm only writing for a Ghanaian audience, or that I'm writing for a world audience. What I've come to recognize as the basic notion of an audience out there is not specific.

Whereas *No Sweetness Here* is wholly Ghanaian and almost wholly rural, my writing has gone through a transition, not necessarily out of Africa, but to a place where, through my own migration – going in and out of Africa – I could see my readers as from Ghana and Africa as well as from the US. Even in *No Sweetness Here,* the notion of migration crept into the last story, 'The Girl Who Can'.

Diplomatic Pounds is almost wholly a reflection of my life outside Ghana. I've never lived permanently outside Africa, but then I go and come often enough for it to impact my own life and my own mind, and therefore my imagination. The stories are what they are because of the life I've been living, not because of a notion of writing for the world. I was in New Orleans, and I was here and there: these stories reflect the life that has been mine for the last 20 years at least.

Maureen Eke: The very first story in *Diplomatic Pounds*, 'New Lessons', signals something autobiographical. You're talking to your niece. This conversation centres upon organising and cleaning up Africa. Again, today in your M. K. O. Abiola Lecture, this question of fixing African problems arose as you looked at independence, the promise to organize Africa, and maybe the lack of success in organizing it. Even in your plays there's a sense of looking back and forward, to the past, to globalization. To what extent do you see history as a theme that runs through your works in general? How does history figure into your work?

Ama Ata Aidoo: I have always believed that yesterday is crucial to everything that we do today and everything we will do tomorrow. The notion that we should be aware of what went on yesterday has always been very important to me.

Vincent Odamtten: I'd like to jump back to *The Girl Who Can and Other Stories* (1997), and the ways in which history is important. The story, 'She-Who-Would-Be-King' strikes me as futuristic, or science fiction, and yet there is a historical element that you pull into the narrative. In the story, as well as in your M. K. O. Abiola Lecture today, you raise questions about women's position. What do you see that gives you hope that we will arrive at the moment you anticipate in 'She-Who-Would-Be-King'?

Ama Ata Aidoo: What gives me hope is that the younger generation – who we may consider crazy, unfaithful, and so on – has energy. The energy with which they are attacking life is very impressive. So I'm almost obliged to hope: it's the imperative to hope for girls' education to yield fruit. What made me do this paper ['Clapping With One Hand, Or A Fundamentally Flawed Management of Post-Colonial African Public Spaces'] is really the reluctance among the leadership for any kind of vision that would add to this energy of the youth. I'm not speaking of the girls only, but the youth. They are not receiving any income; the education systems have virtually broken down; there are no health systems to speak of; and so on and so on with all these disincentives. Looking at the young people, I have a lot of hope: they have all these frustrations and an awareness that among the older generation – the leadership – nobody is caring.

In writing my talk for today, I had to work to be disciplined, to keep the focus on women's marginalization from public spaces, but really I'm aware that it's not only young women who are being denied a future. If we are not careful, we are denying young men too a future, but with this one difference: for the average young man who does have a future, you don't have an equivalent young woman. The future as a statement, as a gift, to the younger generation, does not count in women. When I look around, my question is: where are we taking all of this? If our young men are a casualty, our young women are a double casualty.

Maureen Eke: To conclude our interview, I'd like to return to the topic of artistic creation and which you find less cumbersome to create: the short story or another genre?

Ama Ata Aidoo: Everything is less difficult than the novel! Too many words! Too long! Everything else. Everything – poetry, drama, the short story – is easier than the novel. It takes so much time to write a novel, so much sitting down, so many words. You find yourself going back to find out if something you are saying now is accurate because you don't want to contradict yourself.

REVIEWS

EDITED BY JAMES GIBBS

Amir Tag Elsir *The Grub Hunter*
Translated from Arabic by William M. Hutchins
Harlow: Pearson, (African Writers Series), 2012, 133 pp., £9.30
ISBN 978 0 435 13480 8

In her introduction to the US edition of Tayeb Salih's *Season of Migration to the North*, Laila Lalami observed that the novel was unique in that it was 'written in the author's native language, rather than the colonial one'. Salih explained that he wrote in Arabic 'as a matter of principle'.

We know that some novels have been written in African languages and that Najib Mafouz wrote in Arabic, as have other North African novelists. We also know that many novels written in French or English were uncompromisingly anti-colonial, and we have glimpsed what the choice of language can mean in terms of the dilemma confronting authors. This has been articulated by Ngugi wa Thiong'o in *Decolonising the Mind* and it has led him to write in Gikuyu. The fact that Ngugi is now resident in the USA, where he is lionized for his English-language novels, speaks volumes about the 'balance of power' in publishing and distribution that confronts African writers – and breaks their idealism and resistance.

William Maynard Hutchins and Pearson Publishers deserve credit for the translation and publication of Amir Tag Elsir's *The Grub Hunter*. The volume answers the suspicion that Africans – and writers from all developing countries – have about choice of language. There are obvious reasons for writing in colonial languages and these include earning royalties, gaining access to an international reading public and recognition. Recognition may include winning prizes – that may include a token or a deserved Nobel. The alternative to writing in the colonial language is to remain obscure, trapped within national borders and in a limited distribution market. There is a risk of censorship or self-censorship, of physical restrictions – or worse. This raises the question: Is the desire to do for African languages what Chaucer and Shakespeare did for English a fallacy in the present World Order?

The recently revived African Writers Series and translations like *The Grub Hunter* offer a third way, one that is too feeble to make a major difference, but is, nonetheless, extremely significant. Amir Tag Elsir, it is relevant to note, is an established writer in Arabic, having – since 1988 – published nine novels, a collection of poetry and two biographies. *The Grub Hunter* is not a novice's book: it is the work of a mature novelist who has the self-confidence and experience to lead, mislead and surprise the reader in relating the transformation of an intelligence officer into an author.

This transformation takes place against a background that is a thinly-veiled Sudan during Turabi's hegemony of the early 1990s. The fact that the novel appeared in Arabic in 2010 (ten years after the overthrow of Turabi) and still retains its sharp, satirical edge shows that it was not written in a polemical, topical, documentary manner. As a result, it is not only of interest to those in one country or one epoch, but is relevant in many developing countries that are struggling with post-colonial development pains. Turabi's one-party system was overturned and references in the novel to the prevalence of police surveillance are history, part of a particular political landscape that has been transformed. The novel-within-a-novel and the almost detective novel-like suspense makes this a work to enjoy, and one that will, I hope, lead to calls for the translation of other novels by Amir Tag Elsir.

Incidentally, one commonly accepted perception is dismantled and another reinforced by the rise of Amir Tag Elsir. The claims that writers excel only when they write about what they encounter in real life does not fit *The Grub Hunter* because in this case the novelist is a GP who has consciously researched the life and work of security officers in order to depict them as complex human beings. On the other hand, his writing career illustrates a second commonly accepted perception, namely that creativity runs in families: Amir Tag Elsir is Tayeb Salih's nephew.

The Pearson edition wisely keeps foot-notes to a minimum and the translation is excellent. One can, incidentally, imagine Hutchins' amusement at having to render into English the lines in which the narrator criticizes translations. This emerges in the AWS volume as follows: 'I consider the translation of literature to be an act of betrayal of its truth. All forms of literature should be read in the original language.' Not everyone can read Arabic and this lucid translation is impressive and welcome.

KHALID AL MUBARAK
Playwright, poet

Gordon Collier. ed. *Focus on Nigeria: Literature and Culture*
Matatu 40 (2012), Amsterdam: Rodopi, 496 pp., Euros 105 US$ 142
978-90-420-3572-0

A Matatu is the East African equivalent of the Danfo bus, that chaotic
democratic means of transport that ferries thousands of Nigerians crammed
in as tightly as the wrappers of a newly wealthy woman trader into her
no longer adequate trunk. When I agreed to review the latest edition of
the journal *Matatu* with its theme: *Focus on Nigeria: Literature and Culture*,
I expected a slim envelope to come through the post. Imagine then my
surprise at receiving a hard-backed volume of nearly 500 pages, attractively
bound in a green and white cover that echoes the Nigerian national colours.

Like the vehicle from which it takes its name, this edition is stuffed
with a hodgepodge of scholarly essays, critical perspectives, poetry, an
interview and a short story. Some of the pieces only bear a tenuous link to
Nigeria, but, taking the advice of a popular contemporary Igbo saying, I
will leave the matter of what is written on the bus, and take my seat among
the already seated passengers.

The edition opens with Durotoye Adeleke's essay on the Shakespearean
fool, which tries to find parallels in contemporary Yoruba theatre, but omits
an exploration of any precedent tradition of the fool in 'pre-contemporary'
Yoruba drama. This failure to broaden the scope of discourse is also seen in
Kola Eke's piece on diplomatic leadership in the poetry of Tanure Ojaide,
which seems to draw most of its points of reference from the Bible and
contemporary American Pentecostal preachers. Ojaide's work is the subject
of no less than three of the thirty pieces in the volume, while Adichie and
Achebe appear singly or together in four of the contributions. Given the
burgeoning richness of Nigerian literature, this concentration seems a
missed opportunity. Two contributors are involved in more than one essay
and, given the number of Nigerian literary and cultural academics, this is
a pity.

Like the patent medicine hawkers on the Danfo, many of the essay
titles promise more than they deliver. So having devoured Nwando
Achebe's insightful biography of Ahebi Ugbabe, the only female warrant
chief in Northern Igbo and in the colonial era, I looked forward to
Clifford Nwanna's 'Dialectics of African Feminism, a study of the *Awommili*
Women's Group in Awka'. Nwanna fails to delve deep into the who, what,
where and why of the group, leaving the tantalized reader asking for more:
who for example were the women who led the *Awommili* group? What
motivated them? And why, given that their male patrons are named, are
they left nameless?

There is a similar problem concerning depth with the two contributions
by Nick Mdika Tembo. Writing on *Out of the Masks* by Tracie Utoh-
Ezeajugh, he is silent on the play's strident emphasis on patriarchy, and,
writing on ethnic conflict and the politics of greed in *Half of a Yellow*

Sun, he does not seem to have made use of the reading list that Adichie helpfully provides at the end of her novel.

A consistent characteristic shared by many of the contributions is a limited frame of reference. For instance, Lifongo Vetinde's essay on black filmmakers and Africa's transitional dilemmas makes no reference to Nigerian film. Another recurrent feature is that arguments are not fully developed. This is the case in the essay on Islam and Culture by Anthony Afe Asekhauno and Matthew A. Izibili and in the study of sorcery in Etsako warfare by Asekhanuo and Valentine Ananafe Inagbor – that veers towards the merely anecdotal. Contributors adopt a disconcerting approach towards sources, with newspaper articles and academic research papers given equal weight and cited out of context. See, for example, Tomi Adeaga's essay on the decline of the Nigerian educational system.

The creative writing submissions are of uneven quality, which is a disservice given that there are so many exciting new Nigerian voices in the genres represented.

In spite of these shortcomings, there is much in this volume to attract attention. Michel Olutoyo Olatunji's essays exploring the indigenization of military music in Nigeria and trends in Islamized Yoruba music, Moji A. Olateju's linguistic study of Yoruba local drug advertising, Moses Omoniyi Ayeomoni's analysis of speeches by Nigerian heads of state, and Mohamed Inuwa Umar-Buratai's study of the Durbar and Emirate court art in Northern Nigeria are all interesting riffs on subjects not often explored. My favourite piece was Ode Ogede's fascinating account of the correspondence between Ayi Kwei Armah and his English publisher. There was only a tenuous link to Nigeria: it appears that one of the issues between Armah and his publishers was the payment of royalties from the Nigerian editions of his books! But it was written in refreshingly straight-forward language, and cast fresh light on an often overlooked issue.

Like a journey in a *matatu*, this volume is frustrating, tantalizing and uneven, but definitely worth embarking on.

IKE ANYA
Consultant in Public Health Medicine, London

Dominique Chancé and Alain Ricard (eds). *Études littéraires africaines: Traductions postcoloniales*
Metz: Université de Lorraine, 2013, 172 pp., n.p.
ISSN 0769-4563

Number 34 of *Études littéraires africaines* includes a variety of articles on African literature together with some twenty book reviews. At its heart are seven contributions originally presented at a workshop held in Bordeaux during April 2011, and, as the editors write in the introduction, these reflect current perspectives on post-colonial translation. They analyse ambiguities, and define orientations.

For the editors, and most of the contributors, translation during the colonial period was a tool used to impose western culture on colonized populations, but with the advent of decolonization patterns changed and new trends emerged. The first two articles describe colonial translation practices in Eastern Africa. Nathalie Carré confirms the views that translation was a tool used by colonial masters to dominate indigenous populations, and states that transferring oral material into written texts was a major challenge for translators. In the second article, Xavier Garnier discusses translations to and from Swahili, and shows that during the colonial period almost nothing was translated from Swahili. After independence, translations depended on individual choices, and the number of translations into French remained small: Garnier names only five books translated from Swahili into French between 1959 and 2010. Given that Africa made up a substantial portion of the French colonial empire, translating African literature into French should, he considers, be taken more seriously.

The third and fourth articles focus on Madagascar. Claire Riffard examines the creative approach practised by Jean Joseph Rabearivelo (1903-1937), who translated both into French and into Malagasy. In fact, the eminent translation theorist and practitioner advocates a complete reorientation of the balance in literary exchanges between Madagascar and 'Overseas', advocating intensive translation in both directions and arguing that translation should be regarded as a means of aesthetic liberation. For Didier Galibert, translating in post-colonial Madagascar is influenced by political ideology and by power relationships.

The following two articles deal with the influence of orality in post-colonial Africa, especially in West Africa. Dominique Chancé looks at the novels of Amos Tutuola, and, where others find fault with his English, she identifies an illustration of 'post-colonial translation'. Comparing translations of Tutuola's work by Queneau and Laforest, she comes to the conclusion that Laforest's versions are closer to what the author and his linguistic community express in their own 'English'. For Chancé post-colonial translation has to take into account the historical aspects of the text and its hybridity. In his contribution Abraham Birahima discusses the notion of an 'oral third-text'. It is his view that post-colonial African writers are 'unconscious translators' who move, initially unconsciously, through an 'implicit text' which is oral and composed in an African language. Translating the text produced into European languages becomes a complex, multi-layered task.

Myriam Suhet explores a new and unusual domain of translation (and translation studies) in relation to an African statue in the Musée Quai Branly. He questions the notion of translation as bridging the gap between source and target, and argues in favour of an approach to translation that aims at the 'polyphonic reception' of a piece of art. In this, dialogue between cultures is a crucial factor.

All seven contributions are well researched and well presented. Their central concern, post-colonial translation, is analysed from perspectives that include literature and political ideology, and the papers are united in emphasizing the importance of orality. Though I am slightly disappointed that the volume does not cover a wider geographical area (Central Africa and the Maghreb are not considered), this is a valuable resource for the study of post-colonial translation. The discipline is young, and the attention given in this volume to African languages and to oral literature provide welcome new perspectives.

OUMAROU MAL MAZOU
University of Liège

Laura Murphy. *Metaphor and the Slave Trade in West African Literature*
Athens: Ohio University Press, 2012, 243 pp., $34.95 pbk
ISBN-13 978-0-8214-1995-3

Contrary to critics' claims that African writers harbour an amnesia regarding the slave trade, Laura Murphy argues that African literature represents slavery 'differently' than neo-slave narratives and historical fictions using metaphors that move interiorly 'into the homes of those who lost loved ones or hid from traders, into the landscapes surrounding their communities, even into their very bodies' (31). In *Metaphor and the Slave Trade in West African Literature* Murphy writes that generations of African writers have interpolated metaphors into their novels through the oral tradition 'in a way that allows us to see the transatlantic slave trade's intrusion into the West African imagination of landscapes, memories, and bodies' (74).

Murphy's compelling suppositions perhaps resonate in spaces far more intimately – and traumatically – than do more overt references in protracted narratives especially prevalent in African American literature. The metaphors of the slave trade that Murphy locates in select African fiction are potent reminders that alternative ways to assess slavery and to chronicle its past-to-present transmission exist beyond what non-African slave narratives or historical fictions convey. In Amos Tutuola's *My Life in the Bush of Ghosts*, (1954), for instance, Murphy critiques the childhood fear of slave capture through the concept known as 'the body in the bag' that totally subjugates the individual. In Ben Okri's *The Famished Road* (1991), she views the river that becomes a road that opens out to the world as endemic of globalization, which warns African villagers of the perils that modernity offers. In Ayi Kwei Armah's *Fragments* (1969), she finds disappointment and corruption in colonial and postcolonial rule, as well as shifting emphases on materiality rather than core familial bonds. And in Ama Ata Aidoo's *Our Sister Killjoy* (1977), she reveals how the misogynistic treatment of women is attributable, in part, to slavery's long reach.

Murphy may not be the first to connect cultural tropes in African literature with slavery through the body in the bag motif, the ghosts in the bush, or the figure of the wandering *abiku* child who symbolizes loss. But through meticulous research conducted assiduously on an African Cosmology textual collective, she has recalibrated the equation for how metaphors uniquely constitute slave representation. Whether through snapshots stored in personal memory archives or stories passed along a transgenerational individual or group collective, the African literature in Murphy's study registers slavery's impact more covertly but no less profoundly than in traditional Freytag plot structures. Hence, there is much to laud about her iterations of whispered stories, interviews, folklore, diaries, and individual experiences that recover memories of the slave past in far-flung regions in West Africa.

According to Murphy, critics that decry African writers for not representing slavery more overtly in their fiction subscribe to Pierre Nora's conception of 'duty memory', a form of coercion that forces reliance upon documentation through an official archive so obsessively that it actually results in the opposite effect. Murphy's study is most penetrating when it unbinds sophisticated layering techniques in literature that adhere the corrosive effects of slavery conterminously with colonialism, post-colonialism, and even independence, especially for Ghana and Nigeria.

And yet, given cross-fertilization and proliferation transnationally in neo-slave narratives and/or historical fictions, Murphy's claims to a cleavage between African literature that steeps slavery covertly in metaphors as opposed to slave narratives that do so overtly and protractedly require some qualification. Although Murphy's metaphorical readings are compelling, some African writers employ traits recognizable in historical fiction while historical fiction writers often apply metaphors, allusions, and other features that perform similar functions. Furthermore, a burgeoning community of contemporary historical fiction writers beyond the US has broadened the dimensions of these narratives. Haitian writer Evelyne Trouillot (*Rosalie l'Infame*, 2003) and Canadian writer Dionne

Brand (*At the Full and Change of the Moon*, 1997), for instance, include female revolutionaries that actively participate in slave insurrections.

Examples of what might be construed as cross-fertilization include Tutuola's ghost in the bush and Okri's magical realism, which Toni Morrison and Fred D'Aguiar employ, albeit through different iterations in *Beloved* (1987) and *Feeding the Ghosts* (1997) respectively. And John Edgar Wideman's *The Cattle Killing* (1996) has generated a near cult following among African literature scholars for its associative embodiment of a timeless allegory about the South African Xhosa people whom Murphy briefly cite. When the Xhosa heed a false prophecy to kill their precious cattle in order to drive out white colonialists and to secure a better future, the slaughter backfires, and they suffer ceaselessly through many generations like those we find in Murphy's study of select African literature.

Murphy's analysis of Ben Okri's signification of Tutuola's 'trope of the body in the bag' conjures Henry Louis Gates' 'trope of the talking book' in *The Signifying Monkey* (1988). Gates' reading of the talking book in several slave narratives portends the formation of a black literary discourse by formerly enslaved Africans in Europe and the Americas. Meanwhile, Murphy's transmission of the 'body in the bag' signals coalescence among some contemporary African authors around such metaphors in the service of an omnipresent oral tradition.

This discursive transmission is especially revealing since Olaudah Equiano who participates in both the talking book and the body in the bag inscriptions, reminisces in his *Interesting Narrative* about being placed in a sack upon captivity. This is similar to what Tutuola, Okri and others describe. These examples serve to clarify rather than disqualify Murphy's suppositions, which remain impressive and acutely discerning. Ultimately, Murphy's attention to African writers' liberal application of metaphor gives homage to a tradition whose representations of the slave past perhaps equal historical fiction as an operative counter discursive alternative.

HELENA WOODARD

Associate Professor, Department of English, University of Texas at Austin

---

Eldred Durosimi Jones with Marjorie Jones. *The Freetown Bond: A Life under Two Flags*
Woodbridge: James Currey, 2012, pp. 174, £30.00
ISBN 978-1-84701-055-1

In opening *The Freetown Bond* readers engage with a memoir. Eldred Durosimi Jones, with the help of his wife, Marjorie, has arranged the material for 'A Life under Two Flags' in ten chapters and a briskly informative Appendix. The opening chapters proceed chronologically under titles that sometimes have literary echoes: '1 Early Childhood under the British Flag' and '2 Manhood's Gleam in Boyish Eyes' – a quotation from a school song. However, this book is not intended to be a conventional autobiography. We are not given, for example, a year by year account of Jones's remarkable career or of his growing family. Instead, in an eminently readable volume, we are offered accounts of experiences that reflect a colonial education and a working life spent in a colony moving towards independence and then in a nation state confronting harsh, post-colonial realities.

Chapter 3 is headed 'In the Footsteps of Ajayi Crowther' (Jones, like Crowther, attended Fourah Bay College); Chapter 4 'The Gleaming Spires of Oxford' (Jones was an undergraduate at Corpus Christi); Chapter 5 'Home Pastures'; Chapter 6 'America & New Found Lands', and Chapter 7 'West African Travels'. By the time we reach Chapter 8, 'All Freetown's a Stage', we have long since departed from an arrangement around the chronological, and are faced with a life chopped up into topics. The title of Chapter 8 prepares us for sub-sections on 'Acting – Walking – Broadcasting', and the abrupt title of Chapter 9, 'Books, Words, Causes', indicates even more strongly that the author has been dicing his life. In this chapter, we are even given sub-headings, the first of which is – '*African Literature Today*'. Such is the scale of Jones's achievement and the modesty of his analysis that the 'story' of *ALT*, which Jones founded and then edited for thirty-three years (141) – or 'some thirty-two years' (61), occupies only four and a half pages!

As might be expected, the early chapters contain valuable material on Jones's background and upbringing and can be seen in relation to other accounts by Sierra Leoneans such as *Kossoh Town Boy* by Wellesley Cole or *Creoldom* by Arthur T. Porter. Jones moves on to sketch in the wide horizons opened up by his continuing education and then, in 'Home Pastures', he begins an outline of his working life and of his adult engagement with his native land. His rise in his chosen profession was rapid: he began teaching at Fourah Bay College in October 1953 and was appointed acting head of English in 1956. Other promotions and appointments followed: in 1963, he became a senior lecturer and the following year was made professor. This career trajectory indicates that he was part of an institution that was reacting to nationalist pressures and to Jones's academic achievements. Jones's life was, it becomes clear, entwined with that of the college that became a university and with a new nation. Reading *Freetown Bond* we watch the history of Sierra Leone unfold 'by flashes of lightning' and the book will be mined for first-hand experiences that reflect the participation of a principled intellectual imbued with ideals of public service.

The memoir is separate from Jones's academic publications but shares with them the themes of shifting scholarly interests and an evolving sense of identity. It assumes readers are familiar with – or prepared to pursue – titles such as *Othello's Countrymen* (by 'Eldred Jones', 1965), *The Writing of Wole Soyinka* (by 'Eldred Durosimi Jones', 1973), and *The Krio-English Dictionary* ('prepared by Clifford N. Fyle and Eldred D. Jones', 1980). This journal, *African Literature Today,* was initially edited by 'Eldred D. Jones', later by 'Eldred Durosimi Jones', and later still by Eldred Durosimi Jones with Eustace Palmer. Recognition was subsequently given to the involvement of Marjorie Jones.

In selecting the title for his memoir, Jones highlights his link with his home town. Over the years, he has been offered tempting positions in the UK and in North America, but, unlike a number of other distinguished West Africans, he has centred his life firmly on Sierra Leone and Freetown. Sierra Leone's Independence Day found him lecturing in the US, but he felt the 'bond' and hurried home to share in part of the national celebration. By 1961, Jones was, as this 'clip' suggests, already living on a large map, but he did not let his burgeoning international career cut him off completely from participation in the national rite of passage.

Some of the issues and individuals mentioned in the memoir have already been the subject of longer studies. For example, Jones documents his intervention during the dark days of 1970 when he wrote (from Canada) to Governor General Banja Tejan-Sie urging him to take a stand. He then refers to his next meeting with Banja ('... in London, (he was) dignified, still good humoured but an exile') and he goes on to observe that 'Others met an even more cruel fate' (154). Indeed they did and the 'others' included Mohammed Fauna whose arrest Jones records (152). This arrest and what happened after it has been doggedly investigated by Aminatta Forna – whom Jones also mentions (164), and there will be those who wish the book had devoted more pages to the Fauna case and similar 'disappearances'. However, such events are not the author's main concern in this volume. Having referred to the arrest, reproduced his letter to the Governor and described the London meeting, Jones moves on, as he is entitled to do in a memoir. He focuses on his response to the 'dark days' that was typically constructive: he records that he and Marjorie worked for the National Policy Advisory Committee. Such work does not make headlines nor does it catch the attention of international observers, but it is vital for nation building and is quietly undertaken by the principled and dedicated.

While some may find Jones's involvement in national affairs of consuming interest, others – particularly those intrigued by evolving attitudes – will be fascinated by the trajectory of his career. As indicated by the recitation of book titles, Jones moved from concern with Shakespeare and with the representation of black characters in Shakespeare's plays to the study of Wole Soyinka. He made this a natural progression and, with a glance over his shoulder, inscribed his Soyinka book 'For W.S. *Our* W.S.' With *African Literature Today*, he created a forum for the critical discussion of a new discipline. Through this brief summary and, more clearly through the pages of his memoir, Jones's coming to terms with Africa as a creative continent and his positioning of himself in relation to this new area of study can be traced.

Crucial in this exploration seems to have been the experiences described in the chapter headed 'West African Travels'. This account of his visit to Nigeria is written – and the text we have may draw heavily on one composed at the time – with particular passion and shows that, in 1963, Jones was primed to respond to the creativity of an exciting group of Nigerian artists. With great intensity, he describes his encounters with Ekwensi, Nwapa, Tutuola, Onitsha Market Literature, Soyinka and Beier.

In the section on the Nigerian visit, Jones shares with the reader elements from a conversation he had with Mable Segun about his middle name. Significantly his middle name was not alluded to on the title page of his Shakespeare book where he was simply 'Eldred Jones' – his name suggesting a conjunction of Anglo-Saxon and Celt. Later, when he wrote about Soyinka, he reclaimed Yoruba links by including his 'Durosimi'. Apparently 'durosimi' means 'Wait to bury me' (123) and its choice was explained by the fact that Jones was an *abiku*. Over the years, and on the covers of various books, he has – as tabulated above – come to 'own' and to 'out' his middle name.

Despite the rather sombre note struck by 'Wait to bury me', the memoir is robustly life affirming. High among the values that Jones celebrates in the volume can be found the pleasure taken in making and keeping friends. Central to this theme, apparent as one gets to know the author better and fully present in the final chapter, that is entitled with a nod to Tennyson 'Twilight & Evening Bell', is an awareness of the presence by his side of his closest collaborator, the best of his friends, the most sustaining of his companions, the helpmate who has given him 'tremendous support' – in every aspect of his work (156). Author credits are crucial and names are important; *Freetown Bond* is, of course, by 'Eldred Durosimi Jones with Marjorie Jones'.

JAMES GIBBS
Senior Visiting Research Fellow, University of the West of England

Printed and bound by CPI Group (UK) Ltd, Croydon, CR0 4YY

13/04/2025

14656514-0001